SOCIAL IMPACT ASSESSMENT METHODS

SOCIAL
IMPACT
ASSESSMENT
METHODS

Edited by
Kurt Finsterbusch
Lynn G. Llewellyn
C. P. Wolf

 SAGE PUBLICATIONS   Beverly Hills / London / New Delhi

For information address:

SAGE Publications, Inc.
275 South Beverly Drive
Beverly Hills, California 90212

SAGE Publications India Pvt. Ltd.
C-236 Defence Colony
New Delhi 110 024, India

SAGE Publications Ltd
28 Banner Street
London EC1Y 8QE, England

Printed in the United States of America

Library of Congress Cataloging in Publication Data

Main entry under title:

Social impact assessment methods.

    Bibliography: p.
    1. Social indicators.   2. Technological innovations—
Social aspects—Evaluation.   3. Social prediction.
I. Finsterbusch, Kurt, 1935-   11. Llewellyn,
Lynn G.   III. Wolf, C. P. (Charles Parker), 1933-
HN25.S57   1983   303.4'83   83-17721
ISBN 0-8039-2142-X

FIRST PRINTING

Contents

Introduction

○ ○ ○ ○ ○ ○ ○ ○ ○ ○ ○ ○ ○ ○ ○ ○ ○

LYNN G. LLEWELLYN

○ ○ ○ ○ ○ ○ ○ ○ ○ ○ ○ ○ ○ ○ ○ ○ ○

● The National Environmental Policy Act (NEPA) of 1969 is generally regarded as the legislative mandate for most social impact assessments (SIAs); yet it was not until several years after NEPA was signed into law that a concerted effort was made to bring practitioners together for the purpose of sharing experiences and improving the quality of SIAs. Indeed, perhaps the first such attempt occurred in 1974 at the Fifth Annual Meeting of the Environmental Design Research Association (EDRA 5). The proceedings of the Milwaukee meeting summarized the work of a small but growing group of social scientists engaged in research on the social consequences of nuclear power plants, water resource projects, strip mining, and urban highways (Wolf, 1974). The following year saw the publication of a special issue of *Environment and Behavior* devoted entirely to "the expanding universe of scholarly research and professional practice being directed to the human consequences of environmental modification" (Wolf, 1975: 260). Moreover, a May 1975 workshop held in conjunction with EDRA 6 in Lawrence, Kansas, culminated in the completion of the first partial inventory of methodologies for social impact assessment (Finsterbusch and Wolf, 1977). Since then, of course, the literature on social impact assessment has greatly expanded — in scope, direction, and sophistication. Among the recent books that address social impact assessment methodology are those of Leistritz and Murdock (1981), Tester and Mykes (1981), Soderstrom (1981), and Finsterbusch and Wolf (1981; an updated verson of their 1977 publication).

This book is an attempt to go beyond previous works on methodology — to inventory systematically a broad spectrum of techniques and methods with proven utility. While it would be foolish in the extreme to claim that any book captures the full range of methodologies currently in vogue, this volume does provide an overview and, where appropriate, a critique of major techniques and procedures by researchers who have used them in a variety of settings. Thus we believe that this book will be useful to a diverse audience: first, to members of the academic community, teachers and students alike, interested in the latest research methods in SIA; second, to practitioners whose work as consultants to government and industry necessitates complete familiarity with the state of the art in collecting and analyzing data for inclusion in environmental impact assessments; third, to public officials whose responsibilities include oversight and compliance with NEPA and other environmental regulations; and, fourth, to concerned citizens whose lives may be changed permanently because of their proximity to a flood control project, a new highway, a nuclear power plant, or the like.

The chapters in this volume constitute four major sections: Frameworks and Methodological Approaches, Primary Data Collection Methods, Secondary Data Collection Methods, and Special Methodologies. Included in Part I — Frameworks and Methodological Approaches — is a revised version of Wolf's paradigm for social impact assessment based on more than a decade of research. Wolf discusses each step in the assessment, beginning with the concept of "scoping," and ending with the "management" phase, particularly the determination of oversight responsibilities for mitigation and monitoring. Rather than stating unequivocally what must be done, this chapter outlines a series of tasks that should be completed, but with the proviso that the selection of techniques must be tailored to the special circumstances of particular impact situations. Michael Carley, in the first of two contributed chapters, describes and critiques an array of comprehensive methodologies, many of which involve integrated socioeconomic and environmental approaches. Carley concludes by criticizing the lack of ex post investigations of impact assessments — their predictive validity, structure, and accuracy. Cynthia Flynn and her colleagues provide an in-depth discussion of the mechanics of the Group Ecology Model (GEM) for assessing economic and social change, including public response. The GEM approach has been applied successfully in a variety of settings and has proved to be quite useful in the development of monitoring and mitigation strategies.

Two chapters make up Part II, which is devoted to primary data collection methods. Kurt Finsterbusch leads off with a thorough analysis of survey research, which he maintains has been "underutilized" in SIA for the wrong reasons. This chapter describes how surveys could and should be used most effectively, and then briefly summarizes the major procedural steps in the design, construction, and administration of this valuable tool. Finsterbusch offers guidance to the virgin surveyor, describing many of the pitfalls associated with the technique and where to go to get expert advice. If one accepts Finsterbusch's assertion that surveys are underutilized, then it would be safe to say that the subject of the next chapter — classical ethnography — is virtually unknown in SIA, except perhaps in the context of cross-cultural research. Roy Roper makes a strong case for ethnography, providing a poignant example of its use in assessing long-term family impacts of land acquisition and relocation associated with the Shelbyville (Illinois) Reservoir project. The chapter concludes with a discussion of new analytic methods available to ethnographic researchers.[1]

Part III, devoted to secondary data collection methods, begins with a chapter on yet another infrequently used tool: historical documents. Annabelle Motz feels that such documents provide much-needed information on the setting in which a policy is to be implemented, and the fate of similar policies in other communities. Following a description of various historical documents, Motz illustrates their use in ex post facto impact studies of small communities in Appalachia and in the Arkansas River Valley. Thomas Dietz and C. Mark Dunning follow with a chapter on the assessment of demographic changes associated with development projects. After reviewing recent research on the prediction of demographic changes in impact communities, the authors outline the demographic impact assessment process, focusing on issues important to practitioners. The strengths and weaknesses of computer models that perform demographic impact assessments are reviewed in the final portion of the chapter. In the final chapter in Part III, Michael Carley reflects on the evolution of social indicator research and its relevance to SIA. He first defines social indicators and then discusses the issue of the relationship between objective indicators and subjective responses. Carley later tackles the problem of value weighting from the standpoint of incorporating the preferences of both politicians and concerned citizens, and concludes his presentation with some lessons for SIA.

The final section of the volume is devoted to special methodologies, and includes six chapters covering a broad range of techniques:

• Steve Murdock and Larry Leistritz provide an extensive review of socioeconomic assessment models, specifically: (1) criteria for evaluating models, (2) capabilities and limitations of 13 models now being used in socioeconomic assessment, and (3) factors that should be considered in the development or adaptation of models.

• Rabel Burdge presents a comprehensive review of community needs assessment. His chapter covers such topics as understanding the concept of needs assessment, data collection techniques, interpretation of information, integration of needs assessment information in SIA and related planning activities, and development of a needs assessment report.

● John Lounsbury, Kent Van Liere, and Gregory Meissen argue forcefully for the inclusion of psychosocial assessment in studies of potential social impacts. The focus of their chapter is on attitudes, beliefs, values, intentions, and behavioral responses; a concluding segment underscores some important methodological considerations related to research design, measurement, and analytic techniques.

● Jeryl Mumpower and Barry Anderson provide an in-depth treatment of errors in human judgment: where such errors occur and why, and corrective measures that should be applied in projecting and evaluating impacts. They feel strongly that failure to correct judgmental errors may lead to serious defects in SIAs.

● James Palmer begins his chapter with a compelling rationale for including aesthetic values in the impact assessment process, then reviews current methods used to measure visual quality. How such methods are used to assess visual impacts, incorporating professional appraisals, predictive models and public evaluations, concludes the presentation.

● Kurt Finsterbusch concludes this section, and the book, first with a discussion of the ethical principles that should guide the policy decisions made by public officials, and finally with a review of 19 methods for arriving at policy decisions when multiple criteria are at issue.

As this volume goes to press, indications are that social impact assessment may be fast approaching a critical juncture. Many of the guidelines and regulations designed to broaden the scope of environmental assessments (such as the issuance of Executive Orders calling for community impact statements and assessments of economic and other effects of projects in foreign countries) have been rescinded or reversed. There is also a great deal of uncertainty about the future consequences of a Supreme Court decision (Metropolitan Edison Co. v. People Against Nuclear Energy) that, in effect, places psychological impacts outside the purview of NEPA. At issue also are various social and other effects that cannot be attributed directly to, or linked with, environmental impacts. Will such factors as "involuntary displacement and relocation" and physical barriers that suddenly bisect communities no longer have to be considered in environmental impact assessments? Opinions vary among experts; however, it can be expected that many agencies will take the path of least resistance, something that surely will result in yet another round of court interpretations.

Despite these problems, some encouraging signs also are present. For example, requirements for social impact assessments are now embodied in other policy guidelines and procedural memoranda governing agency decisions. Moreover, agencies must also contend with better informed and more politically active publics than was true when SIA was in its infancy. It follows that SIA practitioners should make every effort to ensure that high standards of objectivity, scientific rigor, and methodological design are maintained throughout the impact assessment process. Without those ingredients, we have no credibility. To this end the editors hope that the present volume contributes in some small way to maintaining that credibility and our stature as professionals.

Note

1. Readers interested in unconventional methods of impact assessment may also wish to consult Szalay (1982), who describes his work with Associative Group Analysis.

References

FINSTERBUSCH, K. and C. P. WOLF [eds.] (1981) Methodology of Social Impact Assessment (rev. ed.). Stroudsburg, PA: Hutchinson Ross.
——— [eds.] (1977) Methodology of Social Impact Assessment. Stroudsburg, PA: Hutchinson Ross.
LEISTRITZ, F. L. and S. MURDOCK (1981) The Socioeconomic Impact of Resource Development: Methods for Assessment. New York: Westview.
SODERSTROM, E. J. (1981) Social Impact Assessment: Experimental Methods and Approaches. New York: Praeger.
SZALAY, L. (1982) "Surveying public images/opinions by associative group analysis," in L. G. Llewellyn et al. (eds.) Social Impact Assessment: A Sourcebook for Highway Planners, Vol. 5. Washington, DC: Federal Highway Administration.
TESTER, F. J. and W. MYKES [eds.] (1981) Social Impact Assessment: Theory, Method and Practice. Alberta, Canada: Detselig.
WOLF, C. P. [ed.] (1975) Social Impact Assessment. Environment and Behavior 7 (September): special issue.
——— [ed.] (1974) Social Impact Assessment. Milwaukee: Environmental Design Research Association.

I
FRAMEWORKS
AND
METHODOLOGICAL
APPROACHES

• • • • • • • • • • • • • •

1

Social Impact Assessment: A Methodological Overview

O O O O O O O O O O O O O O O O O

C. P. WOLF

O O O O O O O O O O O O O O O O O

● While environmental impact assessment has focused mainly on the physical and biological properties of natural environments, social impact assessment (SIA) is concentrated on the distinctively human side of human environments. SIA is about "people impacts" — what we are doing to folks (or failing to do for them) where they live, in families and communities, as a consequence of formulating policies, instituting programs, and building projects. Its aim is to predict and evaluate those impacts before they happen. Unlike the more familiar "evaluation research," which gauges the effectiveness of policies, programs, and projects already in operation, the task for SIA is *anticipatory* research. It seeks to place the expectation and attainment of desired outcomes on a more rational and reliable basis.

The analytic problem of SIA can be modestly stated as learning to make public (and private) decisions that will look good in fifty years, after the evaluative criteria by which they are judged have changed. This "need to know" has arisen because of the unwanted and untoward impacts (side effects and spillovers) of planning approaches that looked promising at the time but did not turn out so well — combined storm and sanitary sewers, the bulldozer approach to urban renewal, and so on.

The "bottom line" question for SIA is "Who benefits and who loses?" (if a proposed action were to be implemented). Since often those who win and those who lose are not the same people, the dissociation of costs (or risks) and benefits creates a problem of equity. Just what the incidence and distribution of social costs and benefits may be in any particular impact situation is a matter for assessment. Getting costs and benefits together, so that those who reap the benefits also bear the costs, is a matter of social justice and social policy.

The goal of SIA is not really different from that of social science traditionally: to understand the causes, conditions, and consequences of social life. As such, it can be argued that SIA is "what we have always done" as social scientists. There are social impacts of ordinary social life and social change, such as of large-scale shifts in demographic structure (rural depopulation, for example). While the content of social knowledge may not differ — and SIA draws freely on all social science disciplines — the occasions and conditions for its application are distinctive. SIA is usually invoked in cases of purposive or planned social intervention, to provide "use knowledge" for impact mitigation and management.

What one *does* in SIA is assess the social impacts. If this seems to belabor the obvious, it must be said that *how* assessments are done varies widely. SIA is a multimethod approach, and its analytic tasks (see Figure 1.1) require assessors to draw selectively from the full range of social research methodologies and techniques. Moreover, each impact situation has unique features, and general methodologies must be tailored to its dimensions. While no one best way has been (or can be) devised to fit all circumstances and cases, there is growing professional consensus and methodological convergence on what may be described as the "main pattern" of assessment steps (Figure 1.1). Essentially this is a "rational problem-solving" schema closely resembling many others in technology assessment, decision analysis, and related fields.

Instrumenting and implementing this series also requires the meshing of analytic and institutional systems. For example, public involvement enters the series at every step in various ways, decisively at some points (for example, impact evaluation). Refining this pattern to a high level of detail and testing it against diverse case experience will be the work of many practitioners over many years. In what follows here, I will briefly sketch the rationale for this series in general methodological terms, indicating some methodologies and techniques that can be usefully employed and illustrating their application by reference to some representative studies.

Assessment Steps	Analytic Operations
Scoping How big a problem is it? How much is enough?	Set level(s) of assessment (policy/program/project). Determine impact area boundaries. Establish time horizons. Develop study design.
Problem Identification What is the problem? What is causing it?	Formulate policy goals, planning objectives. Identify publics and concerns. Perform needs assessment. Determine evaluative criteria.
Formulation of Alternatives What are the alternatives?	Define set of "reasonable" alternatives (corresponding to identified concerns). Determine change agents, instruments. Characterize and describe technical systems; analyze for social (institutional/behavioral) components and correlates. Analyze economic and environmental impacts for secondary social impacts.
Profiling Who is being affected?	Dimensionalize impact categories. Select impact categories. Assign impact indicators. Perform indicator measurements. Compile social profile.
Projection What is it causing?	Explicate "state of society" assumptions. Perform trend impact analysis. Construct dynamic system models. Estimate impact indicator values for alternative plans ("with and without" implementation).
Assessment What difference does it make?	Perform sensitivity analysis for alternative outcomes of alternative plans. Perform cross-impact analysis. Describe and display "significant" impacts.
Evaluation How do you like it?	Reidentify publics and concerns. Reformulate evaluative criteria. Rank and weight preferences for alternatives. Perform trade-off analysis. Identify preferred alternative.
Mitigation What can you do about it? if you do not like it?	Review unavoidable adverse impacts. Identify possible mitigation measures. Perform sensitivity analysis of possible measures.

Figure 1.1 Social Impact Assessment: The Main Pattern

Assessment Steps	Analytic Operations
Monitoring How good are your guesses?	Measure actual versus predicted impacts. Provide feedback of measurements to policy-makers and publics.
Management Who is in charge here?	Devise management plan. Adjust planning objectives, operating procedures, design specifications.
(Bottom Line) Who benefits and who loses?	(All of the above.)

Now, associate and integrate general methodologies, specific techniques, and relevant data.

Figure 1.1   Continued

Scoping

The leading questions here are "How big a problem is it?" and "How much is enough?" In general, the size of the study should reflect the magnitude of the problem, and that cannot be known in advance. The correct scope of assessment cannot be finally decided until after its completion — too late, for most immediate purposes. Although how big a problem it is cannot be predetermined, some of its major proportions and dimensions must be estimated in order to get on with the assessment work. This initial closure must remain provisional and flexible, however, to allow for the learning that is bound to occur if the study is competently done.

In practice, this flexibility is difficult to maintain; deadlines are set and budgets are fixed before the answers are in. These constraints on study resources provide very practical answers to how much is "enough".

Set Level(s) of Assessment (Policy/Program/Project)

The level of assessment is generally determined by the nature of the problem under study. In the case of a development project — a highway, for instance — this would normally dictate that program- and policy-level impacts receive little if any attention.

Determine Impact Area Boundaries

There are two main kinds of impact area boundaries for projects: on-site and off-site. Boundaries should be chosen to enclose the area likely to receive the greatest project impact, although secondary impacts and areas should not be ignored. While usually this will be adjacent to the project site, this is not always the case. For example, the site-specific impacts of the Liard River Hydroelectric Project in northeast British Columbia will probably be far less significant than those 1200 miles downstream, in the Mackenzie Delta. Similarly, project benefits in the form of electric power will be transmitted 1000 miles to the southwest, to the Vancouver region. In this case the impact area extends 2400 miles along river and transmission line corridors, and different types of impacts will occur at different points along this route.

Establish Time Horizons

Temporal as well as spatial considerations enter into impact area delineation. The question here is not *where* an impact is, but *when*. Although prompt impacts may command greatest attention, in cases such as Three Mile Island the delayed (postaccident) impacts were far more potent (Flynn, 1981). If the expected lifetime of a project is used as a convenient time line, special attention should be paid to the "back end," as in nuclear reactor decommissioning and radioactive waste storage. In most boomtown studies, the "bust" side of the boom-bust cycle has been neglected.

Develop Study Design

The problem at this point is to structure the impact study in such a way as to capture the major impacts with the greatest economy of resources. There is now a wide assortment of approaches, frameworks, paradigms, and models for conducting impact studies. The main pattern of assessment steps presented here embodies a systems approach, cutting across and combining institutional systems (such as government agencies), sociotechnical systems (such as building technologies), and social systems (such as communities). Tracing out the consequences of a planned intervention means viewing them in mutual relation.

Problem Identification

What the "problem" is may be a foregone conclusion from a particular standpoint; the task at hand is to open it to question. Upon examination, the "problem" turns out to be a good deal more complicated, and its identification can vary depending upon who does the defining. For example, before the 1973 OPEC embargo, there was only one solution to the problem of energy interruption or shortfall: Increase supply. Since then another possibility has emerged: Decrease demand. Correspondingly, the "energy problem" may be reidentified, from underproduction to overconsumption; alternatives for its solution are likewise altered, for instance, to conservation measures.

Another example is the case of local flooding I encountered in 1970 around Athens, Ohio (Wolf, 1977). One way of stating the problem — the one used by Ohio University and the U.S. Army Corps of Engineers — was "to keep the water away from the people," which was accomplished through the structural (physical) alternative of channelization. Another way of stating the problem — my way — was "to keep the people away from the water," in which case the appropriate (nonstructural) measure would have been a system of floodplain management.

Formulate Policy Goals, Planning Objectives

What are we "solving for" in SIA? A situation, such as a flood hazard, may be viewed as problematic; its removal then becomes the solution. Conversely, the proposed solution may itself appear to pose a problem — as in the Athens case — from the standpoint of habitat destruction and human occupancy. Proposals originate in stated policy goals and planning objectives; these are official definitions of the problem situations and of solutions addressed to them, embodied in legislation such as the National Environment Policy Act of 1969 (NEPA) and the mission statements of agencies such as the U.S. Army Corps of Engineers. In addition, there are the interests of private proponents, whether of superport development in Palau or of housing estates in Podunk. Finally, there are the assessed needs of local publics. Documenting these statements of purpose and their elaboration in programs establishes the ends in relation to which proposals stand as instrumental means.

Identify Publics and Concerns

A wide array of parties and interests are present in any typical impact situation. They provide alternative views of identified problems and proposed solutions, and of evaluative criteria by which to judge them. How the various publics and positions are represented and considered depends on the institutional arrangements for reaching and reviewing decisions. From this participation we can discern some relevant impact categories and potentially affected publics that an impact study must consider. In the Beaufort Sea Hydrocarbons Development case, for instance, public hearing transcripts recorded the various concerns voiced by participants. These were compiled into an "issues list" from which guidelines or "terms of reference" for the impact study were drawn. Identifying publics and their concerns can thus serve as a basis for scoping impact studies (Preister and Kent, 1981). Not all publics and concerns are immediately and systematically recognizable, however, even by the parties themselves.

Perform Needs Assessment

In needs assessment, the interest of the clientele of a public agency or of the community at large provides the starting point. Statutory requirements may dictate that community interests play a part in identifying problems and the formulation of alternatives for their solution. For example, the Community Development Block Grant Program of the U.S. Department of Housing and Urban Development prescribes that funds be allocated to projects designed to serve residents in greatest need. Local citizen groups and planning agencies may have already set these priorities, but in most instances some original data collection, through the use of attitude surveys or some other method, will be required.

Determine Evaluative Criteria

From the preceding we can derive evaluative criteria for judging the consequences of carrying out (or failing to carry out) a course of action, and of calculating the social impacts — benefits and costs — of conditions staying the way they are or changing. These criteria are employed later, in the evaluation step. They represent the different value judgments of the various parties at interest as to the detrimental and beneficial consequences of a planned intervention. These criteria can be expected to change over time, as the emphasis on equity concerns has changed, for example (Lampman, 1974). The prediction of value change is part of the projection step.

Formulation of Alternatives

By definition, rational solutions are relative to problem definitions. The various ways of identifying problems generate a correspondingly wide range of planning alternatives. These may include alternative routes and sites, alternative technologies and project designs, and alternative rates of development (such as construction work force buildup) and uses for a fixed resource such as land.

Define Set of "Reasonable" Alternatives

As the saying, "If it isn't broken, don't fix it" illustrates, the simplest choice of alternatives would be to exercise the "do nothing" or "no build" option. Indeed, there are situations such as beach erosion in which inaction appears to be the most prudent course of action. Proposals are formulated and impact studies are initiated, however, because "doing nothing" seems unreasonable. Even so, it is worthwhile to weigh the expected benefits of a proposal against its projected costs. The "reasonableness" criterion is introduced to limit the range of conceivable alternatives to realistic proportions. One "rule of reasonableness" advanced by the U.S. Department of Housing and Urban Development (1975) was that "alternatives need not extend beyond those which serve the same general purpose of the project being considered."

> For example, if the purpose of the project is to provide housing to a community, then alternatives which provide something other than housing need not be treated. . . . In other words, for projects whose purpose is associated with a specific land use (e.g. housing/residential land use), other land uses (e.g. industrial, open space) need not be considered as "alternatives."

The question naturally arises whether the intended purpose of the project is the one best calculated to meet community "needs."

Determine Change Agents, Instruments

If an alternative is to be implemented, someone must do it, using some available or potential means. Besides resources and equipment, energy development requires some agencies or companies and capital investment, among other things. Which ones, and what their managerial, technical, and financial capabilities, are matters for institutional analysis. If the capability does not currently exist, further impacts may be incurred in the process of creating it. Just as the "receiving" communities are characterized in the profiling step to follow, the proponents should be analyzed in the present one — drawing corporate profiles for sponsors of private development proposals, for example (Michalenko, 1981).

Characterize and Describe Technical Systems; Analyze for Social Components and Correlatives

Although exact specifications of a technology-based proposal may not be known until late in the design phase, after an approval process has been completed, its salient features can usually be discerned in sufficient detail for general assessment. These can then be composed into a "project profile."

Analyze Economic and Environmental Impacts for Secondary Social Impacts

Other categories of impact besides social — notably economic and environmental — generally accompany physical planning projects. These have potential indirect or "secondary" social impacts that should be assessed and that in any case require a social interpretation — employment, for instance. Detailed planning information of this kind may not become available until later in the impact study, but it should be sought out as early as possible, at least in broad outline. The interaction among impact categories is also a consideration in regard to cross-impact and trade-off analysis.

Profiling

Having now gained some impression of what it is that is potentially having an impact, we turn to the question of what it may have an impact on. This is compiled and presented in the form of a social profile at some appropriate scale(s), most often the community, but also, on occasion, the family or region. The question we are asking here is: How much of what kind of impacts on whom? The answer must begin with a baseline measure of the system before proposal-related impacts have occurred. The procedure for profiling is fairly straightforward: First we establish some dimensions and categories of social impact, then we perform some appropriate measures of their current values among various segments of the population.

Dimension Impact Categories

Before deciding what content categories of social impact to examine, it is useful to inquire about the kinds of change that may occur in them. These are impact dimensions such as incidence, distribution, timing, and magnitude of potential impacts.

Select Impact Categories

One way to proceed is to list all conceivable impacts that may impinge on people and then to cluster them according to common properties: health and safety, legal, and so on (Liebermeister, 1978). The resulting typology will provide broad coverage across most institutional areas — family, economy, polity, education, religion, and so on. Identification of functional groups in these areas is a means of tracing organizational and cultural impacts as well (Finsterbusch, 1981). In certain instances the social impact categories of primary interest are mandated by law or regulation. For example, the U.S. Water Resources Council's "social well-being account" (Andrews, 1981) includes: life, health, and safety; emergency preparedness; demographic characteristics; community organization; income, educational, cultural, and recreational opportunities; noise; and aesthetic value. Impacts of greatest interest to local decision makers tend to be in the categories of community services and facilities (sanitation, schools, recreation, fire and police protection, and the like) and fiscal and land use impacts.

Assign Impact Indicators

Once impact categories have been selected, the next task is to assign measures to their salient features. Social indicators research affords many alternatives for measuring an impact category, and indicator selection may be based on the availability, quality, and cost of impact data. Where direct measures are unavailable, "proxy" measures can be used, for example, "community cohesion" as a function of the percentage of homeowners versus renters.

Perform Indicator Measurements

A method of "triangulation" is recommended for measuring impact categories, drawing on attitudinal, observational, and statistical data. The first of these is gathered by interviewing or survey techniques and yields "subjective" measures such as perceptions of community satisfaction and expectations about project impacts. Observational (or behavioral) data provide a reliability check on the consistency of attitudes and actions, for example, whether reported "fear of crime" is followed by the curtailment of social activities. Statistical data, such as census materials, furnish an aggregate baseline for normalizing or contrasting individual and group measures. It is also desirable to obtain time-series data, since the existing state of the system cannot be interpreted without insight into its recent history.

Compile Social Profile

A matrix approach is convenient for summarizing data gathered in the profiling step. In one format (Finsterbusch and Weitzel-O'Neill, 1974) the matrix rows are "quality of life" indicators, such as job satisfaction and pollution exposure, and the columns are "population segments" in various categories — socioeconomic status, racial and ethnic composition, sex, age, place of residence, and so on. Cell entries are the anticipated impacts of a proposal for each indicator and population segment identified. While future states of the system (after impact) are projected in the next step, current values (before impact) can be depicted in the same fashion. The baseline condition is established to separate "normal change" within the population and community from that specific to the proposal; this is the "with and without" (proposal) distinction. The matrix is also useful as a scanning device for detecting the possibly most significant impacts of a proposal, and for diverting study efforts to their closer examination.

Projection

The projection step focuses on the kind and quantity of change in profile features that would occur were one or another planning alternatives to be implemented. This induced change must be estimated against a background of "normal change," or the "without" condition mentioned above. One way of controlling for this is to perform the mental experiment of asking what the social system would be like in the absence of the proposal's implementa-tion. Social systems are dynamic, naturally, and the "without" condition is not one of "no change" or even linear extrapolation.

Explicate "State of Society" Assumptions

"State of society" assumptions are predictions about general trends believed to influence social conditions over the period considered by the study. They must be taken into account in the estimation of changes in the social profile that would occur regardless of the proposal. Such trends as urbanization are usually presented in a highly aggregated form. Because many social impacts are site specific, these general trends must be disaggregated in order to make contact with local conditions (Leistritz et al., 1979). Adding to the uncertainty of these forecasts are trend discontinuities, such as the recent turnaround in migration from rural to urban areas. To allow for these deviations in trend lines, a range of alternative futures or "scenarios" can be postulated, as in the various population projection series computed by the Bureau of the Census. In such cases, the predictive question is what profile changes would result were one or another of these levels to be attained.

Perform Trend Impact Analysis

"Normal change" can interact with proposal-induced change in ways that either intensify or moderate social impacts. Hence the task for trend impact analysis is to estimate the influence of general on local conditions not only "without" the proposal being implemented, but also "with" the proposal. For example, a reservoir development may be proposed in order to meet the future water supply requirements of a growing population. Reservoir development itself may then induct further population growth attracted by recreation opportunities, environmental amenities, or water-using industries. Situations of this kind are sometimes referred to as "self-fulfilling prophesies" — efforts to meet future needs themselves become the stimulus to increased demand (Hollis and McEvoy, 1973).

Another form of trend impact analysis is normative forecasting, in which the planning problem is not merely to provide for anticipated requirements but to realize some vision of a desirable future. For instance, the California Tomorrow Plan (Heller, 1971) describes two future states of the state, California 1 and California 2. The former is the most probable future, given the continuation of existing trends; the latter is a desirable future in which adverse trends, such as land conversion from agricultural to residential use, are abated or eliminated. The problem then is to deflect the trajectory of future development from California 1 to California 2.

Construct Dynamic System Models

To determine future states of the system we must not only project social trends; we must also gain an understanding of the system dynamics that generate them and analyze their principal components.

Estimate Impact Indicator Values
for Alternative Plans
("With and Without" Implementation)

The projection step is completed when the baseline social profile is estimated for the range of trend assumptions and systematically varied with the predicted impacts for each planning alternative.

Assessment

The task for assessment is to compare the potential impacts of the full set of reasonable alternatives under the range of assumptions about future conditions. This is done by predicting differential changes in the current values of impact indicators under alternative trend and plan assumptions, including second-order differentials (changes in the rate of change) caused by cross- and cumulative impacts.

Perform Sensitivity Analysis
for Alternative Outcomes
of Alternative Plans

Covariation is the basic notion in sensitivity analysis, a technique well developed in economics. How much of Y "goes with" a given amount of X, and what change in Y would occur with a certain change in X? As in projection, even if we cannot know the value of X with certainty, we can assume a range of values X might take and then look for systematic variation in Y at different points within that range.

Perform Cross-Impact Analysis

"Cross-impact analysis strives to identify interactions among events or developments by specifying how one event will influence the likelihood, timing, and mode of impact on another event in a different but associated field." We are typically dealing with mutual causal relations in long chains, where one impact can amplify or dampen the effects of others. Second- and higher-order impacts come into consideration here, as do the compound effects, or "synergisms," of cummulative impacts (Danjani and Ortolano, 1979; Grigsby, 1981; Husky, 1979).

Describe and Display "Significant" Impacts

We are now in a position to submit the assessed impacts of alternative plans for evaluation by the various parties at interest. While there are political reasons that assessment results are often poorly utilized, their prospects are not improved by the use of presentational techniques unintelligible to either decision makers or publics. For purposes of public communication, the product is only as good as its packaging. Qualitative analysis of quantitative data is essential. Tables must be converted into more legible charts. A wide variety of display techniques is available in social graphics (Feinberg and Franklin, 1976).

Evaluation

The distinction between "assessment" and "evaluation" is roughly equivalent to that between fact and value, except that the facts in question are "future facts" that have no empirical existence in the present. Whereas in assessment the task is to estimate the possibility of alternative futures, in evaluation their desirability is the issue. Since assessors have no unique privilege in this regard, their role in evaluation is mainly that of facilitators.

Reidentify Publics and Concerns

Over the course of the study new interests and interest groups may have emerged and some old ones may have been missed. Although the series of assessment steps has been presented in linear fashion, in practice there is — and ought to be — a good deal of interplay among them.

Reformulate Evaluative Criteria

Reformulate evaluative criteria in terms of assessment data gathered throughout the study.

Rank and Weight Preferences for Alternatives

Ideally, preferences would be expressed on a single dimension in equivalent units. The analytic situation we face in evaluating alternatives, however, is that of "comparing incommensurables" — apples and rabbits. Hence it is necessary to resort to some ranking and weighting schemes to evaluate different alternatives for different publics. Among the candidate metrics for weighting are the numbers of people potentially affected and the predicted magnitude of impact. Various such schemes are reviewed in a later chapter.

Perform Trade-Off Analysis

To reach this stage there must be at least tentative agreement on the evaluative criteria to be employed and the relative merit of planning alternatives ranked according to them. Techniques of trade-off analysis can be used to clarify the subjective preferences of the parties at interest. The question then is how these respective positions can be unified to produce a single "preferred" alternative. In arriving at this judgment, many concerns not explicitly addressed in the study will enter into consideration, such as the institutional decision rules that govern final selection.

Identify Preferred Alternative

The result of trade-off analysis is the designation of one plan as the "preferred" alternative. Preference ideally would be given to the plan containing the most favorable net balance of beneficial to adverse impacts; no alternative, however preferable, is likely to be free of disadvantages. How preferable the preferred alternative is, therefore, depends also on the availability of mitigation measures for avoiding or alleviating these adverse impacts.

Mitigation

Although the effects of a project should be largely positive, negative impacts of the approved proposal must be accounted for as well. In the past these were simply imposed as the price of what passed for "progress." Now it is understood that just compensation is due those who bear these social costs without sharing equitably in the benefits.

Review Unavoidable Adverse Impacts

The negative impacts of the preferred alternative should have been identified in the evaluation step. Now they must be considered from the standpoint of mitigation. (Modifications to the plan will have taken care of the avoidable ones.)

Identify Possible Mitigation Measures

Appropriate mitigation measures are naturally relative to the nature and extent of the negative impacts. In the case of habitat destruction, for example, the U.S. Fish and Wildlife Service requires that mitigation lands be acquired. Potentially affected communities may also seize upon mitigation provisions as an opportunity for realizing goals unrelated to the specific nature of the proposal. There is no particular reason that mitigation should be in kind, however; impact funds have frequently been allocated to highway construction and other capital improvements, for instance (Moore et al., 1978).

Perform Sensitivity Analysis of Possible Measures

The uncertainty inherent in mitigation suggests the advisability of testing across a range of assumed values. The difference is that here we are trying to anticipate the potential effectiveness of mitigation measures. Of course, the real test can only come after the fact.

Monitoring

The purpose of monitoring is to compare expected against actual impacts; it provides the "after" measure in before-after designs. "Postaudit" studies contribute to this, but often too long after the fact for use in impact mitigation and management.

Measure Actual Versus Predicted Impacts

To ensure comparability of measures in comparing anticipated with actual impacts, the same indicators selected in profiling and then projected should be used as the basis for monitoring. Ideally, the same population would also be sampled, although where population displacement has occurred, such as in reservoir development, it is sometimes impossible to locate the movers.

Provide Feedback of Measurements to Policymakers and Publics

Having determined the correspondence of actual and predicted impacts, these results should be reported to both responsible officials and affected publics. Policymakers can use these to guide any policy adjustments that appear warranted and to improve future program and project designs.

Publics may want to reevaluate their preferences on the basis of these results; this may prove influential in considering future expansion of a completed project, for instance. An excellent example of a community-based monitoring system was the Impact Information Center (now the Community Information Center) in Fairbanks, Alaska, established to monitor local impacts of construction and operation of the Trans Alaska Oil Pipeline. Experience gained from that effort can now be applied to proposals for a parallel gas pipeline.

Management

SIA is not conducted for its own sake, but for its utility in conceiving and conducting socially sound development planning. Assessment results are what managers have to manage. Impact management can be viewed from the perspective of impact- versus project-based assessment. The latter is the more usual; projects are proposed and then their impacts are assessed and mitigated. An equal and opposite view is to take social impacts as the starting point — a social goal orientation — and ensure that project development takes place in conformance with those social criteria. If a high rate of construction work force buildup is expected to have destabilizing community impacts, for instance, it is possible to reduce that rate below what is assumed to be optimum from the standpoint of project management.

Devise Management Plan

An impact management plan should establish oversight responsibility for the "back end" of the assessment cycle — mitigation and monitoring. Since a shift in the locus of control typically occurs between the construction and operation phases of project development, determination of responsibility and capability are often not simple matters. An institutional needs assessment may be useful in determining resource requirements and sources.

Adjust Planning Objectives, Operating Procedures, Design Specifications

The utilization of SIA in policy formation, program development, and project implementation is its ultimate justification. Based on hindsight, policy adjustment, program redirection, and project modification may now appear possible and desirable courses of action.

A Final Word

Not all the steps and tasks outlined above will prove necessary in every assessment. What I have tried to present is a methodologically complete series as a guide. This schema is still undergoing revision and elaboration, although the underlying logic seems about right. By concentrating more on the "why" than on the "how" questions, I hope to have laid a firmer basis for the enlightened use of assessment techniques. Stated in the general terms used here, the discussion is still one removed from the specification of an operational methodology. It remains for assessors now to "associate and integrate general methodologies, specific techniques, and relevant data" adapted to the special circumstances of particular impact situations. This chapter may serve as a point of departure toward that end.

References

ANDREWS, W. (1981) Evaluating Social Effects in Water Resources Planning: First Steps. Washington, DC: U.S. Water Resources Council.

DANJANI, S. and L. ORTOLANO [eds.] (1979) Methods of Forecasting the Reciprocal Impacts of Infrastructure Development and Land-Use. Report IPM-11. Stanford, CA: Department of Engineering, Stanford University.

FEINBERG, B. M. and C. A. FRANKLIN [eds.] (1976) Social Graphics Bibliography. Washington, DC: Bureau of Social Science Research.

FINSTERBUSCH, K. (1981) "The potential role of social impact assessments in instituting public policies," pp. 2-12 in K. Finsterbusch and C. P. Wolf (eds.) Methodology of Social Impact Assessment. Stroudsburg, PA: Hutchinson Ross.

———— and P. A. WEITZEL-O'NEILL (1974) A Methodology for the Analysis of Social Impacts. Vienna, VA: Braddock, Dunn & McDonald.

FLYNN, C. R. (1981) "Impact discontinuity: the case of Three Mile Island." Presented at the 76th Annual Meeting of the American Sociological Association, Toronto, August 24.

GRIGSBY, J. E. III (1981) "Cumulative impact assessment: a case study of the aggregate effects of diversified federal projects on Santa Barbara County, California." Presented at the 76th Annual Meeting of the American Sociological Association, Toronto, August 24.

HELLER, A. [ed.] (1971) The California Tomorrow Plan. Los Altos, CA: William Kaufmann.

HOLLIS, J. and J. McEVOY III (1973) "Demographic effects of water development." Impact of Water Resources Development 1 (July): 24-40.

HUSKY, L. (1979) Analysis of Cumulative Impacts, Western Gulf of Alaska Impact Analysis. Anchorage: Institute of Social and Economic Research, University of Alaska.

LAMPMAN, R. J. (1974) "What does it do for the poor? — A new test for national policy." Public Interest 34 (Winter): 66-82.

LEISTRITZ, F. L. et al. (1979) "A model for projecting localized economic, demographic, and fiscal impacts of large-scale projects." Western Journal of Agricultural Economics 4: 1-16.

LIEBERMEISTER, U. (1978) "Universal checklists in the concept of 'impact trees,' " pp. 133-158 in D. F. Burkhardt and W. H. Ittelson (eds.) Environmental Assessment of Socioeconomic Systems. New York: Plenum.

MICHALENKO, G. (1981) "The social assessment of corporations," pp. 168-179 in F. J. Tester and W. Mykes (eds.) Social Impact Assessment: Theory, Method and Practice. Calgary, Alberta: Detselig.

MOORE, K. D. et al. (1978) Mitigating Adverse Socioeconomic Impacts of Energy Development. Washington, DC: U.S. Department of Energy.

PREISTER, K. and J. KENT (1981) "The issue-centered approach to social impacts: from assessment to management." Social Impact Assessment 71/72 (November-December).

U.S. Department of Housing and Urban Development, Office of Environmental Quality (1975) Environmental Reviews at the Community Level: A Program Guide. Washington, DC: Office for Community Planning and Development.

WOLF, C. P. (1977) "They are filling in the river! Ecology action in Athens, Ohio," pp. 407-433 in A. B. Shostak (ed.) Our Sociological Eye: Personal Essays on Society and Culture. Port Washington, NY: Alfred.

2

A Review of Selected Methods

○ ○ ○ ○ ○ ○ ○ ○ ○ ○ ○ ○ ○ ○ ○ ○ ○ ○

MICHAEL J. CARLEY

○ ○ ○ ○ ○ ○ ○ ○ ○ ○ ○ ○ ○ ○ ○ ○ ○

● Some people argue that socioeconomic impact assessment is basically about political change. Such assessments, for example, "involve political, social, and ethical issues, not the issue of efficient resource allocation" (Ophuls, 1977). Or, "insofar as social scientists concur in a systematic approach to impact assessment, they tend to sublimate the underlying political conflicts inherent in selective availability of public data, and too often falsely reinforce the technical over the political dimensions" (Schnaiberg and Meidinger, 1978). This latter quote, by the way, gives us a good short definition of what we mean here by "SIA methodology," that is, "a systematic approach." These authors' warning about obscuring political conflict is important, but they may be throwing the baby out with the bathwater when they dismiss systematic approaches to SIA. The opposite of "systematic" is "unsystematic," and that hardly sounds like a reasonable approach to complex decisions. Of course, what we are being warned against is being oversystematic, that is, where commitment to an elegant methodological system obscures the overriding political aspects of a development problem.

There have been a few examinations of SIA from a methodological point of view. Flynn (1976) reviewed a number of attempts at developing SIA methodologies and found them woefully lacking because (1) they demonstrated a poor understanding of methodological developments in the social sciences, (2) the scope and usefulness of the methods proposed were seriously overestimated, (3) the enunciation and quantification of impacts was often arbitrary and not done in a useful way, (4) critical areas of SIA were without a developed methodology, and (5) titles of SIA methodologies are usually overblown and misleading. On the methodological point, problems were especially acute in impact quantification, measurement of values, and value weighting and integration of socioeconomic and environmental variables. Flynn gives a number of examples of mid-1970s EIA (environmental impact assessment)/SIA handbooks that border on the ludicrous, and yet she assures us that they are mainstream efforts. Cortese (1979) also examines some recent efforts at SIA (especially within an EIA framework), and draws similar critical conclusions. First, studies often concentrate on the symptoms of impacts (such as crime) and not on the impacts themselves (such as changes in community social structure). This can result in inadequate mitigation measures, where expensive human services are substituted for the possible avoidance of impacts. Second, and echoing Flynn, Cortese finds that many attempts at SIA reflect a poor or nonexistent understanding of social science research methods.

Aside from the newness of the SIA field the main reason for this state of affairs is that most impact studies have to be concerned with the immediate needs of decision making, rather than with methodological development, which requires the more refined criteria governing academic research. This suggests that project-oriented SIAs need the valuable complement of longer-term academic research into what are known as the policy sciences.

Guidelines for Methodological Development in SIA

Given the relative infancy of social forecasting and modeling, it is naive to assume that current attempts at SIA will be able to approximate any refined level of social scientific forecasting. SIA methodology must be designed to *enlighten* and *assist* political choice, not to predict the future. SIA methodology should promote a systematic, orderly approach to the study of development problems. This is important because of contentiousness of policy issues, the vast amount of data that may be involved, and the need to simplify complex reality for busy decision makers. The alternative to this systematic approach is often a loose, unstructured collection of information that mixes up conceptual levels, hides bias in its presentation, lacks any readily graspable perspective on the problem, and so confuses decision makers that they ignore the information altogether.

SIA methodology also assists in problem definition, or locating a decision space, which is the first and often the most important step in impact analysis. Political issues in a development decision seldom emerge cut and dried and ready for debate. Rather, they come to the fore clouded in half fact, fancy, and value predilection. A systematic approach helps to define and, equally important, to redefine the decision space as more facets of the impact problem become apparent.

SIA methodology assists in satisfying the information needs of all the parties to a policy decision insofar, of course, as the policymaking process itself allows a free flow of information among interested parties. Good decisions are based on adequate information and some information is always better than none. SIA is one useful source of information for decision makers and the public.

SIA methodology may be developed in general, that is, applicable to a variety of situations, or tailored to a particular situation. In either case the following factors should be considered:

Data requirements. The methodology must consider what data are realistically required for a sound decision. The SIA is not designed around available data, which may be insufficient. On the other hand, the SIA does not require totally comprehensive data, which might be very expensive to acquire and difficult to manipulate. Relevant data are the key.

Resource capability. The design of the SIA is related to the limited resources that are usually available for analysis, but is not necessarily governed by those. On the one hand, there are certain ethical minimum standards for an SIA; on the other, overly complex methodologies are also less than useful.

Quantification and qualification. Where quantified data are available, they are almost always used, but every effort is made to avoid bias toward such quantified data. Unquantifiable information is featured equally prominently, as in a planning balance sheet, and not obscured by pseudo quantification such as arbitrary value weights reflecting the analyst's bias.

Disaggregation of data. Quantified information is disaggregated, but not to the extent that it becomes too complex to be of use. Where moderate aggregation takes place, disaggregated backup data are available.

Probability of impact occurrence. Where possible it is a good idea to offer some estimation of the probability of impact occurrence (high, medium, low), and the condition under which impacts are likely to occur.

Significance of impacts. Determining the significance of impacts is ultimately a political decision. However, significance is a function of impact magnitude, duration, demographic coverage, diffusion, and local values (Flynn et al., 1982). The methodology should aid this determination as much as possible.

Sensitivity analysis. When there is a large amount of uncertainty inherent in projections, it is a good idea to present alternative values for uncertain variables. These are examined for their sensitivity to variations in the assumptions of the impact assessment.

Robustness measures. When possible, outcomes are ranked. A robustness measure indicates how much change in variables must occur before there is a reversal of ranking in the outcomes.

Hierarchical structure. Information in the SIA is structured hierarchically, leading from an executive review to a general synopsis to detailed data and methodology, with technical information in detailed appendices.

Value assumptions. Value assumptions on the part of the analyst are included in the general synopsis, as well as discussion of the methodological limitations inherent in such analyses.

Mitigation measures. Mitigation measures should regularly be associated with negative impacts, including remedial costs.

Communicability. The SIA is presented in clear terminology understandable to decision makers and laypersons alike, with a format readily discernible to all concerned, and social scientific jargon is confined to the appendices.

Public debate. The SIA is designed, written, and presented in such a manner as to facilitate public debate on important social issues related to development. It is not an analytic exercise offering a determinate solution to a policy problem.

Causal understanding. As much as possible, given its context, the methodology promotes causal understanding.

Validity. Few SIA methodologies have been tested by ex post analysis, that is, as a check that what did happen in a development situation is similar to what was predicted to happen by the SIA. More ex post checks on validity would greatly benefit methodological development.

SIA Methodologies: Introduction

This section looks at attempts to specify fairly comprehensive or general methodologies (procedures) for assessing social impact. It does not review individual methods (such as surveys), but it does evaluate codified methodologies. These sometimes concentrate solely on SIA, but often they involve an integrated socioeconomic and environmental approach. Some methodologies (especially computer-assisted schemes) are confined to forecasting quantifiable, multiplier-linked, demographic and facilities variables. Others attempt to incorporate a broad spectrum of objective data and subjective evaluations and opinions. Some are basically information-organizing techniques, while others propose aggregated value-weighting schemes. Still others stress the community involvement or participatory mode of SIA. All have in common a comprehensive perspective on impacts ranging across a wide array of domains, or subject areas, that influence quality of life. None fills the bill entirely as a model for good SIA, but some offer a practical organizational framework for structuring SIAs, and many have salient points that are usefully incorporated into project-specific SIAs. A consideration of such general methodologies raises almost all the important issues in SIA.

As we review SIA methodologies it quickly becomes apparent that there are roughly two camps. One reflects what can be called a numerical orientation, and the other a participatory orientation. These, of course, are stereotypes marking out the extremes of a continuum of SIA methodological types. As the methodological development of SIA cannot be separated from its political context, so a numerical orientation is only partially distinct from a participatory one, and some SIA approaches are therefore termed combination methodologies.

Numerically Oriented SIA Methodologies

Water Resources Assessment Methodology

The most extensive and comprehensive approach to the development of an EIA/SIA methodology has been undertaken by various researchers for the U.S. Army Corps of Engineers, a long-time sponsor of attempts at SIA and EIA. This is termed the Water Resources Assessment Methodology (WRAM) and is presented in a variety of volumes. Solomon et al. (1977) review a wide variety of previously proposed assessment techniques and evaluate these according to seven screening criteria, which are summarized as follows: responsible to basic principles and standards, comprehensive, dynamic, flexible, objective, implementable, and replicable. Eight method-ologies made it to the final screening and, although none satisfied all criteria, each had salient points that were incorporated in the WRAM approach. The components of WRAM include the selection of an interdisciplinary team, the selection of assessment variables, an environ-mental inventory, impact prediction, impact weighting and scaling, impact evaluation, and documentation of results. The assessment variables are organized into four accounts: environmental quality, economic develop-ment, social well-being, and regional development.

The social well-being (SWB) account for WRAM is divided into 6 main categories and 20 subcategories (Guseman and Dietrich, 1978). These are described by 68 specified variables. The main categories are real income distribution; life, health, and safety; education, cultural, and recreational opportunities and other community services; emergency preparedness (such as for floods); community cohesion; and other population characteristics. For each of the 68 specified variables in the SWB accounts (as for the other 3 accounts), the WRAM reports discuss the definition and measurement of baseline conditions, the prediction of impacts, data sources, and further references. WRAM also proposes a hypothesized transformation function between levels of each variable and a quality (of life) index.

A report on a preliminary field test of WRAM for a water resource project (Richardson et al. 1978) concluded that WRAM's interdisciplinary team approach is of great value, and that the weighted rankings technique provided a useful procedure for selecting assessment variables and for focusing detailed analysis on the most critical variables. In addition, the WRAM team examined the 253 methodologies for assessing impacts that were first considered for WRAM and organized these into a literature review (Canter, 1979).

The WRAM approach is very comprehensive and detailed, and deserves to be examined and analyzed in depth. The experienced reader will appreciate the methodical and systematic approach of WRAM; the wealth of information uncovered in the review process; the attention equally to economic, environmental, and social variables; the emphasis on the interdisciplinary team process; the attention to the "no project" option; and the cautious testing of WRAM. The same experienced reader will also be slightly wary of some aspects of WRAM, such as the extension of a highly quantified approach from EIA to social variables, or the value assumptions implicit in some of the very hypothetical functional curves or transforma-tion functions. The reader will also look with caution at WRAM's highly aggregated proposal for a value-weighting and scaling scheme, and will be wary of such scientific and objective-sounding, but highly value-laden, terms such as a "relative importance coefficient." Nonetheless, for sheer effort, WRAM can hardly be ignored.

The Battelle Social Indicators Model

Another comprehensive approach to SIA methodology proposes to use a set of social indicators to measure predicted social impacts. This is the Batelle model (Olsen et al., 1981), which relates direct demographic and economic impacts through indirect impacts (community structural changes and public service changes) to changes in social well-being resulting in predicted social impacts. These in turn feed back to policy decisions. And in spite of the fact that Olsen et al. recognize the enormous theoretical difficulties past researchers have had in developing quality of life indicators, they do go on to propose fifty factors, or community characteristics, that are essential components of the quality of social life in the United States. These factors are transformed to standard scores by the establishment of a desired goal which may be specified by "qualified experts" or the public as a whole.

Olsen et al.'s (1981) recognition of the difficulties of causation and the necessity for subjective value weighting, and their attempt to structure this highly aggregated model and relate it to SIA, is certainly worthwhile. However, these dynamic models, while having considerable potential, are at present far from useful in the social field. Specification of such models at any sophisticated level can be very difficult because of the complexity of the systems to be simulated and the difficulty of establishing quantitative relationships among variables. Given all the potential problems of the Battelle approach, it does recognize and make explicit the difficulties associated with ascribing causation to indirect social effects, and it is probably most useful as an organizational model for practical efforts at collecting objective data relevant to the SIA.

The Social and Economic Assessment Model

A limited but rigorous approach to SIA is taken by the Argonne National Laboratory with the Social and Economic Assessment Model (SEAM). This is a computerized simulation model designed to estimate some socioeconomic changes that accompany energy and industrial developments (Stenehjem, 1978).[1] SEAM can provide annual estimates of the following data for any county or group of counties in the continental United States:

- population projections by age, sex, and race

- direct employment requirements of most types of energy-related facilities

- secondary employment requirements created by new energy or industrial facilities

- locally available work force from affected and adjacent counties

- numbers and characteristics of inmigrating worker households attracted by the new facility

- housing needs and subcounty spatial allocation of the new population

- public service requirements and costs due to the new population

To date, the SEAM model has been used in a number of studies. In one case it was used to forecast the incremental public costs of new and expanded coal mines in over 200 U.S. counties by 1985, under two differing projected levels of coal extraction. In another study, SEAM was used to study the changes that might occur in a single county in Virginia in which two new coal mines were to be developed. In this case, advisory groups of local residents were established to provide the researchers with important local data and to examine critically the forecasts of the model. The forecasts were then presented to public meetings for further feedback. The main purpose of the exercise was to avoid as many possible negative impacts of the mine development as possible. Note that SEAM is basically a quantitative forecasting model for use as a tool in wider SIA that includes public participation.

Community-Level Impacts Projection Systems

Similar to SEAM is the Community-Level Impacts Projection System (CLIPS) discussed by Monts and Bareiss (1979). Written to help in the assessment of energy-related developments in the state of Texas, CLIPS consists of (1) a large mathematical model translated into three FORTRAN programs and (2) a set of accompanying FORTRAN routines that take the information required, feed it through the model, and generate the results. Like SEAM, the results generated by CLIPS are multiplier-linked projections of selected demographic and facilities variables based on assumptions fed by the user. The authors warn that the output of CLIPS should not be taken literally, but merely as a forecasting guide, and they stress that CLIPS is no substitute for local, on-the-ground planning.

SIMPACT

A third computer-assisted scheme has been developed by social scientists at Arthur D. Little, Inc. Called SIMPACT (simulated impact), the current version was developed during the preparation of an EIA for a proposed $4 billion steel plant, which would require as many as 10,500 construction workers at peak construction period (Huston and DeSouza, 1980). SIMPACT is designed to deal with just such a situation — it quantifies socio-economic and secondary environmental changes that occur in a defined region when a large-scale facility locates there. SIMPACT was recently examined by Oak Ridge National Laboratories and accepted for use in U.S. coal gasification projects.

SIMPACT involves four linked models: economic and demographic, community planning, fiscal, and environmental. These models each consist of a series of equations that predict a range of socioeconomic and environmental variables. The model is run once for each year under construction, once for each region, and for the construction and operation phases of the project.

The economic and demographic model is concerned with predicting these classes of variables: production, and then, in turn, employment, and then inmigrating population based on employment opportunities. Variables in the community planning model include an interesting and potentially useful distinction between privately financed and publicly financed infrastructure. Private infrastructure includes the factories, offices, and stores associated with the secondary economic activity, as well as the homes, apartments, and motels required to house the inmigrating primary and secondary workers. Public infrastructure, on the other hand, consists of schools, police stations, fire stations, streets, water supply and sanitation facilities, and solid-waste landfills. The model calculates data for each infrastructure category, and for floor space, construction costs, and land areas.

The fiscal model draws on solutions from the economic and demographic and community planning models, and analysis is performed at the municipal level. For the purpose of the fiscal model, the municipal data solutions are aggregated to a school district, county, and multicounty levels, and analysis involves three sequential stages: revenue, cost, and budget. In the first stage, the increased revenue that will be generated by the new economic and demographic activity is computed. In the second stage, the operating and capital costs associated with providing the public infrastructure demands created by such activity are determined; and the capital costs are then annualized and added to operating costs to give total annual costs. In the third stage, the net budgetary change is calculated by comparing revenues to total annualized costs.

Finally, the environmental model focuses attention on the physical environmental problems created by the primary facility. Most important are the pollutant-concentration levels at the property line of the plant site. However, the regional air-quality impacts of the secondary economic and demographic activity will also be considered. The environmental model of SIMPACT is designed to project the air emissions and water-effluent loadings resulting from secondary developments, while the water-consumption, solid-waste generation, and land-use projects have already been analyzed in the community planning model. The environmental model, while recognizing a three-stage environmental analysis procedure — including changes in the ambient air and water quality and the effect of the changed ambient quality on life, health, and property — goes no further than amount of pollutants discharged. The reason is that the second stage — the so-called dispersion or diffusion modeling — is highly site specific and cannot be incorporated within the structures of a system such as SIMPACT, while modeling at the third stage is still in its infancy.

The proposers of SIMPACT recognize the practical difficulty of their task, and they are the first to note the limitations of the model. These include the need to rework the application of SIMPACT to adapt it to the specific characteristics of each project, which can only be done after local interviews with planners, contractors, and local representatives. They also recognize that systems models are no panacea for planning problems, and contain rigidities not present in qualitative approaches. They argue that SIMPACT helps link economists, sociologists, planners, architects, engineers, and financial analysts to a systematic mode of analysis. This is a worthwhile objective in its own right.

The BOOMH Model

This computer model is an extension of the BOOM1 model, developed at Los Alamos Scientific Laboratory to help assess the local impacts of rapid development of U.S. coal reserves (Ford, 1976). The purpose of BOOMH (a subsector of BOOM1 concerned solely with housing) is to help industry and government decision makers anticipate the probable effects of various impact-mitigating strategies thought to be of assistance in dealing with housing shortages and other problems in boomtowns (Rink, 1980).

The model focuses on two aspects of the boomtown housing market: supply and demand for temporary and permanent housing, and the use and value of land. For each aspect the model makes a series of explicit assumptions, for example, under permanent housing there are eleven key assumptions, one of which is "market price of housing rises and falls in response to variations in the vacancy rate." For temporary housing and for use and value of land there are another series of assumptions. All the assumptions are linked in a complex series of supply-and-demand loops for their interrelated effects on one another.

The BOOMH model was tested for the oil sands boomtown of Fort McMurray, Alberta, for the years 1971-1979. Parameter estimates were obtained from discussions with local officials, and from secondary sources such as the census. The driving input to the model was taken as the expected employment of construction and permanent workers. Impact-mitigating strategies were also specified, such as company-sponsored development of permanent housing, advanced planning of town infrastructure, and the provision of job-site dormitories for 85 percent of construction workers at all times.

The validation run of BOOMH demonstrated that it was reasonably successful in tracking population growth and housing supply and demand for Fort McMurray during the test period. Any discrepancy between BOOMH predictions and actual occurrence is the result of the very kind of political and social factors that cannot be modeled with any reasonable certainty. The BOOMH model was also run to explore other hypothetical housing policy options for Fort McMurray. Here it was able to demonstrate the negative impacts that might have occurred in the boomtown, had there not been a reasonable degree of advanced planning. In this case, the BOOMH model proved that it not only anticipated a real boomtown situation with reasonable accuracy, but that it would prove useful in exploring broad policy options for helping avoid boom-and-bust cycles in such towns.

Texas Assessment Modeling System

The Texas Assessment Modeling System (TAMS) is of particular interest because it is an attempt to adapt an existing computer model to a new setting. The authors of TAMS (Murdock et al., 1980) argue quite rightly that model adaptation will be an increasingly important mode of analysis for the following reasons:

(1) Model development is increasingly expensive and thus difficult to justify to sponsoring agencies.

(2) Adaptation provides an opportunity to expand and refine a model's structure and capabilities beyond that possible in an initial model development effort.

(3) Model adaptation provides the means to pursue the replicative principles basic to science, for the long-term improvement of all modeling efforts.

TAMS is an adaptation of the North Dakota Regional Environmental Assessment Program's (REAP) models, and is used to provide baseline and single- or multiple-project impact projections for six regions in east Texas. These regions correspond to functional economic areas, which are the trade areas of larger cities in the region. Outputs of TAMS include business activity, personal income, employment by type, population by age, sex, housing demand, school enrollments, criminal justice service requirements, medical service requirements, and public sector costs and revenues. Reports on these outputs are available at the regional, county, and municipal levels for each output area. In addition, these outputs can be combined into any one of six submodels: economic input-output, cohort survival, economic-demographic interface, residential allocation, service requirements, and fiscal inputs. These are described in detail in the associated literature (Murdock et al., 1979a, 1979b).

Especially interesting for the purposes of this chapter are the considerations required in the adaptation of the model. The first problem encountered was incompatibility of software, especially language, between the computer systems. The second was the need to adapt the structure of the model to suit the particular requirements of the new region. For example, the 13 industrial sectors of the original had to be expanded to 27 to reflect the east Texas economy. The third problem was that computer experts capable of writing the original program were also essential for revising and adapting the program to new needs. The fourth problem was the difficulty in validating a model that was originally written for other purposes. For example, when an error became apparent, was it the fault of the original model formulation or the adaptation?

The authors of TAMS draw some useful general conclusions. First, it is very important to spend adequate time and resources in evaluating which computer model will be adapted. Such time is never wasted, even though there may be pressure to get started as quickly as possible. Second, it is necessary to have a truly interdisciplinary team to adapt the model. Third, although model adaptation can save a sponsoring agency money, it should not be oversold, because adaptation will require considerable time and effort. Fourth, a client or user advisory group is recommended whenever possible. Finally, good communication between the original developers and the adapters is essential for successful adaptation.

Participatory and Combination SIA Methodologies

There has been some debate in the SIA field in the recent past over its presumed role in the decision-making process. The numerical school tends to perceive SIA as a social scientific exercise aimed at predicting the effects of change by applying the skills of various academic disciplines, such as economics, sociology, anthropology, and statistics; in other words, supplying needed information to enlighten decisions. Other people, however, see the most important task of SIA as mobilizing public involvement in the decision process — a participatory role. In fact, valid and valuable SIA can ill afford to ignore either role. The opinions and reactions of residents in the study area, and of other individuals concerned with a project, are essential to an understanding of the objective data generated by social scientific analysis. Such opinions and reactions are gathered not as a public relations exercise, but rather to ensure concerted public participation in the assessment process, which means an essential two-way flow of information and interaction between the public and the developer or government agency. The public response and the attitudinal information generated by such a process are important for bringing the SIA closer to an elusive social reality that can be mirrored only partially by numerical analytic techniques.

Public participation also helps all the actors in the decision process put some measures of priority, positive or negative direction, and sensitivity to the various factors in the assessment problem. Most important, citizen participation promotes the intensive public debate that leads to healthy political decisions. A useful perspective attempts to combine the social scientific and participatory roles of SIA. Such a dual orientation gives due recognition to the importance of what Bish (1976) calls "time and place specific information," that is, the varieties of information that reflect a complex social world but that are not necessarily amenable to statistical manipulation.

Participatory Approaches

An emphasis on a pluralistic decision process is apparent in work by Torgerson (1980), who argues that the predominant tendency in many current efforts at SIA can be characterized as "elitist" in that the orientation is technocratic, with the analyst assuming the role of an expert engaged in detached scientific inquiry. Such elitist impact assessors emphasize objective data, ignore social conflict, and give only a token nod to public involvement in the process. Torgerson suggests that this elitist stance arises out of a functionalist orientation in sociology, that is, one based on the assumption that communities have monolithic, discernible social goals, the degree of attainment of which can be measured. This orientation is rejected in that the workings of the social system may well be about the systematic promotion of certain value stances at the expense of others, that is, about pluralistic rather than monolithic social processes. Instead, a participatory mode of SIA is proposed that recognizes the value orientation of the SIA researcher, and the necessarily ambiguous, or subjective, nature of studies of social phenomena. This ambiguity means that intuitive judgments will always be present in an SIA. In the participatory mode active public participation is viewed as essential to the SIA process, and as the *right* of affected parties. Such participatory impact assessment is itself an educative social process that may change society. The final assessment arises not from some formula-derived numerical calculation, but from intergroup conflict and cooperation over development proposals.

Such arguments and warnings about the political nature of SIA are important. Torgerson advises a high degree of suspicion of the role and value of seemingly "objective" methodologies. His emphasis on participation is not just strong, but in fact constitutes the cornerstone of his argument for an SIA process that becomes almost one with the pluralist political process itself. This is an embracing and laudatory role for SIA. It is worth noting, simply as a matter of balance, that the political process is in turn enlightened by the objective and subjective data gathered as part of the SIA process, and such routine data collection procedures also serve a valuable role in the complex mosaic that constitutes political decision making.

A different approach to SIA is taken by Freudenburg (1978), who argues that in the past, SIA approaches have often ignored or glossed over the study of the informal social networks and relationships that go a long way toward defining the nature of the affected community. Ignoring these relationships has meant that very important social consequences of development have also been ignored by SIA researchers. Freudenburg is especially interested in the sociological study of boomtowns that experience rapid development due to new energy-extraction and power-generation projects. In boomtowns, he suggests, rapid change destroys, or irrevocably alters, mechanisms of social control and social caring that had previously characterized the town. This may lead not only to diminishing the quality of the community for many people, but more specifically to substantial increases in "social pathology rates" such as crime and drug abuse.

Why these important changes and impacts in informal social networks are often ignored in SIAs is a matter of conjecture. The reason is unlikely to be malicious, but rather some combination of time and resource constraints and the sheer difficulty of doing so. Certainly it is not possible for all SIAs done by a consultant-researcher to include continuous monitoring or lengthy visits to the affected community over a period of many years. On the other hand, Freudenburg is right that these are vitally important issues and that the patterns and lessons that emerge in one boomtown (or in any other assessment problem) should give us guidance in similar future developments. This points to an important role for the academic community interested in SIA: the long-term study and monitoring of the social impact of large development in communities where such development is taking place.

Project Huntly

One case in which this role has been taken up is at the University of Waikato in New Zealand, where Project Huntly is studying the socioeconomic impact generated by the process of locating, designing, and constructing a large power station in a small town comprising a variety of socioeconomic and racial groupings, including a sizable population of native people. The Huntly Project began in 1975 and has a main objective of gathering information that would assist planning for similar future projects (Fookes, 1979). Huntly is a recently completed seven-year monitoring project that studied such topics as land and housing, local authority administration, demography, traffic generation, provision of services, recreation, employment, community attitudes and stress, and minority racial groups. Of special interest in a lengthy project of this type is the ability to compare resident expectations with actual events for a variety of population subgroups. In addition, Huntly has established a data base of 98 variables that may prove useful for examining some relationships between construction activity and postulated impacts. Huntly also payed attention to the concept of monitoring itself, and provides information on the possibilities and pitfalls of this important aspect of SIA (Krawetz, 1981a, 1981b).

The No-Action Alternative Approach

This approach to impact assessment was developed by the Transportation Research Board of the U.S. National Research Council (Lane et al., 1979a, 1979b). The approach is based on the argument that (1) the "no-action" option in transportation planning has been ill defined and is therefore confusing, (2) the "no-action" option has not been integrated into the assessment process, and therefore (3) comparative information about alternative transportation investments has not been intelligible to decision makers. "No-action alternative" refers to the "without-the-project" projection familiar to SIA researchers, but not often applied with the degree of rigor recommended here. In this case a very clear definition of no-action means no new planned investments, but rather the maintenance of existing facilities and services, the completion of committed projects, and the continuation of existing policies. The authors stress that other similar terms, such as "without-the-project," "no-build," or "do-nothing" may mean something similar but only serve to confuse the issue because they are not clearly defined.

The no-action methodology argues that the no-action alternative should serve as a benchmark for all further analysis in impact assessment and evaluation, and it provides a means of structuring the assessment process. More specifically, there are three roles for this benchmark function: (1) to identify and predict the impacts of the no-action alternative, (2) to compare the impacts of the no-action alternative to the other alternatives under consideration, and (3) to assist in determining costs and selecting the appropriate alternative.

The no-action methodology is considerably more than a commitment to using the no-action alternative as a benchmark for impact assessment. It is also one of the most comprehensive surveys available of impact assessment techniques for a set of thirteen categories of potential impacts.

In the Lane et al. reports, the techniques are arrayed in a series of tables reflecting each of these impact categories. As the authors put it, this is to illustrate the range of techniques available, or the lack of techniques. The techniques are organized into a series of steps, which are designed to elicit the magnitude, incidence, and significance of impacts (Lane et al., 1979b: 40):

(1) Identify and forecast project attributes causing impact.
(2) Identify and forecast external factors influencing impact.
(3) Identify and forecast intervening factors influencing impact.
(4) Determine magnitude of impact.
(5) Identify and forecast receptors of impact.
(6) Determine incidence of impact.
(7) Identify and forecast standards, norms, or values related to the impact.
(8) Determine significance of impact.

For each step, within each impact category, there is a series of assessment techniques listed, and this is referenced to an alphabetical compendium of assessment techniques. For each technique there is a general description, a list of the necessary inputs and likely outputs of the application of the technique, a short (and sometimes critical) comment, and literature references. There are 68 techniques listed, and in fact the vast majority are useful for (1) environmental assessment (food chain analysis, noise exposure analysis, pollutant migration analysis), (2) economic analysis (housing market surveys, trade area analysis, economic base analysis), or (3) transit planning (public transit submarket index, right-of-way cost ratio technique, flow modeling). Some techniques are specifically for SIA, but, as may be expected, there is nothing new or startling: community input, community profile, field survey, projective attitude survey, quality of life indicators (Battelle), or social capacity indicators. The comments on each technique are fair and do not overinflate the analytic capacity of each approach.

Conclusion

There are other methodological approaches to SIA, including that presented in Chapter 3 of this volume, but those described above suffice to give us a good picture of current thinking in the field, either as comprehensive, generalist approaches, or offer particular insights or advantages in data collection, organization, or manipulation.

There are equally many diverse problems hindering the methodological development of SIA techniques. As mentioned at the beginning of this chapter, some of these problems relate to the political nature of resource development, and thus to SIA. For example, however sophisticated computer models might become, they cannot take into account all the worldwide political ramifications that may affect projects. The BOOM1 or BOOMH model could not anticipate the combination of political and world market forces that caused the demise of tar sands oil projects in northern Alberta. Nor are important intangible social factors — for example, sense of community in preboom towns — readily reduced to the quantification required for simulation modeling. These complicated problems having to do with the relationship between methodology and values or politics are well discussed elsewhere (Carley, 1980; O'Riordan and Sewell, 1981).

From a methodological point of view, if there is one overriding hindrance to development of SIA, it is a lack of attention to the ex post examination of impact assessments themselves. Such examinations would serve to check on the validity, structure, and accuracy of the SIA forecasting models in comparison with actual events. The reasons for this lack of attention are no doubt partly institutional, insofar as many SIA researchers are planners rather than model builders per se, and their clients are businesses and governments with immediate needs for SIA information. By the time the actual forecast year is reached, the problems of the short-term future are far more pressing than any examination of past mistakes, and people's attention has moved on to the next SIA problem. Besides, what politician or civil servant wants to come up with money to study yesterday's issues and problems? The next election is too pressing for that.

This, however, does not diminish the patently obvious advantages of ex post studies of SIA forecasting efforts. It also suggests the importance of closer ties between academic researchers and planners. Fortunately, there have been a few good ex post SIA studies, and we can anticipate more. Examples include Project Huntly (Fookes 1979; Krawetz 1981a, 1981b), the postlicensing studies of power stations in the United States (Denver Research Institute et al., 1982), and similar power station studies in the United Kingdom (Power Station Impacts Research Team, 1979). It is essential that efforts to improve methodology be based on the practical lessons of past experience.

References

BISH, R. L. (1976) "The assumption of knowledge in policy analysis," in P. M. Gregg (ed.) Problems of Theory in Policy Analysis. Lexington, MA: D. C. Heath.

BOWEN, P., J. DEVITT, J. HOLDEN, G. LEONARDSON, K. McMANUS, and L. WENNER (1979) Social Impact Assessment for Forest Planning and Decision-Making. Missoula, MT: U.S. Department of Agriculture, Forest Service, Northern Region.
CANTER, L. W. (1979) Water Resources Assessment — Methodology and Technology Sourcebook. Ann Arbor, MI: Ann Arbor Science Publishers.
CARLEY, M. J. (1980) Rational Techniques in Policy Analysis. London: Heinemann.
——— and A. WALKEY (1981) "Exploring some key elements in SIA," in F. J. Tester and W. Mykes (eds.) Social Impact Assessment: Theory, Methods, and Practice. Calgary, Alberta: Detselig.
CORTESE, C. F. (1979) "Rapid growth and social change in western communities." Social Impact Assessment 40/41: 7-11.
Denver Research Institute and Browne, Bortz, and Coddington (1982) Socio-economic Impacts of Power Plants. Palo Alto, CA: Electric Power Research Institute.
FLYNN, C. (1976) "Science and speculation in social impact assessment." Social Impact Assessment 11/12: 5-14.
——— et al. (1982) An Integrated Methodology for Socioeconomic Impact Assessment and Planning. Seattle: Social Impact Research.
FOOKES, T. W. (1979) Monitoring Social and Economic Impact: Huntly Case Study. Waikato, New Zealand: Huntly Monitoring Project, University of Waikato.
FORD, A. (1976) User's Guide to the BOOM1 Model. Los Alamos, NM: Los Alamos Scientific Laboratory.
FREUDENBURG, W. R. (1978) "Toward ending the inattention: a report on social impact and policy implications of energy boomtown developments." Prepared for the annual meeting of the American Association for the Advancement of Science.
GUSEMAN, P. K. and K. T. DIETRICH (1978) Profile and Measurement of Social Well-Being Indicators for Use in the Evaluation of Water and Related Land Management Planning. Vicksburg, MS: U.S. Army Engineer Waterways Experiment Station.
HUSTON, M. C. and G. R. DeSOUZA (1980) "SIMPACT: a system to forecast impacts of growth and development," in Computer Models and Forecasting Socio-Economic Impacts of Growth and Development. Edmonton: University of Alberta.
KRAWETZ, N. M. (1981a) Overseas Energy Projects and Huntly. Waikato, New Zealand: Huntly Monitoring Project, University of Waikato.
——— (1981b) Implications for Development Planning. Waikato, New Zealand: Huntly Monitoring Project, University of Waikato.
LANE, J. S., L. R. GRENZEBACK, T. J. MARTIN, and S. C. LOCKWOOD (1979a) The No-Action Alternative Research Report. Washington, DC: Transportation Research Board, National Research Council.
——— (1979b) The No-Action Alternative Impact Assessment Guidelines. Washington, DC: Transportation Research Board, National Research Council.
LEISTRITZ, F. L. and S. H. MURDOCK (1981) The Socioeconomic Impact of Resource Development: Methods for Assessment. Boulder, CO: Westview.
MONTS, J. K. and E. R. BAREISS (1979) CLIPS: Community-Level Impacts Projection System. Austin: Center for Energy Studies, University of Texas.
MURDOCK, S. H., L. L. JONES, F. L. LEISTRITZ, and D. R. ANDREWS (1980) "The Texas Assessment Modeling System (TAMS): a case study in model

adaptation," in Computer Models and Forecasting Socio-Economic Impacts of Growth and Development. Edmonton: University of Alberta.

MURDOCK, S. H., F. L. LEISTRITZ, L. L. JONES, D. ANDREWS, B. WILSON, D. FANNIN, and J. DE MONTEL (1979a) Texas Assessment Modeling System: User Manual. College Station: Texas Agricultural Experiment Station, Texas A&M University.

———— (1979b) Texas Assessment Modeling System: Technical Description. College Station: Texas Agricultural Experiment Station, Texas A&M University.

OLSEN, M. E., B. D. MELBER, and D. J. MERWIN (1981) "A methodology for conducting social impact assessments using quality of social life indicators," in K. Finsterbusch and C. P. Wolf (eds.) Methodology of Social Impact Assessment. Stroudsburg, PA: Hutchinson Ross.

OPHULS, W. (1977) Ecology and the Politics of Scarcity: Prologue to the Theory of the Steady State. San Francisco: Freeman.

O'RIORDAN, T. and W.R. SEWELL (1981) Project Appraisal and Policy Review. New York: John Wiley.

Power Station Impacts Research Team (1979) The Socio-Economic Effects of Power Stations on Their Localities. Oxford: Department of Town Planning, Oxford Polytechnic.

RICHARDSON, S. E., W. HANSEN, R. C. SOLOMON, and J. JONES (1978) Preliminary Field Test of the Water Resources Assessment Methodology (WRAM): Tensas River, Louisiana. Vicksburg, MS: U.S. Army Engineer Waterways Experiment Station.

RINK, R. E. (1980) "Boomtown system dynamics: the BOOMH Model," in Computer Models and Forecasting Socio-Economic Impacts of Growth and Development. Edmonton: University of Alberta.

SCHNAIBERG, A. and E. MEIDINGER (1978) "Social reality vs. analytic methodology: social impact assessment of natural resource utilization." Presented at the annual meeting of the American Sociological Association.

SOLOMON, R. C., B. COLBERT, W. HANSE, S. RICHARDSON, L. CANTER, and E. VLACHOS (1977) Water Resources Assessment Methodology (WRAM): Impact Assessment and Alternative Evaluation. Vicksburg, MS: U.S. Army Engineer Waterways Experiment Station.

STENEHJEM, E. J. (1978) Summary Description of SEAM: The Social and Economic Assessment Model. Argonne, IL: Argonne National Laboratory.

TORGERSON, D. (1980) Industrialization and Assessment: Social Impact Assessment as a Social Phenomenon. Toronto: York University.

3

An Integrated
Methodology
for Large-Scale
Development Projects

○　○　○　○　○　○　○　○　○　○　○　○　○　○　○　○　○

CYNTHIA B. FLYNN, JAMES H. FLYNN,
JAMES A. CHALMERS, DAVID PIJAWKA,
and KRISTI BRANCH

○　○　○　○　○　○　○　○　○　○　○　○　○　○　○　○　○

● The ability of planners, administrators, project managers, and the public to use social impact assessment (SIA) information has developed rapidly during the last few years. The process of creating and publishing an Environmental Impact Statement (EIS), and holding public hearings based upon the EIS information, has made a great deal of technical and planning information available to people who were previously without such resources. EISs have become data bases for project planning and management, not merely ends in themselves. EIS methods have developed to the point that they are a valuable administrative resource. This has been the result of a number of concentrated efforts to improve the focus, scope, and accuracy of work in the field.

As the concerns of various social groups have been more clearly expressed, socioeconomic variables have assumed a new importance, both for those directly affected by proposed developments and for those responsible for anticipating and mitigating project-related consequences. Numerous refinements have been made in the ways that economic/ demographic (E/D) effects are analyzed. Several highly sophisticated and computer-based E/D models have been developed to provide detailed descriptions and forecasts of the size, composition, and spatial distribution of demographic and economic effects. Based on such information, the demand for housing and public facilities and services can be estimated and much of the data for fiscal impact assessment can be assembled.

The concerns of the involved parties, however, have gone well beyond an interest in the geographical and institutional distribution of project-related effects, even while everyone recognizes how important these impacts are. People want to know who is going to be affected and what the costs and benefits will be for groups in the local communities. The evaluation of a project is no longer the exclusive work of developers, planners, hearing boards, or judges. Local groups, intervenors, project proponents, and neutral commentators are all ready to make their own distribution and evaluation of project-related effects, often based on a very subjective point of view. In a number of cases, these people also are willing to involve themselves in the planning and siting process, even, on occasion, to the point of litigation. An ability to deal with the public response has become extremely important both for proponents and opponents, not only in terms of public participation and public relations, but also in terms of the economics of project development.

An ideal conceptual framework for social impact assessment uses an integrated approach that covers the whole range of social effects, including public response. Such an approach is extremely useful in siting projects, and in the design of mitigation plans and monitoring programs. In addition, it allows for the identification of the objective changes due to the project, the distribution of those effects to functional social groups, the determination of the groups' evaluation of those effects, and an overall evaluation of the significance of the proposed action. This chapter describes the design of one such approach.

Basic Conceptual Framework

The local effects of a project occur in a geographical area defined as the study area. The size of the study area is necessarily arbitrary, but any area that will receive significant impacts should be included. A project will produce noticeably different impacts in one study area compared to another because the socioeconomic contexts of study areas differ markedly. The project-induced effects will interact with different dynamic patterns and trends of change in each study area.

An accurate baseline description is essential to understanding what the study area will be like in the future without the project, and how the proposed project will affect the future life of the residents. An adequate SIA must take into account the social and economic changes that are already under way and that will occur in any event. It is, after all, the difference between the "without" project alternative and the "with" project case, at the same future point in time, that describes an impact. It is often useful for heuristic purposes to compare the future without the project to current conditions, but current conditions are not used in the actual impact assessment.

Four variables are central to understanding the social and economic effects of the project on the area where it will be located: (1) the size of the project-related work force residing in the study area, which determines employment and income; (2) the amount of project-related materials, equipment, and services purchased in the study area; (3) the project-related taxes accruing to the local taxing jurisdictions; and (4) the noneconomic project characteristics, such as those that may affect health and safety, traffic, or the natural environment. These four variables can be characterized as "driving variables," since they drive the remainder of the analysis. They represent the major exogenous inputs that induce social and economic changes in the study area.

The total employment and income effects are important in their own right. They are also important because they represent the demand for labor, which, in conjunction with the local supply of labor, determines the labor force migration necessary to balance local labor market conditions. Net migration due to the project, in the form either of inmigration or reduced outmigration, will be the principal determinant of project-induced population change. Population change will, in turn, affect housing demand and settlement patterns in specific communities. Once the direct and indirect income, taxes, and population changes have been estimated, the effects on the public sector can be determined. Changes in both revenues and the demand for facilities and services can be discussed.

Finally, changes in the social structure of the study area may be expected to result from the changes outlined above. New groups may appear, existing groups may be displaced, the characteristics of existing groups may change, and patterns of interaction between groups may be affected. Because the causal linkages for social structural effects are not understood as well as are the linkages among the more obvious components, social structure effects are discussed in greater detail below.

All of the previously summarized affects are observable changes in the socioeconomic environment that can be studied independently of the value systems of local residents or of observers. For the sake of clarity, we have sometimes referred to these as objective changes. It is well recognized, however, that defining the objective change associated with a project is only part of what is required. Equally important is a description of what these changes mean for those persons affected by them, and how group responses will influence the social structure of the study area. This requires explicit consideration of the values of affected groups in order to understand their evaluation of the socioeconomic effects and their overall evaluation of the project. Such research provides the essential information for understanding locally based public response to a project.

Overall, then, the objective and subjective changes produce a projected "with-project" social and economic system, which can be compared to the baseline social and economic system over time. The differences between these two systems are the socioeconomic impacts of a project. This conceptual framework represents a straightforward set of cause-and-effect relationships. Its great utility is that it links the direct effects of building and operating a facility to a probable set of responses in the study area. It does this by combining the more established methods and approaches of economic, demographic, and fiscal impact assessment with a new examination of those connecting links to "social social" effects (Freudenburg, 1978). Thus an integrated chain of socioeconomic causation has been conceptualized, one that links groups in the local study area to the project-induced effects. The framework is shown schematically in Figure 3.1.

Methods Used to Estimate Major Effects

Identification of the Study Area

There is no doubt that the socioeconomic portion of the assessment is considerably simplified if the boundaries of the study area coincide with political jurisdictions, particularly counties. This is because secondary data are readily available for such areas. However, to define the local study area properly, the critical question is, where will significant socioeconomic changes take place?

Any area that will receive significant impacts should be included in the study area. Since the driving variables determine the magnitude of the

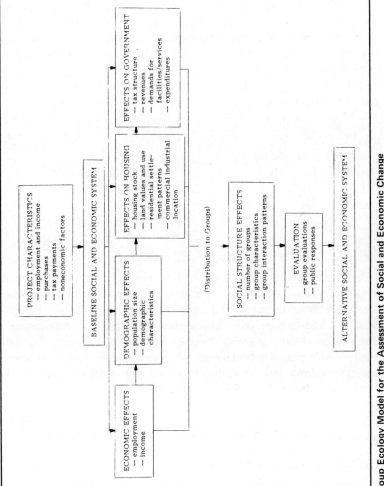

Figure 3.1 Group Ecology Model for the Assessment of Social and Economic Change

impacts, the geographical distribution of the driving variables determines the geographical distribution of the impacts. Thus the study area should coincide as nearly as possible with those areas that will receive project-related employment, income, taxes, and any other significant effects. The study area may need to be expanded somewhat if the sociopolitical role of the project is significant in an adjoining area, although such an addition complicates the analysis.

Economic Effects

The premise of the economic analysis is that the economic activities of the project — the direct employment at the project, the purchase of goods and services for the project, and other market effects of the project (such as the consequences of tax revenues) — will cause additional economic activity in the study area. The determination of the total project effects on employment and income in the study area requires the quantification of both the direct project activity and the additional induced nonproject activity. In order to control for the unknown future effects of inflation or deflation, all dollar calculations are made in constant dollars.

Work force characteristics. An analysis of socioeconomic effects resulting from the construction and operation of a project requires specific information about the project-related work force. For the construction period, information on worker characteristics (local/nonlocal status, family accompaniment, location within the study area) is based on the following: interviews with union business agents, project management and contractor personnel; realtors; apartment, mobile home, and motel managers; construction worker studies, including surveys of other projects; and an examination of secondary employment data for the study area.

For the operations period, employment projections made by the project management and the findings of other similar operations are examined. Access to numerous case histories of industrial developments and the current human resource requirements for the operation of similar facilities provide good corroborative data for making estimates for operations period employment.

BASIC EMPLOYMENT AND INCOME

Direct basic. The first of the three components of total project-related basic income and employment is designated as "direct" basic income and employment. Workers employed in the actual construction and operation of the project are referred to as "direct" basic employees; the income they earn is "direct" basic income.

The income and employment of these workers is discussed in two ways: (1) on a place-of-work basis, to show the number of jobs and the amount of income generated by the project and the effects of these jobs on the study area economy; and (2) on a place-of-residence basis, to show the number of area residents employed at the project, their income, and the effect on the study area labor force. The determination of direct basic income and direct basic employment by place of work is derived from project employment and wage data. The determination of direct basic income and employment by place of residence in the study area requires information about the wage rates and residential locations of the direct basic employees.

Indirect basic. The second component of total project-related basic income and employment is referred to as "indirect" basic, the earnings and employment resulting from the purchase of goods and services in the study area for project construction and operation. The amount of indirect basic income produced by a given value of purchases is determined by the ratio of indirect basic income to product value added locally, which varies according to the type of goods and type of establishment involved in the transactions.

Observations regarding indirect basic employment cannot be made directly. Few workers (or their employers) recognize that such jobs are the result of purchases made for the construction and operation of the new facility. Consequently, primary data on local purchases are converted to local employment and income figures using a ratio technique. The resulting estimates are then scrutinized to determine whether any local data exist that contradict or refute the derived results.

"Other" direct basic. The third component of total project-related basic income and employment is referred to as "other" basic. This category of basic income and employment accounts for such additional changes in basic employment and income as wage-induced or fiscally induced employment effects.

In the case of wages, it is often suggested that the higher wages paid at the construction site may attract workers from lower-paying jobs. If those workers cannot be replaced, or if the resulting higher wage costs render the lower-paying activities unprofitable and they subsequently cease to exist, the resulting reduction in income and employment would be considered a reduction in "other" basic employment.

The second possibility is that the large tax revenues paid by a major industrial development may generate public sector employment. However, it is important to distinguish this "other" direct basic employment in the government sector from nonbasic government employment that results from the multiplier effect of basic income. Most public sector employment (such as in schools or sanitation and police services) is a direct function of economic and demographic conditions. In some cases where there are tax windfalls, however, new services are provided that result in additional public sector employment. Only if there has been an increase in government employment beyond that expected to accompany associated population, employment, and income growth would part of the government employment growth be classified as "other" direct basic.

Total basic employment and income. Total basic employment and income is the sum of the three basic components — direct basic, indirect basic, and other direct basic.

NONBASIC EMPLOYMENT AND INCOME

Nonbasic employment and income, the final components of project-related employment and income effects, result from the expenditure (and re-expenditure) of basic income in the local economy. The amount of project-related nonbasic employment and income in the study area economy is determined by the interaction of two factors: (1) the amount of "effective" basic income created by the project, and (2) the size of the nonbasic-to-basic employment and income gammas for each sector of the local economy. Both of these factors are influenced by the study area's economic characteristics.

Effective basic income. Two principal factors affect the amount of effective basic income that results from a project: (1) the residential location of the workers earning the basic income, and (2) the magnitude of their outside financial commitments (such as the maintenance of a household outside the study area). The effects of these factors are analyzed by dividing the project-related basic workers into four groups: nonmovers, movers accompanied by families, movers unaccompanied by families (or single), and daily commuters from outside the study area. The basic income of each of the four groups is weighted so that its effect, in terms of generating induced economic activity in the study area, will be commensurate across groups. The resulting weighted income estimate is referred to as "effective" basic income.

Because multipliers are based on the consumption patterns of average local residents who are principally nonmovers, nonmovers serve as the standard for defining effective basic income; all of their income is treated as effective (that is, their income is weighted by a factor of 1.0). Data outlined by the *Consumer Expenditure Survey* (U.S. Bureau of Labor Statistics, 1973) are utilized to estimate the proportion of income spent in the local area by the remaining categories of workers compared to the amount spent by nonmovers. Averages in this survey include annual family expenditures for major items (shelter, clothing, health care, and recreation) by income bracket. Examination of the study area economy and discussions with workers, local planners, and area residents are used to estimate the percentage of expenditures that are local for each of the major consumer items.

For example, some proportion of the project-related income is usually earned by daily commuters who live outside the study area. These daily commuters generally spend a smaller proportion of their income in the local area than do resident workers earning the same income who live full time in the study area. Therefore, the presence of the daily commuters reduces the effect of the project-related basic income on the local economy by diminishing the amount available for multiplication. To account for this, the project-related basic income earned by daily commuters is adjusted (weighted by a fraction less than 1.0).

Gammas. Effective basic income is converted to personal income (by place of residence) by adjusting for transfer payments, social security payments, and the like. Sector-specific gammas for a recent year are developed by (1) splitting employment by sector into its basic and nonbasic components using the four-digit Standard Industrial Codes; and (2) dividing the nonbasic component of each sector by the total personal income for that year. If the data for these detailed analyses are not available, average gammas can be used. Anderson and Chalmers (1980) have derived region-, order-, and sector-specific gammas from a regression analysis of the empirical relationships that have actually occurred in 988 counties west of the Mississippi.

The sum of the four components of project-related employment and income — basic, indirect basic, other direct basic, and nonbasic — is the total employment and income created in the study area by the construction and operation of the project. These data are presented on both place-of-work and place-of-residence bases, given assumptions based on labor force availability and commuting patterns.

In general, if the demand for labor in the study area will be growing faster than the local supply, it is assumed that the indirect basic, other basic, and nonbasic workers are movers. On the other hand, if the demand for labor will be sluggish relative to local supply, the indirect basic, other basic, and nonbasic workers are assumed to be nonmovers who would otherwise be unemployed or move out of the area. In intermediate cases, a mix of movers and nonmovers is assumed.

Note that local hires (nonmovers) are impacts of the project. If these employees are currently employed, then inmigrants are required to fill their current positions when they are hired on the project (unless very significant changes in labor force participation or productivity are projected). If these employees are excess unemployed, it is presumed that eventually there will be outmigration (often of the young) without the project to balance the supply and demand of labor (Long and Hansen, 1979). This implies a smaller baseline population size and demand for services than for the current population.

The final step in the estimation of project-related economic effects is to calculate the ratios of total project-induced employment and income to direct basic employment and income. These ratios are what are commonly referred to as employment and income "multipliers"; rather than just making an a priori assumption about the size of the multipliers, these are calculated by taking into account the characteristics of the local economy. The multipliers thus calculated provide the basis for estimating project-induced effects over the entire study period, based on the annual series of direct basic employment.

Demographic Effects

The determination of project-related demographic effects is keyed to estimates of basic and nonbasic employment associated with the facility. Two sources of population change are considered: (1) increases due to the inmigration of basic and nonbasic workers and their household members, and (2) increases resulting from the diminished outmigration of local residents and their household members.

Population increase due to inmigration is composed of movers and their accompanying household members. The estimated distribution of the basic and nonbasic jobs among the four categories of workers is based partly on local labor market conditions and commuting patterns, and partly on survey data assembled for similar projects (for example, see Malhotra and Manninen, 1979). Average family size for the direct basic construction workers is also based on construction worker survey data, while family size data for direct operations workers, indirect and other basic workers, and nonbasic workers are based on state- or locality-specific census data.

Workers and their household members who would normally have outmigrated during the project period to obtain employment, but who stayed because they found work in project-related jobs, constitute the second component of project-induced population change. In those cases where the baseline study shows that a study area will experience decline or little growth and where it will be characterized by outmigration, it is assumed that the majority of the jobs obtained by local residents (nonmovers) will prevent outmigration that would otherwise have occurred. The associated demographic effects are calculated using the same methodology as for inmigration.

Housing and Settlement Pattern Effects

Increased demand for housing results from the inmigration of workers and their accompanying household members or through the retention of local residents who would otherwise have outmigrated. Information on family accompaniment and preferred housing type (single-family dwelling, shared rental units, mobile homes, and so on) is used to generate estimates of the increased demand for housing units due to the project.

This demand is compared to the estimated supply under the baseline scenario in order to project whether any additional units (by type) will be required as a result of the project. In many cases, information from previous construction worker studies can be combined with information about local settlement pattern trends in order to estimate the probable location of the housing demand.

Infrastructure, Local Government, and Public Service Effects

This section focuses on the jurisdictional units in the impact area, the revenues and expenditures for affected government agencies and public service areas, and the cost, availability, and quality of public services. A proper fiscal impact assessment is central to this section of the research since it provides the basis for mitigation and the design of monitoring work, if such efforts are required. The basic approaches to fiscal impact assessment are discussed in Burchell and Listokin (1978).

Measurement of the impacts of the project on public services requires a detailed analysis of the revenue flows from project-related sources to local government jurisdictions. Changes in tax bases and tax rates must be estimated. Included in these estimates are increased revenues from the project itself (property taxes, business taxes, sales taxes on purchases, and the like), the induced effects on residential and commercial property values, and differentials in tax revenues generated by project-related taxpayers compared to average-income taxpayers in the impact area. Previous research shows that if project employees earn significantly more (or less) income than the average worker for a specific jurisdiction, they will also pay a larger (or smaller) amount in local taxes.

Following an examination of the direct revenue effects, local expenditures are estimated for each jurisdiction. Special emphasis is placed upon those areas most often identified as vulnerable to impacts from large-scale industrial development — schools, public safety, and transportation. The areas of public safety and transportation (roads) must include special consideration of commuter effects when there are significant numbers of commuters estimated. Other infrastructural components that may be examined separately include general government administration (legislative, judicial, planning, and so on), water and waste-water treatment facilities, solid waste disposal, utilities (telephone, electricity), fire protection, hospitals, physicians, emergency services, mental health facilities, parks and recreation, and libraries.

This basic approach typically utilizes an "average cost" methodology for fiscal impact assessment. It also identifies any special needs for facilities or other capital costs. These needs are estimated using state or other applicable standards for service levels, which are usually stated on a per capita basis (for example, average water use per day per capita). The impact population can sometimes be accommodated by current or planned excess capacity. However, any potential "marginal" costs can be important issues for local jurisdictions, in particular when local government financing faces the prospect of severe restrictions.

Finally, the analyses of government and public services are assessed in terms of a cost/benefit format. This approach describes project-related effects for both revenues and expenditures. The distribution of these two categories of fiscal impacts will not be equal, due to jurisdictional boundaries, and there may very well be tax windfalls to certain jurisdictions. This does not imply that other relatively less fortunate jurisdictions will necessarily experience absolute negative fiscal impacts. Positive or negative fiscal impacts are evaluated separately in terms of a consistent cost/benefit methodology for each significant jurisdiction.

Social Structure Effects

Social structure effects are identified by describing major functional social groups at the beginning of the study period, the characteristics of the groups, and the major features of the relationships among the groups. A premise of this approach is that relationships among people in a community are structured and that community residents form functional and interacting groups that can be identified and described. This approach was derived from the human ecology literature, and we have called it the Group Ecology Method (GEM; see Flynn and Flynn, 1982).

The aggregation of study area residents into groups has three principal objectives: (1) to identify groups that are discernable to study area residents — groups are defined such that residents can easily discuss the composition of the community; (2) to define groups that accurately reflect the functional organization of people within the study area, so that residents can easily describe the economic, political, and social relationships within the community; and (3) to identify groups that will experience differential effects (economic, demographic, housing, or fiscal) as a result of the project, or for which the evaluation of project-related effects is unique.

Based on a review of the literature on community organization, social structure, and large-scale project effects, seven attributes have been identified that seem most critical to the description of the groups and the social structure, and to the definition of the social effects of a major project:

(1) size of the group
(2) livelihood of group members
(3) demographic characteristics
(4) geographic location (residential and occupational)
(5) property ownership characteristics
(6) dominant attributes and values toward growth, environment, community participation, zoning, and planning
(7) patterns of interaction among group members (cohesion)

A profile of each major group in the study area is developed on the basis of these seven attributes. This is done by examining secondary data and by interviewing key informants. Because the purpose of these profiles is to explicate the social structure and to provide a basis for the analyses of project effects, the modal (average) characteristics of each group are described, along with an indication of the group's diversity.

The patterns of interaction among group members are examined for three spheres of activity — economic, political, and social relationships. For instance, for each pair of groups in the study area, we can ask how these groups relate to each other politically. Are they allies or competitors? Does one of the groups dominate the other when political decisions are made? What are their historical interrelationships on political issues? Similar questions can be used to describe the economic and social interaction patterns among the groups. The sum of all such patterned interactions provides an operationalized description of the social structure of the study area.

Once the groups within the study area are identified and characterized and the relationships among the groups defined, these characteristics must be projected into the future, assuming that the project is not built. The primary variables that can be used to project changes in the social structure are changes in the demographic compositions of the groups, changes in the economic structure of the study area, and national trends that will affect the study area (for example, increased labor force participation rates for women or declining agricultural employment). There are many other variables that will affect social interaction patterns in the future if the project is not built, but unless these can be defined clearly, they cannot be used in the baseline projection.

In order to project conditions *with* the project, the economic, demographic, housing, government, fiscal, and public services effects of the project are distributed among the groups. For instance, those groups that will benefit from project-induced reductions in outmigration can be identified. Those that will be affected by changes in traffic can be pointed out. Those that will disproportionately benefit from tax effects can be delineated. Projected changes in the profiles of the groups and in the relationships among groups are then described and the role of the project in those changes is determined.

Thus the overall strategy in attributing changes in social organization to the proposed project is to distribute project effects to groups, estimate the resulting changes in group profiles, and then forecast the changes that new group profiles would be expected to have on patterns of political, social, or economic interaction among groups. To the extent that the number of groups, group profiles, or group interaction patterns are different from the baseline projection, the proposed facility will be said to have caused a change in the social organization of the study area.

This technique has been used successfully both for post hoc and projective studies. In the postlicensing studies for the Nuclear Regulatory Commission (Mountain West Research with Social Impact Research, 1982), the twelve study areas were disaggregated into their component groups, each group was profiled at the beginning of the study period (generally, when the project was announced), and changes in each group over the study period were related to other project impacts. For instance, at the Calvert Cliffs (Maryland) Nuclear Power Plant, blacks received nearly a quarter of the basic employment and more than a quarter of the nonbasic employment. These jobs paid significantly more than their previous employment as agricultural day laborers, improved their job skills so that they could be hired on other construction projects in the area, stemmed the rate of outmigration for young male blacks during the construction period and dramatically increased the rate when the construction was completed, and permanently altered the social and economic interaction patterns of blacks with other groups in the study area (Flynn, 1982).

In a technical report for the Interdisciplinary Team for the U.S. Forest Service on the Social and Economic Effects of the Proposed Ski Development at Early Winters (Social Impact Research, 1981), the four major groups in the in the Methow Valley were profiled, and baseline projections of the group characteristics and interaction patterns were made. The primary effect of the ski resort would be different for each group. Briefly, the rural quality of the valley would be diminished for all groups. The "longtime residents" would become a smaller proportion of the population, would not benefit directly from the employment or income generated by the resort, but would retain significant political power. The "mainstream newcomers" would be the primary beneficiaries of the tax and income effects of the resort, as they own the majority of the tourist-related services. This group would be expected to grow in size and influence. The "alternative lifestyle newcomers" would have additional sources of short-term employment if they needed it, which might enable the more economically marginal people to stay in the valley. The value of the "seasonal residents'" property would increase because it would be used in the winter as well as the summer. Finally, there would be a new social group in the valley, "seasonal workers." Research at other ski resorts indicates that this group has a profile that is very different from any of the other groups in the valley, and that it would be difficult to integrate members of this group into the existing social structure.

Evaluation and Effects

The social effects described so far occur regardless of the point of view of the observer, and are referred to, for simplicity, as the objective effects of the project. However, the evaluation of the project's objective effects is based on the impacts of the project on each group, and on each group's evaluation of the significance of those impacts over time. The determination of the significance of both the specific and overall effects is based on the size, magnitude, importance, duration, extent, and diffusion of the impacts, and on the preexisting values of the groups. Thus, if we think of giving 200 new ski resort jobs to one of the groups mentioned above, the significance would be quite different depending upon which one of groups was selected. Each group's summary evaluation of the project is analyzed in light of its own perception of the risks (including safety and environmental issues) and benefits.

Taking into account the objective changes associated with the project and the subjective evaluation of those changes by affected groups, the analysis concludes with a final statement of the project's social and economic importance to the study area as a whole. Such an analysis is critical for understanding the public response to the project. In both of the examples cited, the projects either were or would be significant in the study area and would be evaluated as such by study area residents. In the ski resort case, the differential distribution of project effects and the different value systems of the groups imply that the public response to the proposal would be divided.

Conclusion

The conceptual framework reported here represents a relatively simple set of cause-and-effect relationships. The great utility of the Group Ecology Method is that it links the direct effects of building and operating a facility to the probable social and economic responses in the study area. The GEM approach does this by combining the established methods of SIA research with new conceptual links to the "social social" effects. Thus an integrated chain of social and economic causation has been described, one that links functional groups in the local study area to the project-induced effects.

The approach to social impact assessment described here is based upon the premise that changes in a study area can be adequately described only when a causal link can be made between the project-related effects and the characteristics of local areas. The methodology employed in this approach used many theories and techniques that were developed during the last decade. It goes further in a number of instances by refining the accepted methodologies.

One of the most important advances of this approach is in its conceptualization of the functional group as the basic component for defining social change. This allows the study team to make an accurate description of the impact area social structure and to distribute the project-related effects in a way that was not possible prior to this development. Such an approach also allows a much better understanding of the socioeconomic context within which issues are raised in response to the project.

References

ANDERSON, E. J. and J. CHALMERS (1980) Spatial Interaction and the Economic Hierarchy in the Western United States. Tempe, AZ: Mountain West Research, Inc.

BURCHELL, R. W. and D. LISTOKIN (1978) Fiscal Impact Handbook. New Brunswick, NJ: Center for Urban Policy Research.

DUNNING, C. M. (1982) "Construction work force characteristics and community service impact assessment." Water Resources Bulletin 18, 2: 239-244.

FLYNN, C. and J. FLYNN (1982) "The Group Ecology Method: a new conceptual design for social impact assessment." IAIA Bulletin 1, 4: 11-19.

FLYNN, J. (1982) "Socioeconomic impacts of nuclear generating stations, vol. 2: Calvert Cliffs case study." NUREG/CR-2749. Prepared for the U.S. Nuclear Regulatory Commission.

FREUDENBURG, W. R. (1978) "A *social* social impact analysis of a Rocky Mountain energy boomtown," Presented at the 73rd Annual Meetings of the American Sociological Association, San Francisco.

LEISTRITZ, L. and S. MURDOCK (1981) The Socioeconomic Impact of Resource Development: Methods for Assessment. Boulder, CO: Westview.

LONG, L. H. and K. A. HANSEN (1979) "Reasons for interstate migration," in U.S. Bureau of the Census, Current Population Reports. Series P-23, No. 81. Washington, DC: Government Printing Office.

MALHOTRA, S. and D. MANNINEN (1980) Migration and Residential Location of Workers at Nuclear Power Plant Construction Sites. Seattle: Battelle Human Affairs Research Centers.

—— (1979)Socioeconomic Impact Assessment: Profile Analysis of Worker Surveys Conducted at Nuclear Power Plant Construction Sites. Seattle: Battelle Human Affairs Research Centers.

Mountain West Research, Inc. (1977a) "Construction worker survey." Prepared for the Bureau of Reclamation, Tempe, AZ.

—— (1977b) "Economic/demographic assessment manual." Prepared for the Bureau of Reclamation, Tempe, AZ.

—— (1975) "Construction worker profile." Final report. Prepared for the Old West Regional Commission, Tempe, AZ.

———— with Social Impact Research, Inc. (1982) "Socioeconomic impact of nuclear generating stations, summary report on the NRC post-licensing studies." Prepared for the U.S. Nuclear Regulatory Commission, Tempe, AZ; Seattle.

MURDOCK, S. H., S. WEILAND, and F. L. LEISTRITZ (1980) "Selecting socioeconomic assessment models: a discussion of criteria and selected models." Journal of Environmental Management 10: 241-252.

———— (1978) "An assessment of the validity of the gravity model for predicting community settlement patterns in rural impacted areas in the West." Journal of Land Economics 54, 3: 461-471.

Social Impact Research, Inc. (1981) "The social and economic effects of the proposed ski development at Early Winters." Prepared for the U.S. Forest Service, Region 6, Portland, OR.

TOMAN, N. E. et al. (1977) "A fiscal impact model for rural industrialization." Western Journal of Agricultural Economics, 1, 1.

U.S. Bureau of Labor Statistics (1973) Consumer Expenditure Survey Series. Washington, DC: Government Printing Office.

U.S. Department of Commerce, Bureau of the Census (1979) Projections of the Number of Households and Families: 1979-1995. Washington, DC: Government Printing Office.

II
PRIMARY DATA
COLLECTION
METHODS

• • • • • • • • • • • • •

4

Survey Research

○ ○ ○ ○ ○ ○ ○ ○ ○ ○ ○ ○ ○ ○ ○ ○ ○ ○

KURT FINSTERBUSCH

○ ○ ○ ○ ○ ○ ○ ○ ○ ○ ○ ○ ○ ○ ○ ○ ○ ○

● Surveys are the bread and butter of sociologists and many other social scientists. They provide not only self-reported external facts about respondents, but also a record of inner feelings, attitudes, and opinions that cannot be obtained efficiently in any other way. Again and again policies that are based entirely on observables or statistical records miss the mark because they are not properly tailored to what people really want. For example, a county government planned to enlarge a two-lane road to four lanes to improve the access to and from a community on the suburban fringe. It assumed that this was what the residents wanted and was dumbfounded when it encountered loud and widespread protests. The community wanted to keep its partly rural ambiance even at the cost of slightly longer travel times. Decision makers need to know what people like and dislike and how they will respond to government actions, and surveys usually are the best way to get this information.

It should be pointed out that surveys have their own set of methodological problems and work best when used in conjunction with other sources of information. Nevertheless, they are generally the best method for finding out the characteristics and attitudes of a population and a rich source of information for SIAs.

Uses of Surveys in SIAs

Government actions supposedly address the needs of citizens. Surveys may be required to determine the extent and distribution of these needs.

Accordingly, the provision of services at the community or county level is often guided by a community needs assessment survey (see Chapter 11 for an extended discussion of needs assessment). Generally, needs assessment surveys ascertain the need for and attitudes toward various types of government programs and expenditures. Together with agency statistics, these surveys can guide public expenditures. They can also help assess the community impacts of large construction projects.

The most typical use of surveys in SIA is to determine the attitudes of area residents and/or potential facility users toward the project alternatives. Community members have a chance to voice their attitudes toward alternatives in public hearings, but hearings provide very biased readings of public opinion. Properly performed surveys are infinitely superior to hearings and are a valuable aid to decision making.

Another use of surveys in SIAs is to determine some of the policy's impacts and people's responses to them. If parking fees are raised will people carpool? If a dam is built will the displaced farmers buy other farms, shift out of farming, retire, or move away? Who are the people displaced and what are their resources for coping with relocation? How will a new low-income housing project affect nearby middle-class residents? Surveys are needed to answer these questions so that the project can be designed to better fit the situation and mitigate problems.

Finally, surveys can be the source of weights to be used in evaluating alternatives. The various physical, economic, and social impacts cannot be reduced to a common measure. They must be subjectively traded off against one another when alternatives are ranked. Surveys can establish the priorities of specific groups and the general public and describe their attitudes toward the alternatives.

Conducting Surveys for SIAs

Space does not allow this chapter to serve as a text for survey procedures. The reader should consult survey texts for complete descriptions of survey methods (Babbie, 1973; Cornog, 1982; Dillman, 1978; Labaw, 1980; Moser and Kalton, 1972; Sudman and Bradburn, 1982; Warwick and Lininger, 1975). In this section survey procedures are evaluated for their relevance to SIAs.

A survey consists of the following tasks:

(1) clarifying the purpose or goals of the survey

(2)   identifying the survey population
(3)   selecting the sample
(4)   planning the survey
(5)   selecting the method of implementation
(6)   designing the questionnaire
(7)   testing the questionnaire
(8)   administering the survey
(9)   coding and keypunching
(10)   analyzing and presenting the data

It should be noted that a questionnaire has its own impacts. Surveys do not just find out what people think and feel, they also start people thinking and feeling; this is especially true of SIA surveys. At the time of the interview many people will not have opinions, or at least not clear ones. The interview process itself will cause some of them to form or clarify their opinions. In other words, the survey is an event that changes the respondents by making them somewhat more informed and sometimes more opinionated. In some instances crystallization of attitudes can affect the acceptability, indeed the very future, of the project.

Survey Goals

Surveys are used to test hypotheses, determine the characteristics of populations, explain why people act the way they do, understand causal influences, identify consumer or voter preferences, and explore new topics of investigation. The main purposes of surveys in SIAs are to describe populations, register their opinions, and predict their responses. These objectives do not require very complex survey designs. They are relatively straightforward and can be pursued by relatively inexperienced survey researchers. Descriptions of populations usually include the following characteristics of individuals or families: age, sex, education, occupation, income, marital status, length of residence, need for services (and the project), and sometimes race, ethnicity, place of birth, father's occupation and education, occupational history, memberships, networks, trips, and leisure activities. Descriptions of the population also include their attitudes on relevant topics. Related to attitudes are opinions on proposed govern-ment actions and their various alternatives. Finally, surveys are used in SIAs to predict the responses of populations to proposed changes. Citizens often predict their own responses inaccurately, thus other methods for predicting their responses must be utilized, such as reviewing how citizens responded in similar past cases. Nonetheless, one should not try to predict people's responses without at least finding out what people think they will do.

The Survey Population

Seldom is the survey population readily identified in SIAs. Ideally, the survey population should encompass the population that will be affected. Most SIAs involve a geographically located government action — often involving construction on a site. The survey population would include the neighboring communities that would experience significant construction impacts. Exactly what communities are included involves an arbitrary judgment, because no one can tell when impacts shade from significant to insignificant. Furthermore, the classification of subpopulations is often arbitrary to a degree. For example, classifying residents into the categories of "neighboring" and "nonneighboring" is arbitrary, though traditions for this type of decision are developing (for example, a quarter-mile band on both sides of proposed highways is commonly identified as neighboring because highway noise exceeds normal background noise in built-up areas for about this distance). Since the geographic boundaries of the survey population and subpopulations are at least partly arbitrary, the researcher is advised to review his or her research plans with community leaders and spokespersons for interested parties to ensure the legitimacy of the survey sample.

For nongeographically located government actions, such as the national 55 mph speed limit, the survey population may be the entire nation or entire categories of people such as hunters, licensed drivers, people over 65, or farmers. The categories of people should be selected on the basis of an impact model for the government action that identifies affected groups.

Sampling

Surveys almost never involve the entire population. Normally, they involve a random sample drawn from the population. A later section will review sampling theory and practices, because they warrant extended discussion. This section is devoted to a discussion of one sampling method, map sampling, which is particularly well suited to SIAs for facility construction.

When facilities are constructed, maps and areal photographs are important data sources for the SIA. They can also be used for a sampling frame from which the sample is randomly selected. For facilities such as highways, transmission or pipe lines, and airports, the affected area cu across geopolitical boundaries. Most lists of populations are organized geopolitically and are difficult to use for sampling in these SIAs. Detail maps and areal photographs can identify all structures within various distances of the proposed facility. Except in central cities, multiunit dwellings can be easily identified, visited, and numbered for the number of dwelling units. All dwelling units in the impact area can be assigned numbers and a random sample drawn using a table of random numbers. A few garages or barns might get included in the sample, but nonetheless the sample should be useful for personal interviews or "leave and pick-up" or "leave and mail-back" questionnaires.

Survey Plans

Decisions must be made regarding the type of survey and the survey schedule. The four basic types of surveys are cross-sectional, trend, cohort, and panel. Almost all surveys for SIAs are cross-sectional, but the growth of substantive knowledge in SIAs would benefit greatly from trend and panel studies. A *cross-sectional survey* takes place at one point in time. By the time the SIA is published, however, many parameters may have changed. Trend, cohort, and panel surveys provide data on changes over time. They provide data management and comparability problems that probably would be too taxing for most inexperienced researchers, but they generally are far superior to cross-sectional surveys. A *trend survey* studies the same general population at several points in time. The individuals within the population (for example, a student body) may change and a new sample drawn each time, but each sample represents the same population at different points in time. In SIAs a particularly valuable trend survey would study a community population before, during, and after the construction of a major facility. To date we know surprisingly little about how attitudes of community citizens change over these project stages. A *cohort survey* studies the same specific population but draws new samples each time. The name comes from the practice of studying the same age cohort over time, such as those born in 1930 or the graduating class of 1970. It could also apply to a varied age group that shared a common experience in time, such as the founders (first-year residents) of a new town. The *panel survey* studies the same people repeatedly. It is the ideal longitudinal study, but even modest amounts of attrition can greatly weaken the reliability of the findings and tracking costs are likely to be high.

Almost all surveys in SIAs are cross-sectional and this practice is likely to continue. Nevertheless, I recommend the greater use of trend and panel surveys, because public opinion on public projects or policies can shift significantly in a short period of time. On the other hand, if a cross-sectional survey is to be used, its scheduling must be carefully planned. If the survey is conducted too early most community residents will be poorly informed. If the survey is conducted after opinions have fully formed, it may be too late to help decision makers avoid pitfalls and to plan widely accepted alternatives.

I suggest that the cross-sectional survey be converted into a trend analysis by dividing the originally planned sample into two halves and interviewing one half as early as possible and the other half as late as possible. The preliminary analysis of the first sample can feed into the project plans before they become set. The comparison between the two samples can indicate the direction in which public opinion is moving. On the other hand, the two samples can be combined for the bulk of the analysis. If possible, two additional interview waves (using smaller samples, if necessary) during and after the construction of the facility or after implementation of the program are recommended. The comparison of public opinion at different stages of the project would contribute greatly to our understanding of social impacts.

If one can conduct only a cross-sectional survey, one can attempt to obtain longitudinal data by asking respondents not only about their current situations and attitudes, but also about their past ones. Answers to questions about the past are less accurate than answers to questions about the present, but the directions of trends can be ascertained by comparing the two. Respondents could be asked to recall their original reactions to the project when they first heard about it as well as their current attitudes. It must be remembered, however, that the sample being studied is a probability sample of current residents and does not represent the population at the earlier time, some of whom may have moved away. If the project has been completed, respondents can be asked about their before and after opinions. One must be extremely cautious in interpreting the results as trends, however, unless one has been able to question a sample of those who moved away.

Survey Method

The five major survey methods are (1) face-to-face interview, (2) telephone interview, (3) self-administered questionnaires in groups, (4) leave and pick-up questionnaire, and (5) mail questionnaire. The mail questionnaire is the least expensive but also produces the lowest response rates, often in the unacceptably low range of 30-50 percent. At the other end of the continuum, the face-to-face interview is the most expensive but generally produces the highest-quality information and may be necessary for long or complex questionnaires. The interviewer can see that the questions are properly understood and the answers properly expressed. He or she can probe the answers, find out why people answer the way they do, and ask open-ended questions. The interviewer also serves as a motivating force for completing the questionnaire even if it is long and/or difficult. Normally response rates exceed 70 percent for face-to-face interviews, though response rates have been dropping in the past decade. The presence of the interviewer, however, does have one disadvantage. Respondents will tend to answer in ways that they believe the interviewer will approve. This bias also exists in other types of surveys, but to a lesser extent.

The telephone interview has most of the advantages of the face-to-face interview but costs much less and is becoming the preferred method for many survey researchers if the survey is not too long. Since 98% of households in the United States have telephones, non-subscribing is not a very serious problem (U.S. Department of Commerce, 1981: 562). Groves and Kahn (1979) make a strong case for the attractions of telephone surveys. Sampling random telephone numbers and administering the questionnaire are relatively easy, and response rates are very close to response rates for personal interviews. Groves and Kahn found that differences in question comprehension and missing data were small.

An excellent manual for conducting effective telephone surveys (and mail surveys) is Dillman's *Mail and Telephone Surveys: The Total Design Method* (1978). He claims that by using his method he and other researchers obtained an average response rate of 91% for 31 telephone surveys (mostly in the state of Washington). His method is detailed and cannot be presented here. It involves efforts to reward respondents based on exchange theory; efforts to minimize the costs to respondents in time, effort, and psychological discomfort; and efforts to maintain trust. These principles are used to shape practically every detail of the survey operation.

The other three survey methods involve self-administration of the questionnaire. The first of these has respondents fill out the questionnaire in groups. The fieldworker distributes, explains, and collects the questionnaires and answers questions. His or her presence assures a high response rate. The second method of self-administered surveys also involves some personal contact. The fieldworker distributes and collects the questionnaires, usually at the respondents' homes. The visit by the fieldworker substantially increases the response rate. The last method is the mail questionnaire, which, as mentioned above, seldom produces a sufficient response rate unless the respondents have something to gain by returning their answers, for example, when the survey serves as a ballot on an issue of importance to the respondent.

Most SIAs estimate the social impacts of a potential project or program on a community or region and gather information on public attitudes toward the proposed action. In these settings SIA researchers must get to know the community; face-to-face interviews greatly aid this objective. On the other hand, most SIAs have very small budgets compared to the information they are asked to produce. Normally, the budget forces the researchers to use telephone interviews or self-administered questionnaires. If this is the case, it is strongly recommended that the pretesting of the questionnaire be conducted in part in face-to-face interviews or, better still, that a preliminary exploratory survey of a small sample (40-50 respondents) be conducted face-to-face. The telephone interview or self-administered questionnaire would then build on the preliminary study. The advantages of the telephone and self-administered surveys are apparent, but they cannot take the place of fieldwork.

Questionnaire Design

It is easy to ask questions, but it is not always easy to ask useful questions. The art of questionnaire construction, although seemingly simple, is actually very technical and complicated. A later section provides a set of guidelines for questionnaire construction, but survey textbooks should also be consulted. Some example questionnaires that can be used as models can be found in Campbell et al. (1976), Marans and Wellman (1978), and Gilmore and Duff (1975). Even with all these aids, however, inexperienced survey researchers are urged to have their questionnaires reviewed by more experienced researchers. Incidentally, it is common even for experienced survey researchers to have colleagues review their question-naires, because what is an absolutely clear question to one person can be interpreted in logical but unexpected ways by another person.

Testing, Administering, and Processing the Survey

Once constructed, the questionnaire normally is pretested on a compara-ble population to determine whether questions are properly understood and whether they elicit the kinds of information desired. The pretest also provides responses to open-ended questions that can be used to create the categories for closed-ended questions in the final form of the questionnaire.

It is recommended that surveys for SIAs be conducted in cycles (Finsterbusch, 1977) rather than in a linear fashion proceeding from questionnaire design to interviewing to analysis. Once constructed and pretested, the questionnaire should be used on a small random sample of the target population and quickly analyzed in a preliminary way. The findings could then be used to add to and modify the questionnaire before surveying the remainder of the sample. Too often researchers learn the important issues the survey should examine only when they reach the analysis stage. If the survey is conducted in cycles, appropriate midcourse corrections in the questionnaire can be made after the first cycle. In SIAs one cannot leave to future research the study of the issues that arise in the course of the research.

There are numerous administrative aspects of surveys for which helpful advice can save time, money, and heartaches. Discussions of these issues are left to the survey textbooks, except for three quick items. First, be sure to set up a reliable system for protecting confidentiality. Second, supply training for the interviewers in which the questionnaire is carefully explained and the interviewers can practice giving the interview. Finally, develop procedures that ensure accountability. Interviewers have been known to fill in questionnaires themselves without ever going into the field. A check-up telephone call to a random sample of respondents is one method of addressing this problem.

The processing of the questionnaire principally involves constructing a codebook, coding, keypunching (or use of scanners), computing new variables, and creating a working data file. Professional expertise may be necessary in order to make sure that the data file can be easily amended and manipulated in the necessary ways.

Analyzing the Survey

The major purpose of SIAs is description, hence the major analytical tool is simple frequency distributions that show the percentage of respondents with various characteristics and attitudes. Also important are the comparisons between various groups of respondents on their characteristics and attitudes. For example, how do the distributions of attitudes of farmers differ from the distributions of attitudes for local merchants, town residents, and lumbermen? Special expertise is not necessary for these analyses.

Seldom do SIAs require complex multivariate analyses, but these methods can add to our understanding of public responses to public actions and should be used more often. For example, a multiple regression analysis can show the extent to which support for the project can be explained by the variables in the study and can roughly sort out the relative importance of each of those variables for predicting support. Professional expertise is required for properly conducting and interpreting multiple regression techniques, because assumptions about linearity, independence, and additivity must be taken into account. This expertise is widely available, however, so the need for statistical expertise is not a significant barrier to using multivariate analyses in SIAs.

Sampling Theory and Practices

The concepts of probability and random sampling are the keys to keeping survey costs low (a requirement in many SIAs). *Probability* is the expected proportion of occurrences of a particular outcome out of numerous repetitions of an event. For example, the probability of a flipped coin coming up heads is .5. However, it is very unlikely that 500 heads will occur in 1000 flips of a coin. It is likely, however, that the number of heads will be close to 500, and the difference between the actual proportion and the expected proportion decreases on the average with the number of flips. These statements illustrate the fact that almost all samples contain some error in representing the population from which they are drawn, and the error on the average decreases with the size of the sample. In other words, the researcher must trade off accuracy and sample size in planning surveys.

Unless target populations are under 2000, they should be sampled rather than studied in their entirety. Even many populations of less than 2000 should be sampled for SIAs. The amount of error introduced is usually within acceptable ranges for descriptive studies with samples of only 500 respondents unless precise comparisons between means for numerous subpopulations are needed. Even samples of 40 or 80 can provide a rough reading of population characteristics and attitudes when they are used cautiously (for a discussion of the utility of surveys of small samples, see Finsterbusch 1976a, 1976b, 1977).

A sample of 100 provides sufficient accuracy to be taken seriously. The .95 confidence interval lies about .1 above and below the population proportion. It takes 300 more respondents to cut this interval in half and another 1200 respondents to cut it in half again. Since SIAs require mainly

TABLE 4.1   Typical Sample Sizes for Studies of Human
             and Institutional Populations

Number of Subgroup Analyses	People or Households		Institutions	
	National	Regional or Special	National	Regional or Special
None or few	1000-1500	200-500	200-500	50-200
Average	1500-2500	500-1000	500-1000	200-500
Many	2500+	1000+	1000+	500+

SOURCE: Sudman (1976). Reprinted by permission.

descriptive statistics (simple frequency distributions and bivariate tables) and seldom use complex multivariate analyses, samples of 400 or 500 should be sufficient in most cases, and even a sample of 100 would be sufficient if the survey is not going to have a critical role in the decision process. We must emphasize that selecting sample sizes is a matter of judgment. Sudman (1976) recommends larger sample sizes than I have proposed based on his observation of several hundred studies (see Table 4.1). He also reviews a technical method for determining the optimum sample size (Sudman 1976: 99-102, 231-233) drawn from Schlaifer (1959). The reader should consult these works for a full discussion of the issues in sample size selection.

The second key concept in sampling methodology is *randomness*. In a random sample all members of a population have an equal probability of being chosen for the sample. This attribute of samples is extremely important because the statistics used in analyzing the results are applicable only if the sample is random. Nonrandom samples must be used in certain situations, but they have the disadvantage of containing some unknown amount of bias and thus they surround the survey findings and interpretations with a shroud of uncertainty.

To draw a sample one needs a list of all elements in a population. The list or the materials, such as maps, areal photographs, and directories, that are used to identify the elements of the population constitute a *sampling frame*. For surveys in SIAs the population usually consists of individuals or households, each of which is given a unique number. Numbers are then obtained from a list of random numbers and matched with the list until the appropriate size sample is selected. Normally, if a person's number comes up more than once, he or she is counted only once in the sample (sampling without replacement), though counting individuals more than once is legitimate. The above procedure procures a simple random sample.

It is usually practical to modify the above procedure in various ways that should not invalidate the randomness of the sample. These modifications create *equal probability samples.* A commonly used equal probability sample is the *systematic sample with a random start.* Once the sample size is determined, it is divided into the population. The quotient (i) determines the number between sample members on the population list. Every i^th person is selected after the first person is randomly selected from the first i persons. This procedure produces identical results to the simple random sample unless the list contains a rhythm that coincides with the selection rhythm.

Multistage cluster sampling is another practical modification of simple random sampling. Sometimes the creation of a population list is impossible or inordinately expensive. The researcher first samples clusters of individuals and then samples individuals within the selected clusters. For example, in drawing a sample in a city a researcher might randomly select 100 blocks and then randomly select 5 individuals or households in each block to obtain a sample of 500. This is a popular method because it greatly lowers costs. It has the disadvantage, however, of somewhat less accuracy than the simple random sample, because it is subject to multiple sampling errors— one at each stage—and the sampling error is larger at each stage than in a single-stage random sample because the sample sizes are smaller at each stage.

Another important modification of simple random sampling is *stratified sampling.* Whenever groups of very unequal size are to be compared in the study the population should be divided (stratified) into relevant groups and the same size sample can be drawn randomly or systematically from each group. This procedure oversamples from small groups and undersamples from large groups, so the overall results are biased. This bias can be removed by weighting the results for the subpopulations in accord with their proportion of the total population.

An example of use of a stratified sample would be a study of university opinion of an honor system that involved a sample of 200 students, 200 faculty, and all administrators from department chairpersons up to the president. A random sample of the university community would be swamped by students and would catch very few administrators. In this case an overall opinion for all members of the university averaged together would be meaningless, but the stratified sample would provide meaningful results. This illustrates the fact that stratified sampling is vastly superior to simple random sampling in many situations. Stratified sampling violates the sacred principle of equal probability sampling, but the results can be made to conform to the results of equal probability sampling as long as the probability of selection in each stratum is known so that appropriate weights can be used to correct the sampling biases.

It is often wise to combine multistage cluster sampling with stratified sampling. For example, the blocks in a multistage cluster sample might be stratified into (a) adjacent to or bisected by the proposed highway, (b) nonadjacent but within a five-minute drive to a highway entrance, and (c) remaining blocks. Forty blocks in each category would then be randomly selected and five individuals randomly selected in each block.

When the sizes of clusters in a multistage cluster sample are very uneven it is advisable to modify this sampling technique by the principle of *probability proportionate to size*. In the first stage of sampling each cluster is given a probability of being selected that is proportionate to its size — large clusters have higher probabilities. In the second stage, however, a set number of individuals are selected regardless of cluster size. Each individual in the population ends up having the same probability of being included, but the chances are very different at each stage. Members of populous city blocks have a relatively high probability that their block will be chosen, but a relatively low probability that they will be chosen if their block is chosen.

All of the above procedures are cases of probability sampling. They are valid bases for scientific surveys. Sometimes nonprobability samples are used in applied research, but they are risky. Three types are common: ad hoc, judgmental, and quota sampling. *Ad hoc samples* are drawn from ad hoc collections of people such as shoppers at a shopping center or people attending a meeting. These samples might be convenient but they are unrepresentative of any larger population. The *judgmental sample* is one selected by the interviewers, who are instructed to obtain a representative sample by interviewing some students, housewives, businessmen, blue-collar workers, salespeople, clerical workers, and professionals while varying age, sex, race, and ethnicity. This technique leaves too much room for judgment to be scientific; the *quota sample* reduces this problem. For quota samples the interviewer is given prearranged categories and a predetermined number of interviews for each category. These specifications are based on the known characteristics of the target population. Within the specified quotas the interviewer is supposed to select representative cases. The quotas reduce interviewers' judgments but do not eliminate them.

Principles for Questionnaire Construction

(1) Provide clear introduction and instructions. The questionnaire should start with an introduction (or cover letter) that explains the purpose of the survey, identifies the sponsor, and describes the confidentiality of the responses. Furthermore, throughout the questionnaire sections or sets of questions should be introduced by statements such as "Now we would like to ask some questions about . . . " or "In this section, we would like to learn about . . . ." It is important to orient the respondent — to give him or her a sense of the general purpose of the questionnaire and the specific purpose of sections of the questionnaire. The respondent should also be instructed carefully on how to answer the questions.

(2) Use global and specific questions. Every concept to be measured by survey questions should be analyzed into its components. For many concepts, a global question will be asked to indicate the concept and specific questions will be asked to indicate the dimensions of the concept. In fact, it may be prudent to use more than one question to indicate a single dimension of a concept. The measurement of attitudes, in particular, normally requires several questions on the same dimension. When several questions are used to indicate a dimension of a concept or the concept itself, they are often aggregated into an index. For example, community satisfaction might be indicated by the global question "On the whole, how happy are you with living here in [name of community]; would you say you're very happy, pretty happy, or not too happy with the community?" On the other hand, community satisfaction might be indicated by an index score aggregated from several questions about the services, friendliness, and taxes of the community, and the opportunities there. In fact, both methods would probably be used and compared.

(3) Use questions about both objective and subjective factors. Surveys ask people to report their circumstances, statuses, experiences, behaviors, beliefs, thoughts, judgments, and attitudes in the past, present, and future. By identifying objective or observable factors of individuals — their statuses, circumstances, experiences, and behavior — the researcher can classify individuals into groups for comparison on other items. For many SIAs age, sex, education, income, family status, race, occupation, length of residency, ownership or rental of housing, location, previous residence, place of work, and organizational membership are especially important for this purpose. Most of these data are obtained by straightforward questions. Subjective characteristics of individuals, beliefs, thoughts, opinions, and

attitudes can be difficult to elicit accurately because the questions must be simple while the subjective characteristics are complex. Generally several questions are used to probe a single attitude or belief in order to catch some of its nuances. For example, the question "Do you believe in God?" would be followed up by several questions for those answering yes such as "Do you believe that God intervenes in history?" Even four or five questions only scratch the surface of the individual's complex belief system about God, the environment, the public project, prospective community changes, and so on. Nevertheless, they should be sufficient for usefully categorizing respondents for purposes of comparison and analysis.

(4) Ask clear questions. The researcher can shoot too high and thereby miss entirely. If he or she attempts too much in a single question, some respondents will be confused and the results will be unreliable and therefore unusable. Some questions are unclear for some respondents because they contain concepts that have unknown or ambiguous references. For example, if a judgment or opinion is sought by means of the question "Do you think the federal government is spending too much money to protect the environment?" some respondents have no idea how much the government spends and thus cannot give an informed opinion. For the sake of clarity the question could be preceded by a statement on the amount that the government does spend. If, on the other hand, the purpose of this question is simply to record an attitude about governmental concern about the environment, then the respondent's ignorance is much less of a problem.

(5) Ask short questions. In an effort to be precise, the researcher is tempted to load the question with information and clarifying phrases. At some point clarifications increase the length and complexity of the question too much and the clarity decreases. Questions should be as short as possible or respondents will be irritated. Short, clear, and easily interpreted questions are the ideal.

(6) Ask only one question at a time. Since respondents give only one answer to a question, each one must be a single question. Double questions are frequently asked by inexperienced survey researchers. For example, "Do you think that the agency's relocation program provided equitable compensation for your home and useful assistance in finding a new one?" is an obvious double question. Others may be more subtle, so examine carefully questions with "and" in them.

(7) Use closed-ended questions. Closed-ended questions supply lists of answers from which the respondent can chose his or her answers. Open-

ended questions let the respondent verbalize an answer without cues. Open-ended questions can provide insights that might not emerge from closed-ended questions. Nevertheless, closed-ended questions are generally preferable except during the exploratory stage of the study. The answers to open-ended questions are much more difficult to interpret and analyze because various respondents might be answering a question in very different ways. For example, when asked "What do you like most about your neighborhood?" one respondent may say "friendly neighbors" and another "its convenient location." The second respondent may have thought that the question referred to the physical aspects of the neighborhood; if a list of answers had been read to him or her that included "kind of neighbors," he or she might have selected that answer. Seldom do open-ended questions provide one with information that can be easily interpreted. As a general rule it is much better to ask several specific closed-ended questions about attitudes toward aspects of one's neighborhood than to ask "What do you like about your neighborhood?" To construct closed-ended questions, however, one must repeat questions from previous surveys or ask open-ended questions in the pretest to get the categories for the closed-ended questions.

(8) Ask positive questions. Introducing a negative into a question always increases the chance of a misunderstanding. Some respondents will miss the negative and those who notice it must take an additional mental step in answering it. One should not always ask questions about positive actions, but should ask positive questions. For example, it is easier for respondents to agree or disagree with "The mayor should oppose the proposed interstate highway plan" than with "The mayor should not support the proposed interstate highway plan." It is all right to use oppose instead of support, or disagree instead of agree, in questions, but "not" should be used sparingly.

(9) Avoid biasing terms in questions. First, emotionally charged questions and words should be avoided. Emotionally charged adjectives such as "radical" or "unfair" or nouns such as "abortionists" or "racists" should be deleted or replaced with tamer terms. Second, when respondents are asked to agree or disagree with statements, the statements should not be identified with a group or person but should stand on their own. Third, mentioning only some of the alternatives biases answers. Mention all or no options. "Do you favor the Lanham or Seabrook or another location for the plant?" prejudices the answer toward the Lanham and Seabrook locations and prejudices the answer against the no-build alternative. Fourth, the type of scale used for answers can bias them. For example, a seven-point scale

ranging from very positive to very negative is less biasing than a scale consisting of "very positive," "fairly positive," "slightly positive," and "negative." Finally, questions that elicit answers that cast the respondent in a negative light will produce biased answers. For example, "Have you ever cheated on your income taxes?" is not likely to obtain honest responses from many respondents.

(10) Use tact in asking embarrassing questions. As a general rule, sensitive or embarrassing questions should come near the end of the questionnaire to allow for the development of rapport, trust, and survey momentum. The income question is always sensitive and is usually one of the last questions. It can be made less discomforting for the respondent if he or she is given a card with four to six income categories on it, listed by letter. The respondent can then tell the interviewer the letter of the appropriate income category. No income figures are ever mentioned and the respondent is made less anxious. There are similar ways to desensitize many other questions, and all questionnaires should be reviewed for tact and sensitivity before going to the field. Small changes are important. To have to say no to "Do you work?" is more unpleasant than saying no to "Do you have a job at present?" One approach to sensitive questions is to ask them indirectly. Instead of asking "How prejudiced are you?" the interviewer asks a number of indirect questions, such as "Would you be upset if a black with the same income and education moved in next door?"

(11) Push respondents off the fence. Interviewers must be tactful, but they must also be pushy. Many people do not have strong opinions on subjects and prefer to remain inoffensively neutral. They have to be prodded into positive or negative categories even if their preferences are slight. Seven-point scales provide ample opportunity for respondents to indicate the intensity of their attitudes and make it easy for them to get off the fence. Of course, respondents who remain neutral after prodding should be scored as neutrals; "don't know," "not applicable," and "no answer" are also necessary categories for many questions.

(12) Concretize questions. As a general rule a concrete question about concrete behavior is preferable to abstract questions about subjective responses. Most researchers prefer the question "How often did you attend church in the past month?" to the question "How religious are you?" Attitudinal questions tend to be tricky and allow too much leeway for respondents to misrepresent themselves. Questions about behavior are not

immune to problems, but they tend to produce more usable results than attitudinal questions.

(13) Ask multiple attitudinal questions. SIA surveys necessitate some attitudinal questions on the proposed action and its consequences. The general rule is that more than one question is necessary for indicating an attitude unless it is a very simple attitude. It is usually advisable to ask a set of carefully planned questions that explore the major dimensions of the attitude and that can be constructed into an index. Some indexes simply add up the degree of favorable support for each item in the index. For example, a community satisfaction index might be constructed by summing the evaluation scores for schools, police, job opportunities, leisure opportunities, costs, and quality of social relationships. Other indexes involve Guttman scales, in which the questions form an order such that answering a question positively almost invariably means that all questions below (or above) it are also answered positively.

(14) Ask only appropriate questions. Many questions should only be asked of respondents who answered a previous question in a certain way. For example, "Did you vote in the last election?" is followed by "Who did you vote for?" for those who answer yes and "Who did you favor?" for those who answer no.

(15) Lay out questionnaires aesthetically and effectively. Avoid cramping the questionnaire, because this turns off respondents. Lay out the questionnaire so that little or no coding is needed to prepare it for keypunching. Answers should be precoded if possible.

Conclusion

Surveys can contribute greatly to SIAs. They are generally the most effective way of describing the characteristics of a population and providing comparisons among subpopulations. They can be conducted inexpensively by using samples as small as 100 and by using telephone surveys or mail questionnaires.

Finally, researchers with little survey experience can conduct successful surveys if they follow the many suggestions presented in this chapter and consult survey textbooks. For the best results, however, survey experts should be consulted, because surveys can be tricky. In sum, surveys are a valuable research tool for social impact assessments. Government agencies that serve the people need to listen to the people they serve, and surveys are the best method of listening.

References

BABBIE, E. R. (1973) Survey Research Methods. Belmont, CA: Wadsworth.

CAMPBELL, A. et al. (1976) The Quality of American Life: Perceptions, Evaluations, and Satisfactions. New York: Russell Sage.

CORNOG, J. R. (1982) "Development and administration of community surveys," in L. Llewellyn et al. (eds.) Social Impact Assessment: Sourcebook for Highway Planners. Report FHWA/RD-81/029. Washington, DC: Federal Highway Administration, U.S. Department of Transportation.

DILLMAN, D. A. (1978) Mail and Telephone Surveys: The Total Design Method. New York: John Wiley.

EZEKIEL, M. and K. A. FOX (1967) Methods of Correlation and Regression Analysis. New York: John Wiley.

FINSTERBUSCH, K. (1977) "The use of mini surveys in social impact assessments," pp. 291-296 in K. Finsterbusch and C. P. Wolf (eds.) Methodology of Social Impact Assessment. Stroudsburg, PA: Hutchinson Ross.

——— (1976a) "The mini survey: an underemployed research tool." Social Science Research 5 (March): 81-93.

——— (1976b) "Demonstrating the value of mini surveys in social research." Sociological Methods and Research 5 (August): 117-136.

GILMORE, J. S. and M. K. DUFF (1975) Boom Town Growth Management: A Case Study of Rock Springs-Green River, Wyoming. Boulder, CO: Westview.

GLOCK, C. Y. (1967) Survey Research in the Social Sciences. New York: Russell Sage.

GROVES, R. M. and R. L. KAHN (1979) Surveys by Telephone: A National Comparison with Personal Interviews. New York: Academic.

HYMAN, H. H. (1955) Survey Design and Analysis. New York: Macmillan.

JESSEN, R. J. (1978) Statistical Survey Techniques. New York: John Wiley.

LABAW, P. J. (1980) Advanced Questionnaire Design. Cambridge, MA: Abt.

MARANS, R. W. and J. D. WELLMAN (1978) The Quality of Metropolitan Living: Evaluations, Behaviors, and Expectations of Northern Michigan Residents. Ann Arbor: University of Michigan.

MOSER, C. A. and G. KALTON (1972) Survey Methods in Social Investigation. New York: Basic Books.

MUELLER, J. H. and K. F. SCHUESSLER (1961) Statistical Reasoning in Sociology. Boston: Houghton Mifflin.

PEARSON, E. S. and H. O. HARTLEY (1966) Biometrika Tables for Statisticians, Vol. 1. Cambridge: Cambridge University Press.

ROSENBERG, M. (1968) The Logic of Survey Analysis. New York: Basic Books.

SCHLAIFER, R. (1959) Probability and Statistics for Business Decisions. New York: McGraw-Hill.

STOUFFER, S. A. (1962) Social Research to Test Ideas. New York: Macmillan.

SUDMAN, S. (1976) Applied Sampling. New York: Academic.

——— (1967) Reducing the Costs of Surveys. Chicago: Aldine.

———— and N. M. BRADBURN (1982) Asking Questions: A Practical Guide to Questionnaire Design. San Francisco: Jossey-Bass.

U.S. Department of Commerce, Bureau of the Census (1981) Statistical Abstract of the United States, 1980. Washington, DC: Government Printing Office.

WARWICK, D. P. and C. A. LININGER (1975) The Sample Survey: Theory and Practice. New York: McGraw-Hill.

WISEMAN, F. (1972) "Methodological bias in public opinion surveys." Public Opinion Quarterly 36: 105-108.

5

Ethnography

O O O O O O O O O O O O O O O O O

ROY ROPER

O O O O O O O O O O O O O O O O O

● Ethnography, as one of the behavioral sciences, has been used widely
in diverse studies of individuals, neighborhoods, communities, societies, and
cultures since the middle of the nineteenth century. Ethnography is
embedded in and ultimately concerned with cultural interpretation, thereby
distinguishing it from fieldwork methods per se and other on-site observer
approaches. Traditionally, ethnographers have studied small-scale societies
firsthand by immersing themselves into the daily routines of their members.
The unique advantage of such participant observation in anthropology is
the development of contextualized understandings of people's cognitions
and behaviors by virtue of placing the researcher among the people being
studied.

Ethnographers generally do not sample populations and behaviors in the
formal, statistical sense since they eventually become acquainted with most
community residents and rely on firsthand, intimate data. They are
concerned with underlying patterns and issues and less with the generalizability of data to a larger grouping of individuals. Anthropologists carry out
their research in what has been typified as a relatively unstructured, free-
ranging, and exploratory manner. The style of study is natural history
(Arensberg, 1961), and it contrasts with the more rigidly controlled
procedures of laboratory experimentation, structured interviewing, and
statistical analysis.

While the problem under investigation dictates the specific methods of
investigation, ethnography can be a most valuable and distinctive tool of the
theoretical and applied anthropologist when faced with social impact

assessment on localized groups of people, especially those in agrarian settings in the United States and abroad. The contextualized knowledge derived from ethnography, a basic strength of this element of anthropology, can be used to inform the overall assessment process from its initial profiling phase through long-term monitoring. Furthermore, a broad interpretive paradigm such as cultural ecology focusing on cultural and ecosystem adaptation can aid in integrating ethnographic field research with data acquired by survey, historic, and demographic analyses.

In dealing with the cultural adaptations of specific cultures and ecosystems, ethnographic research has followed two main roads: (1) the comparison of the adaptation of similar cultures or similar technological systems to different environments, and (2) the comparison of the adaptations of different cultures to similar ecosystems (Kottak, 1982). Researchers also have employed ethnography in a cultural ecology framework for assessing specific cultures and ecosystems, particularly with respect to the consequences of water resources development and similar projects in agrarian cultures throughout the world. Such projects often necessitate land acquisition and human relocation. In agrarian societies land is a major, if not *the* major, economic and social resource. Land serves as the basis for occupation, a medium of social exchange, power, and status for contemporary and future populations. In this context, ethnography would describe the full cultural meaning of land. It would illustrate how routine life events (births, marriages, deaths, retirement, and migration, for example) are linked with land transfers, inheritance, land use, and succession (Bennett, 1982). This type of contextualized knowledge is usually missing when government and corporations intervene in local cultures and ecosystems with their projects. With ethnography's tendency to be part natural history focused on individual adaptations to particular situations, it becomes a natural for use in social impact assessment (Alland and McCay, 1973: 163-170). Ethnography can help discover and integrate findings on the multiple consequences of change programs, as illustrated by studies of irrigation projects of agrarian societies that detected worsening health conditions instead of enhanced food production. In the passages that follow, ethnography's use in dynamic profiling and dealing with the fallacy of aggregation will be illustrated with reference to research in the Midwest.

Dynamic Profiling

Wolf (1974: 22) notes that the purpose of profiling is to develop a set of social baseline data, in effect, a "before" measure of the impact situation in anticipation of project-induced changes. Most baselines or profiles, unfortunately, suggest an essentially static condition prevailing prior to major project development. The assumption is that stable adaptation exists, and in spite of the temporary disruption induced by a project, a reemergence of a new stable solution can be expected in the postproject period. These static, rubberband models derive from long-standing research traditions. Pospisil (1979: 140) details their emergence in ethnography:

> I suspect that because of the brevity of the current single period
> of ethnographic research some anthropologists have produced
> chimeras of "static primitive societies," "structural equilibriums,"
> and false typologies of social groups (households, families, bands,
> hunting groups) which if studied over time would appear as
> temporary phases of a single type of dynamically viewed group.

Ethnographers working with the historical demography of family, household, and domestic groups have produced exciting discoveries regarding the temporal nature of social and family patterns of organization (for example, see Sharlin, 1977; Vinouskis, 1977). A concurrent application within social impact assessment will be reviewed shortly.

Identification of Differentially Affected Groups

Ethnography can further contribute to the complex social impact assessment process by aiding in the identification of impact area boundaries, special affected communities, and types of affected people. It can also reveal their concerns. Such disambiguation of project impacts would thereby avoid the "fallacy of aggregation," wherein the special impacts on a minority group (cultural or social) are submerged within a regional assessment (Wolf, 1978: 185). For example, West (1975: 96) reviewed the Environmental Impact Statement (EIS) of a coal gasification facility in which the social impacts were addressed only in terms of the entire northwestern New Mexico area. Attention was not given to the specific effects on the coal, land, and water resources of a cultural and social minority, the Navaho. Reconstruction of the histories of settlement, agriculture, railroads, and even mining can lead to a recognition of the heterogeneity of most smaller, rural communities and how new developments have differential impacts on different sectors of their populations. Various researchers have noted that those most adversely affected by relocation are the poor, long-term residents, and the elderly.

The fallacy of aggregation often leads researchers to view the most vocal group, minority or majority, rich or poor, as one with influence. But project success is based on a careful balancing of needs and values across diverse population elements, an inherently political process. Disambiguating local political controls and elites is not an easy matter. While routine informant interviewing, surveys, and secondary data analysis may reveal community concerns and the positions of groups relative to the issues, these methods generally do not provide an appreciation of how these groups are organized and interrelated, and how they apply their influence via social and economic alliances. Planning documents, official releases, and newspaper accounts rarely disclose the fashion in which decisions are actually made. Ethnographic detailing of actual decision making reveals the systemic organization in which these groups are embedded, together with the interest groups vying for self-serving distributions of the social costs and benefits that accrue in any project. Accounting for real decision processes thereby helps in identifying the various affected groups and communities. It is then only a short step to effective integration of these groups into the decisional structures regarding mitigation and long-term control over their destinies.

Family Impacts of the Shelbyville Reservoir

An ethnographic account (tempered by a cultural ecology framework) of selected long-term family impacts of land acquisition and relocation caused by the Shelbyville Reservoir specifically reveals how ethnography can be sensitive to the timing of life events, how disruptions to social and cultural schedules can affect families, and how social networks (kinship or not) may serve to facilitate adaptation to forced change.

Lives Through Time

Acquisition of the land for the Shelbyville Reservoir in east central Illinois began in the mid-1960s. Some of the multiple impacts have been reduction in arable lands supporting cash-grain agriculture and other activities, residential relocation, lessened economic diversification, new lifestyles, and occupational changes. All of these have great impact on family life. Generally, water resource projects are designed and implemented with little regard for local social and cultural schedules of personal and familial development. By contrast, the research sought to discover how routine events within the family were related to residential relocation and loss of occupation induced by lease termination and land acquisition. These occurrences were interwoven with the family members' occupational careers, retirement plans, availability of local lands for rental or purchase, and perceptions of responsibility for the economic well-being of the next generation. The study's analytical goal was to describe, ethnographically, the family's adaptive processes within a matrix of external local conditions influenced, in part, by the reservoir development. The following is a summary of one extended family's experiences with the Shelbyville Reservoir development (see Roper and Burdge, 1982).

In the mid-1960s, this family of tenant cash-grain farmers lost about one-third of their total acreage when the U.S. Army Corps of Engineers acquired lands near the Kaskaskia River for the Shelbyville Reservoir. A few years later, their tenant lease was terminated by the farm manager. This event threw the family onto a land market already tighter than normal. Competition for land was fierce because of the prior acquisitions, relocations and reestablishment of neighboring farms, and the accompanying perception of acute land shortage. The family had to choose between reestablishing a farm or moving into a wage-oriented form of subsistence. The latter alternative was perceived as a most unwelcome change to their traditional farm activities. Much more important, however, the latter alternative meant that would never have an appropriate "estate" (homes, land, equipment, and personal heritage) to pass down to their children. They thought less in the egocentric terms of individual adult careers than in terms of generations of interlocking family careers.

This family has since reestablished a viable grain-farm operation, family owned and family operated. However, as illustrated below, the changes associated with the reservoir development had a "ripple effect" for over fifteen years within the extended family. After the lease termination, they knew it was useless to search for a replacement farm because they had insufficient unencumbered capital to make a purchase or even a down payment. To complicate matters, there was no other similar-sized farm available for rent at the time.

The family's eventual success was possible only by heavy reliance on its extended family network dispersed throughout the county. Other units were not affected by the project and maintained their ability to act as "buffers." The network provided interim housing, direct financial aid, backing for loans, and use of farm equipment and grain storage facilities. The family's operation was reestablished in the beginning by a combination of acquiring and renting available lands regardless of location in Shelby county. This created a most inefficiently arranged farm, however. The reacquisition of physically contiguous farmland was possible through competitive replacement of other, older farmers who either retired or died. It is significant that nearly all these older farmers were related to this nuclear family by marriage or birth. Decades are often required to bring plans for establishing a large farm to fruition since land transfers and farm consolidations are dependent upon retirements and deaths, both naturally occurring events in the personal and family life cycles. The crucial lesson is that this process of competitive replacement is bound in time to these cycles and cannot be accelerated to accommodate adaptation to development. Many of the other families displaced by the reservoir were not able to manage the complex reestablishment process successfully, and, hence, left farming altogether.

Adaptive Capacity of Social Networks

Ethnography contributes to social impact assessment by making the familiar terrain of social network functioning more clearly known, as in the Shelbyville Reservoir project, where the financial problems associated with land acquisition were muted by inter- and intrafamilial reliance on overlapping social networks. In this particular example, these social interconnections were not considered by the Corps in the planning and execution of land acquisition and residential relocation. Rather, an atomistic model of human relationships based on the current legal requirement for dealing with each residence as independent from all others was employed. One unquestioned assumption of this model was that all families were equal in their ability to adapt to forced relocation. It goes without saying, however, that the resources families have at their disposal vary by such macro-level indicators as socioeconomic status. Additionally, variations occur by stages in the life cycles of people, families, and corporate groups, and even location within the impact area. For instance, those families who lived closest to the river lost part or all of their property. In contrast to the model's supposition that adequate, external compensation occurred, our research indicated that the extended networks of kith and kin were primarily responsible for providing sufficient resources to cushion the move itself. Such resource packages consisted of cash gifts, loans, use of cars and trucks, machinery, grain storage facilities, and direct labor inputs. The long-term issue of farm reconsolidation was also dependent on these social networks. In most if not all cases where a farm operation was affected, resources provided by the change agency were not well suited to the problems at hand. No pre- or postdevelopment study of the social parameters of the project was ever undertaken by its local, state, or federal sponsors.

Proximity to the reservoir reduced the economic resiliency of these supportive social networks as functional units. Some families suffered economic shortfalls after relocating because the families constituting their network of interrelated families also lost land, relocated, or provided help to others who had been affected earlier in the project's history, inhibiting the transference of resources in times of additional need. Those family networks located at least a few miles away from the acquisition lines appeared to be relatively unaffected by the project. Consequently, they could provide help to displaced members.

New Analytical Methods

The ethnographer employs a variety of methods for obtaining and analyzing materials in social impact assessment. For example, personal network and kinship models, resource exchange paradigms, knowledge of dominant and subcultural traditions, and occupation-specific domestic and corporate developmental cycles are frequently utilized. Two relatively new methods have significant implications for applied (and theoretical) ethnography. The first, computer assistance, reduces the time required to aggregate and perform preliminary reviews of verbal and numerical data (see Heise, 1981; Sonquist, 1977). The second, use of stochastic models, helps in the linkage of individual with group phenomena through time, a problematic aspect of most behavioral science research.

Computer-Assisted Ethnography

Two major drawbacks in performing applied ethnographic research are the time and resources required to do an adequate job. The project sponsors typically contract the research without considering the differing logistic and data acquisition requirements of ethnographers, sociologists, demographers, and economists. In social impact assessment, ethnographers usually have inadequate time. Now the application of emerging computer technologies to typical ethnographic tasks can shorten the time required to produce ethnographic reports.

Aside from the multitude of routine word-processing software and hardware packages that have virtually revolutionized text handling in modern societies, only a few advances have been of direct aid to ethnographers. Experimental computer programs (EUROP and EURE-KA), developed at the University of Illinois in connection with the Comparative Ethnography of Functional Uses of Literacy (CEFUL) project (see Hill-Burnett, 1978), are capable of aiding the ethnographer in imposing a broader perspective on ethnographic text data, discovering dimensions inherent in the observational and interview situations, as well as supporting the retrieval, storage, and typing tasks. In the CEFUL project, ethnographic observations were recorded in notebooks after each observation episode. These notes were then entered into computer files via a text editor in an elementary format with less than a dozen special codes or flags. These individual text files were merged and formatted for the text retrieval program (EUREKA) by its compiler (EUROP). The programs make available a frequency and locational list of every word within the combined text files. The full texts of all separate input files (the ethnographic episodes) remain available for on-line search, inspection, and printing.

Major features of the programs include the following: (1) the ability to interact with the growing data bases through "queries," the results of which can be stored independently for later use; (2) the full text of each episode, as noted above, remains retrievable — no intermediate coding procedure can "wash out" meaningful data and relationships; (3) the index is inclusive of all terms instead of consisting of a restricted coding structure; (4) each document is divided into such "contexts" as ethnographer, title (objective details of episode), and paragraph and sentence; and (5) the ability to browse through full or restricted sets of contexts. In essence, the programs allow the ethnographer to construct text data bases, specific to all or components of the project, usable in an iterative fashion as the research matures. If adapted to the newest generations of personal computers with state-of-the-art compact hard-disk storage, the programs could become a true field tool reducing much drudgery. At present they are dedicated to PDP-11 mainframes and large disk storage.

Returning to social impact assessment, it is often important to discover, through interviews and observations, attitudes and beliefs on various issues of residents near a river slated for impoundment, and whether these differ by residential location. For example, a typical concern of downstream residents is the ability of the reservoir authority to control river height after reservoir construction. Upstream, few people are so concerned. Downstream, where land acquisition is usually minimal, issues of fairness and compensation adequacy often surface with less frequency than in the proposed reservoir basin. With the text from interviews, ethnographic observations, and even ancillary sources such as newspaper articles stored in the program format, rapid inspection for locational differences in attitudes and beliefs could be accomplished. Where population parameters are subordinate to the isolation of themes of potential political conflict, the program could facilitate rapid thematic analysis, leading to greater accuracy in the subsequent selection of respondents and interview items (see Krippendorff, 1980).

Probabilistic Stochastic Models

Anthropologists have begun to explore these models in an attempt to account for intracultural diversity arising out of individual choice and temporal change (Thompson, 1970; Fjellman, 1977). Beuchler and Selby (1968: 63-66) and White (1973), using hypothetical data, have demonstrated the utility of Markov models for investigating the developmental cycles of domestic groups on Andros Island in the Bahamas and predicting the future distributions of household types. In White's genre of research, one can specify the likelihood that a household of a specific type at time T (present) will remain the same or be transformed in a specified way at time T + 1 (some future time interval) by examining the matrix of transition probabilities.

Returning to the example of the farm family whose operation was disrupted by land acquisition, probabilistic stochastic models of sociocultural processes could have been employed to determine if project developments led to changes in rate and direction of change (Thompson and Roper, 1980). Project-specific consequences might have been differentiated from existing sociocultural trends. An ideal strategy would be to develop dynamic, baseline models of agrarian, domestic cycles in non-affected areas and compare these with cycles actually noted in residential units near the reservoir. Assuming a series of controls on such variables as the type of farm operation, family size, and stages in family and domestic cycles, one might specify how the reservoir led to fewer three-generational farm operations within a given area, thereby linking the individual household data with information on larger numbers of units.

By extension, it is possible to observe differences in transition probabilities across populations differentially affected by water resource projects that require a modification of current land tenure arrangements. One might find that the dissolution of the classic "farm family" was already occurring at a rapid rate, and that, at a county level, the water project may have actually retarded its dissolution by forcing a reemergence of dependence on kinship networks for farm establishment and consolidation. It is obviously crucial to be able not only to specify that changes take place when agrarian populations are affected, but also to specify the direction and rate of these changes.

Contextual Experience

McCoy (1975: 371) and Finsterbusch (1980: 13) note that the ethno-graphic reporting style per se can be beneficial for social impact assessment because it has the potential of communicating objectively discovered human impacts in language that planners and decision makers can easily assimilate. The statistical presentation of supporting data through charts, tables, and graphs may not demonstrate the same sensitivities to humans undergoing forced social change. It is easy to understand how ethnography has become equated so widely with empathy. From the days of Franz Boas and the "historical method," ethnographic fieldwork has been the backbone of anthropological inquiry, and

> by its very nature fieldwork is particularistic in its concentration on a specific problem among a specific people, in a specific location, and in a specific time period [Rohner, 1977: 118].

Well-crafted ethnographies are necessarily based on contextual experi-ence and demonstrate the intercontingencies of natural, human, and cultural events through time, as well as an awareness of the ecological contexts in which they occur. Earlier models of ethnographic fieldwork assumed static conditions existing prior to a culture's contact with outside groups, and conducted historical reconstruction through interviews with elderly informants combined with archaeological, linguistic, and occasion-ally physical data. However, significant developments in the ability of the behavioral sciences to handle psychological, social, and cultural phenomena diachronically rather than synchronically have occurred. New approaches in life cycle, human development, and aging research incorporate changes over time (for example, see Bertaux, 1981). They have great potential in promoting understanding of project-specific consequences for agrarian populations since household, corporate, and personal events are usually affiliated with issues of land tenure.

Perhaps most significant for developing contextualized, ethnographic knowledge of agrarian populations subjected to forced social change comes from the interdisciplinary analyses of American family changes over time using historical sources. Not only is the approach useful in developing dynamic baselines in social impact assessment, the implicit message concerns the danger of taking too short a time perspective when viewing social change within the family or other social group. Gordon and Hareven (1973: 393-394) comment on this work:

Instead of focusing narrowly on structural and institutional definitions of change in the family, they investigate the interaction between the family and social processes: kinship and migration, changing patterns of parental authority and filial autonomy, patterns of family adjustment to urban life, changing conceptions and practices of social space within the family. These approaches transcend the more traditional concern with the isolated household unit and family structure. . . . They focus instead on relationships, processes of exchange and the interaction in the family and society. "Family" is seen, therefore, as a series of relationships, rather than as static units. These relationships change not only over time, but also within the same historical period, in response to different social conditions, as well as within the . . . lives of individuals.

Examples of this interdisciplinary work may be found in Hareven (1971a, 1971b, 1975), Hareven and Vinouskis (1978), Gordon (1973), Demos (1970), and Laslett (1974).

Conclusion

This chapter has explored a few specific areas where ethnographic research could be used to good advantage in social impact assessment. Ethnography will contribute to future social impact assessment by making available to planners information on how populations actually live and function through time. Dynamic baselines based on research in similar populations will help in the determination of how to plan for mitigating the impacts attendant on the disruptions of these bundles of exchanges and interactions in families, nuclear and extended, and communities. The promise of ethnography is still in close contact with people as well as a knowledge of the broader contexts of social and cultural existence. This may help do away with the cultural arrogance so often revealed in large- and small-scale development projects, both at home and abroad.

References

ALLAND, A. and B. McCAY (1973) "The concept of adaptation in biological and cultural evolution," pp. 143-178 in J. J. Honigmann (ed.) Handbook of Social and Cultural Anthropology. Chicago: Rand McNally.
ARENSBERG, C. (1961) "The community as object and as sample." American Anthropologist 63: 241-264.

BENNETT, J. W. (1982) Of Time and Enterprise: North-American Family Farm Management in the Context of Resource Marginality. Minneapolis: University of Minnesota Press.

BERTAUX, D. [ed.] (1981) Biography and Society: The Life History Approach in the Social Sciences. Beverly Hills, CA: Sage.

BEUCHLER, H. and H. SELBY [eds.] (1968) Kinship and Social Organization. New York: Macmillan.

DEMOS, J. (1970) A Little Commonwealth: Family Life in Plymouth Colony. New York: Oxford University Press.

FINSTERBUSCH, K. (1980) Understanding Social Impacts: Assessing the Effects of Public Projects. Beverly Hills, CA: Sage.

FJELLMAN, S. M. (1977) "The Akamba domestic cycle as Markovian process." American Ethnologist 4: 699-713.

GORDON, M. [ed.] (1973) The American Family in Social-Historical Perspective. New York: St. Martin's.

―――― and T. K. HAREVEN [eds.] (1973) The New Social History of the Family. Journal of Marriage and the Family 35 (special issue).

HAREVEN, T. K. [ed.] (1975) The History of the Family in American Urban Society. Journal of Urban History 1 (special issue).

―――― [ed.] (1971a) Anonymous Americans: Explorations in Nineteenth-Century Social History. Englewood Cliffs, NJ: Prentice-Hall.

―――― (1971b) "The history of the family as an interdisciplinary field," pp. 211-226 in T. K. Rabb and R. I. Rotberg (eds.) The Family History: Interdisciplinary Essays. New York: Harper & Row.

―――― and M. A. VINOUSKIS [eds.] (1978) Family and Population in Nineteenth-Century America. Princeton, NJ: Princeton University Press.

HEISE, D. R. [ed.] (1981) Microcomputers in Social Research. Sociological Methods and Research 9, 4 (special issue).

HILL-BURNETT, J. (1978) "Developing anthropological knowledge through application," pp. 112-128 in E. M. Eddy and W. L. Partridge (eds.) Applied Anthropology in America. New York: Columbia University Press.

KOTTAK, C. P. (1982) Anthropology: The Exploration of Human Diversity. New York: Random House.

KRIPPENDORFF, K. (1980) Content Analysis: An Introduction to Its Methodology. Beverly Hills, CA: Sage.

LASLETT, P. (1974) "Introduction: the history of the family," pp. 1-90 in P. Laslett (ed.) Household and Family in Past Time. London: Cambridge University Press.

McCOY, C. B. (1975) "The impact of an impact study: contributions of sociology to decision-making in government." Environment and Behavior 7: 358-372.

POSPISIL, L. (1979) "The Tirolean peasants of Obernberg: a study in long-term research," pp. 127-143 in G. M. Foster et al. (eds.) Long-Term Field Research in Social Anthropology. New York: Academic.

ROHNER, R. P. (1977) "Advantages of the comparative method of anthropology." Behavioral Science Research 12: 117-144.

ROPER, R. E. and R. J. BURDGE (1982) Family Life-Cycle Disruption in Rural Communities: The Case of the Lake Shelbyville Reservoir. Research Report 166. Urbana: Water Resources Center, University of Illinois.

SHARLIN, A. N. (1977) "Historical demography as history and demography." American Behavioral Scientist 21: 245-262.

SONQUIST, J. A. [ed.] (1977) Using computers in the social sciences. American Behavioral Scientist 20, 3 (special issue).

THOMPSON, R. A. (1970) "Stochastics and structure: culture change and social mobility in a Yucatee town." Journal of Anthropological Research 26: 354-375.

THOMPSON, R. W. and R. E. ROPER (1980) "Methods in social anthropology: new directions for old problems." American Behavioral Scientist 23: 905-924.

VINOUSKIS, M. A. (1977) "From household size to the life course: some observations on recent trends in family history." American Behavioral Scientist 21: 263-287.

WEST, B. J. (1975) "Navajo coal development impact study: a social impact statement," pp. 95-107 in W. D. Bliss (ed.) Symposium on Environmental Effects on Behavior. Bozeman: Montana State University and Environmental Design Group of the Human Factors Society.

WHITE, D. R. (1973) "Mathematical anthropology," pp. 369-446 in J. J. Honigmann (ed.) Handbook of Social and Cultural Anthropology. Chicago: Rand McNally.

WOLF, C. P. (1978) "The cultural impact statement," pp. 178-193 in R. S. Dickens, Jr, and C. E. Hill [eds.] Cultural Resources: Planning and Management. Boulder, CA: Westview.

——— (1974) "Social impact assessment: the state of the art," pp. 1-44 in C. P. Wolf (ed.) Social Impact Assessment. Milwaukee: Environmental Design Research Association.

III
SECONDARY DATA
COLLECTION
METHODS

• • • • • • • • • • • • • • •

6

Historical Documents

○ ○ ○ ○ ○ ○ ○ ○ ○ ○ ○ ○ ○ ○ ○ ○ ○

ANNABELLE BENDER MOTZ

○ ○ ○ ○ ○ ○ ○ ○ ○ ○ ○ ○ ○ ○ ○ ○ ○

● "Past Is Prologue" is engraved at the entrance of the National Archives of the United States. These words express the raison d'être for the study of historical documents. Documents provide knowledge of people and places. They enable people engaged in social impact assessment to learn about the setting in which a policy is to be implemented and the fate of similar policies elsewhere. These findings guide the researcher's estimation of the impacts of social changes.

In this chapter, an overview of historical documentation is presented in several steps, explaining what historical documents are, why they are used in social impact assessment, how they are found, and how they are used. Two social impact assessments that depended heavily on the use of historical documents are then described. Finally, the advantages and disadvantages of using historical documents are discussed.

What Are Historical Documents?

Generally speaking, any artifact — a building, a work of art, a manuscript, or a bill of lading — is a document or record of the past that tells a story about a way of life. For example, homes are documents, the style and vintage of which tell social impact assessors about their residents and the age of the community. Similarly, bank financial statements, telephone directory listings, and newspaper ads are documents revealing the economic status of an area and the kinds of services offered there.

Because the concept of historical documents is so broad, I have chosen to limit its usage in the following pages to any written communication from the past.[1] Such documents as maps, biographies, accounting ledgers, and newspapers — to name but a few — constitute valuable resources of raw or primary data for use by persons engaged in social impact assessment.

Historical records are either statistical or narrative (Shyne, 1975). *Statistical* historical documents are largely composed of figures, for example, sales receipts, bank statements, voting records, statistical reference books, and surveys. They have the advantage of readily lending themselves to quantitative analyses. When similar records are maintained over a long period of time they provide what Webb and his associates (1966) refer to as a "running record" or a "continuous historical document." Records such as the U.S. Census enable researchers to identify changes over time by dealing with data diachronically.

In contrast to statistical historical documents, *narrative* historical documents — such as autobiographies, minutes of meetings, legal documents, and letters — require a different type of analysis of their contents, an analysis that is more subject to personal interpretations and definitions of situations. Their utility depends on the assessor's needs for the information and insightfulness. Some narratives are one-time accounts or "episodes" (Webb et al., 1966); others, such as letters written over a period of time, enable the researcher to trace changes.

Statistical and narrative historical documents differ in terms of the document writer's intended audiences. Personal historical documents, such as diaries and family photo albums, are meant for specific individuals or groups. These documents are generally found in the possession of private individuals or historic societies. Papers produced for offices or public usage are called public historical documents. Exemplifying this genre are institutional reports and records, fictional and nonfictional popular literature, scientific studies and reports, and mass media magazines.

What, then, are historical documents? They are the innumerable statistical and narrative writings from both the distant and recent past intended for private or public audiences. The writers of these documents — as private parties or public officials — wrote them to meet their own needs, not those of social impact researchers. Yet today's social researcher uses these documents to gain understanding of the area that is subject to change and to relate it to the larger society.

Documents are not an end in themselves; rather, they are the raw materials that serve as means to ends. Secondary analysis helps social impact assessors anticipate the potential impacts of a policy on people who are likely to be affected by the policy. Historical documents provide information for identifying communities and delineating boundaries, describing community life, profiling communities, and analyzing community contexts. They are useful in naming key people, organizations, and industries. Further, they make it possible to discern patterns and processes of change.

How Historical Documents Are Located

Unlike social researchers who collect raw data that are uniquely appropriate to their studies, users of historical documents are faced with the problems of determining which records exist, which are available to the researcher, and which are relevant. Identification of documents that can be collated or analyzed as raw data generally involves turning to sources different than usual bibliographic references.

Sources that indicate the content and location of computerized data provide a wealth of information about specific communities. For example, publications such as *Computer-Readable Databases: A Directory and Data Sourcebook* (Williams, 1976) and *Social Science Data Banks and the Institute for Water Resources* (Motz, 1974) identify the locations of data banks and the nature of their contents.

Specialized indexes are also of utility to social researchers. Among the noteworthy ones are the *Vertical File Service Catalog* (which lists leaflets, pamphlets, and mimeographed materials), *N. W. Ayer and Son's Directory of Newspapers and Periodicals* (which lists printed media in American towns and cities), and the *Monthly Catalog of U.S. Government Publications* (which lists publications from the government's executive, legislative, and judicial branches).

Besides seeking out reference sources, a very useful procedure for researchers is to telephone, personally visit, or write to request copies of documents. Frequently persons contracted provide referrals to others familiar with records or to people who collected data of potential use to impact assessors. In this way researchers acquire familiarity not only with persons who know what is available, but also where the records are, whether they may be borrowed, and from whom they may be obtained. Locating specific publications is often a major task. A check of periodical indexes at a public library is a first step. Two particularly valuable indexes are the *Social Science Citation Index* and the *Subject Guide to Books in Print.* The former is composed of three parts enabling researchers to locate subjects, titles, and authors of journal articles and selected books. It also indicates footnoted references contained within any given publication and places in which the given publication has been subsequently cited. The latter provides subjects, titles, and authors of books currently available for purchase.

Of tremendous value in locating where particular publications are housed are two Library of Congress sources and data banks containing bibliographies. The former, entitled the *Library of Congress Subject Catalog* and the *National Union Catalog*, list books by subject and author, respectively. Both indicate which libraries house each reference. Among the latter, two data banks — the Smithsonian Science Information Exchange and the Lockheed DIALOG — are widely used by social researchers.

Abstracts of journals and books enable researchers to determine whether the content of a publication is relevant to the impact study. There are volumes of abstracts for each of the social sciences as well as of dissertations and theses from hundreds of universities.

How to Use Historical Documents

Given the vast array of historical documents that exist, a first step is to assess those that are available and carefully select the ones that appear most relevant to the research problem. Seven tasks are involved in this step:

(1) List possible sources of useful documents.
(2) Identify which sources are available and what documents they contain.
(3) Select sample copies of documents from each source.
(4) Study the copies for potentially useful information.
(5) Develop systematic techniques for analyzing the contents of each record.
(6) Determine the utility of the data for researching impacts on the study area.
(7) Evaluate whether further analysis of each data source is worth the time and effort for the returns anticipated.

After this step is accomplished, the researcher is in a position to select the sources to be used and to proceed to read and analyze them. This step is facilitated by answering the question, What do the documents reveal about:

(1) population groups, lifestyles, and leadership roles in the general area of study;
(2) social institutions — their kinds, interrelationships, and changes;

(3) the interdependence of socioeconomic and interest groups;

(4) how individuals and communities cope with problems, issues, and changes; and

(5) the boundaries to the area where the social affects of the project are likely to be significant?

On the basis of tentative answers to the above questions, the researcher can select one or more data sources for intense analysis. The contents of historical documents can be analyzed in two ways: systematically, according to formal replicable procedures; or subjectively, for reported facts and an intuitive understanding. The former involves an explicit methodology, which is described here.

A major step in the systematic study of historical documents is sampling. Standard sampling procedures are followed whenever possible for selecting documents or portions of documents (Nachmias and Nachmias, 1976; Babbie, 1979). However, it is unlikely that the universe of historical documents from which the sample is to be drawn will be complete. Therefore, the sampling has to be adapted to the particular situation. Researchers have to develop rationales for selecting the sources to be used. The rationale for sample selection must take the following factors into account:

(1) The existence and availability of sources comparable to a given source (this is important for establishing the reliability and validity of the data).

(2) The advantages and disadvantages in selecting samples of a given source from particular years or days and months in given years (consideration must be given to whether "typical" or "atypical" time periods provide more valuable data).

(3) The completeness of records, in two senses: (a) internally, in that the record contains all the data it is intended to contain; and (b) externally, in that all the records of a given type are available (incomplete records bias samples in ways similar to low response rates on a survey).

(4) The degree of comparability of a series of records from a given source (similar forms are not comparable if people filling out the forms interpret questions differently).

(5) Cost and other practical considerations.

While consideration of the above factors is important in justifying the sample selection, the quality of the documents calls for careful scrutiny. As Shyne (1975) points out, users of historical records should know about the procedures used in the collection of raw data, the organizational and political context in which they were collected, and staff capability. It is important, too, to know how the original data collectors defined terms and whether changes in their definitions occurred over time. If, for example, two documents refer to "blue-collar workers," are the same occupations included in the term?

Eliciting Impact Area Information

Social impact researchers approach historical documents with a desire to learn about the organization of the area as a dynamic social system. Historical documents provide data that enable reconstruction of the area's past and tracing its development through time. Armed with knowledge of typical patterns of community life gleaned from the social science literature, they can investigate whether these typical patterns also apply in the impact area and, if not, why not.

Using Historical Documents: Examples

This section presents my experiences in using both narrative and quantitative documents in two studies of communities along waterways. One was an ex post facto social impact analysis of small towns along the Arkansas River (Motz, 1977). Its objective was to assess the effects of the McClellan-Kerr Navigation System on those towns. The second involved learning about many small towns and villages exposed to the flooding of an Appalachian river for flood control planning purposes (Motz, 1979).

An early step for each study was to take "windshield tours" of the areas and formally and informally interview people. Return visits and more interviews were made midway through and toward the end of both researches. Through these contacts a broad range of records, including minutes of public hearings, dissertations, economic reports, and anthropological and sociological case studies not available outside the area of study, was acquired. These local materials were supplemented with publications from the Library of Congress and university libraries.

I have selected four types of historical documents drawn from local and national repositories for detailed discussion: maps, telephone directories, newspapers, and *Dun and Bradstreet* reference books.[2]

MAPS

It is important to obtain maps of the area when starting a community study: ordinary travel maps, Rand-McNally atlas maps, and more specialized maps from libraries, government agencies, and planning commissions.

I used these maps to learn about the surroundings of the proposed project in terms of the following factors:

(1) accessibility to the area and its communities by train, highways, and airlines;

(2) natural and human-made barriers separating the area and its communities from one another and the world;

(3) names and sizes of cities and towns within the area;

(4) the distribution and concentration of people throughout the area and, more specifically, in relation to the project's location;

(5) the proximity of the study area to capitals, county seats, and various public institutions; and

(6) the presence of natural resources (or natural hazards) or governmental, industrial, or other installations that distinguish the area or portions of it from other places.

Besides making it easier to locate each community in relation to its immediate neighbors and the region, map information was particularly useful in connection with choosing sample settlements for intensive case study analysis. For example, Appalachia maps show mountainous ranges forming a natural barrier between river communities and other communities. This makes it relatively easy to identify flood-prone areas. On the other hand, Arkansas River maps show no such marked separation between communities. The task of identifying flood-prone settlements is more difficult.

In both studies, information from maps was recorded on index cards under community names. The data recorded included population size, county name, nearest political seat of power, and neighboring communities. Distances between proximate towns were noted for the length of the river included in each study. Additional recorded data came from detailed maps from specialized agencies; for example, highway commissions provided maps showing the proximity of houses to one another, churches, mines, or other important landmarks.

TELEPHONE DIRECTORIES

Telephone directories provide very interesting information about study areas. They are helpful in determining how far a community extends (what I call the "geographical reach of the community"). The phone company's division of the book designates the formally recognized sections of the area and names communities not listed in other sources. In some rural areas, the addresses of subscribers often are in smaller communities neighboring the town whose name is used for the section of the phone book. In this way, a major settlement and dependent satellite communities can be identified.

Phone books also are useful in disclosing businesses and services offered in small towns. (Sometimes they offer the only way to learn about small businesses such as home beauty salons and auto garages — provided they have telephones!)

Another procedure for using phone books, particularly in small places, is to help discern community ties. I have traced the frequency with which given surnames appear in a cluster of communities. For example, in a directory covering a 20-mile radius, I found the name Sender appearing 10 times with Pineville addresses, 18 times with Walnut addresses, and 5 and 2 times, respectively, with Locust Hill and Elm addresses. These figures suggest that (a) the Senders are an extended family; (b) they probably originated in Pineville or Walnut; and (c) the yellow pages and other directories may have more information about the family.

Phone directories can also be used to compare communities to each other and to compare population, occupations, and businesses in a community over time. However, this type of historical document has certain limitations. Not everyone has a telephone, nor is everyone listed. Further, people with the same name are not necessarily related. Nevertheless, phone directories complement and supplement other historical documents.

NEWSPAPERS

Knowing that I must rely on documents as major data sources. I always look for local community newspapers. A tour of the Arkansas River valley indicated that only a small number of communities have such papers. (This was borne out by a check through the *Ayer Directory.*)

Further, where there are papers, local publishers often do not maintain complete archives, nor can they inexpensively provide copies of existent papers.

With the help of the *Ayer Directory* and the Arkansas State Historical Library (which subsequently provided reels of microfilms of newspapers), I found communities that had papers available over continuous periods of time. Their existence and availability became important criteria in my selection of sample cities for intensive analysis.

Initial reading of the papers fostered (a) clarification of the study's objectives, (b) acquaintanceship with the communities, (c) development of insights that guided my selection of the issues to be studied, and (d) understanding of these communities as having lives that persist through time regardless of population changes.

I wanted to capture the dynamics of each of the small cities being studied to see how it evolved over a period of decades and to compare it with others. The newspaper research had to answer several questions:

(1)   What are the boundaries of each city in the sample? (Does it have clearly defined political boundaries? Is the city a center with a reach that goes beyond city, county, or even state lines?)

(2)   What is the nature of the community's social organization? (What political, economic, and social groups does the community support? How do people become leaders? How are the leaders and groups interlocked?)

(3)   What is the quality of life in the community? (What services are provided? By whom? For whom? What are the levels of living of the people in the community?)

Answering these questions involved (a) selecting a sample of papers for content analysis, (b) conceptualizing each question and operationalizing the concepts, and (c) devising coding procedures for recording the response to each question. A few brief examples that communicate the sense of the process are presented below.

Once the sample cities and the newspapers were selected, I chose to study 1950, 1960, and 1970 newspapers appearing two weeks before and after Christmas and two weeks before and after July 1. The rationale was that the decennial years complemented U.S. Census data. Further, the preholiday period disclosed a large number of names, organizations, and community activities; the postholiday period showed a "more usual" picture of local conditions. Also, more ads and accounts about outlying communities ("locality places") as well as the sample cities ("local places") appeared at those times.

Since the objectives of the ex post facto study were to note the nature of community interrelationships over time and to see how the construction of the waterway system impinged on these communities, key concepts included "community interaction," "boundaries," "institutions," and "leadership." These were operationally indicated by references to social institutions (for example, recreational, economic, and religious), leadership, and voluntary associations, as well as festive activities, crises, and daily routines.

The analytic procedures took two major forms, namely, recording statements about narrative items and statistical coding. For the first, activities, issues, and the like were noted on cards, which were then sorted and categorized. The information then was extrapolated to form a picture of the community as a social system. In addition, at the time that items were noted, they were also statistically coded in terms of a number of concepts. A sample of papers was coded by all coders as a reliability check.

The dual approach of analyzing and interpreting the narrative data and coding the newspaper contents statistically provided a great deal of information about each community's development over the thirty-year period. Editorials, letters to the editor, ads giving prices of homes and other necessities, articles reporting the movement of job seekers or people moving up on the job, and accounts of internal rivalry as well as intercommunity conflict all contributed to the picture of each sample city. Local perceptions of external events, life careers, the role of the absentee-owned corporations, social and economic crises, and turning points associated with economic development or the loss of leaders were traced. Thus newspaper content analysis afforded a view of community life and institutions at given points in time and diachronically.

Despite the riches that newspaper content analysis offers, I was always cognizant of its shortcomings. These small-town papers relied on volunteer reporters for much of their information and therefore reflect their interests and biases. Besides the reporters, publishers and editors (frequently one and the same person or family members) and advertisers also color what is printed. Nevertheless, when the selective orientation and minimal coverage of these newspapers are recognized, they serve as a very important tool for study of an impact area.

BUSINESS CREDIT RATINGS

Business credit ratings can be used to address questions about community power relations and stratification. Monthly *Dun and Bradstreet* reference books provide extremely valuable information on business and industrial firms in innumerable towns and cities throughout the United States. The name of each business is listed alphabetically. Beside each name information is provided on the type of business; the date it was established or changed to current control or management; its estimated financial strength and credit rating (from "high" to "limited"); names of bank heads; and, if a branch company, name and location of parent organization.

The procedure followed in analyzing these lists of firms consisted of (a) determining which years and months would be used, (b) locating the book containing the appropriate year, month, state, and town; (c) developing a typology of businesses; (d) classifying businesses by type; and (f) checking which businesses were in the sample city for ten years or less. The raw data were put into tables for each city and for 1950, 1960, and 1970.

By recording the rating of each firm within the sample cities it was possible to describe the economic infrastructure of each city. The data showed which types of businesses predominated, whether they were locally owned or not, their age, inventories, and managerial changes. Comparisons by decades were made, including whether family-owned stores persisted, folded, or sold out. Tables were constructed that showed the entry and exit of branch companies in each city.

Dun and Bradstreet provides a picture of the local economy, the nature of the businesses and industries that are the sources of livelihoods for people in the area. These books reveal the part played by local businesses and industries and by outside firms. The credit ratings suggest the success of businesses over time and relative to one another. However, other data sources must be used in conjunction with these references for a more accurate picture. Certain types of small businesses or ones with limited credit potential generally are not included. On the other hand, as illustrated by a community that appeared to have a concentration of strong corporate enterprises, the data present a biased picture: Many of the listed companies used this community as their address, while the bulk of their operations were elsewhere! Cautious of these biases, I found the *Dun and Bradstreet* reference books valuable in terms of economic and social organization of the study areas. These documents permit comparison of cities at any given time period and over time. This type of comparative economic analysis serves to accentuate both the similarities between communities in the study area and the uniqueness of specific places.

Advantages and Disadvantages
of Historical Documents

Like every source of data used by social impact assessors, historical documents have both many strengths and weaknesses as research tools. Of their strengths, research methodologists are prone to emphasize their economy (Selltiz et al., 1976; Babbie, 1979). In addition to being less expensive than fieldwork or surveys, they are economical in terms of time, personnel, and travel. The savings are even greater when the historical documents are collected by others on a continual basis (as are the credit rating documents and newspapers). Thus archives provide single data or continuous data solely for the costs of procuring copies of the records.

There are yet other practical advantages. Although some documents require permission of the writer, many do not. Generally this enables the social scientist to maintain the ethical norms of research, such as the protection of subjects' privacy rights. Also, the researcher does not have to set up appointments, contend with broken ones, do the research during working hours only, and so forth. This means a saving of time and a freedom to use time when and how the researcher sees fit.

In addition to the practical advantages, historical documentation has definite benefits for the conduct of research itself. The documents — particularly narrative ones — enable researchers to familiarize themselves with the study area so that they can appreciate its *zeitgeist* (climate) and what people in the community take for granted (Schutz, 1975). The understanding of the local assumptions of study area residents is essential in trying to forecast the effects that a project will have.

Besides these phenomenological advantages, historical documents both provide baseline data and, when collected over time, make possible the analysis of trends. Trend analysis, of course, is considered an essential part of impact analysis for forecasting the future of the area.

Another advantage in using historical documentation is that the documents frequently contain information and/or an orientation that is refreshingly novel and a source of rich insights (Lin, 1976). Being written for other than the purposes of the social impact assessment, documents such as life histories, muckraking reports, and other narrative descriptions of events direct research attention to circumstances, people, and conditions that would otherwise be ignored.

Yet the use of historical documents also has disadvantages. The careful collection of documents, the pursuit of procedures akin to fieldwork, and the time thorough reading and analyses take are all costly. More important, in terms of research procedures, the questions of validity and reliability are difficult to answer. Are the materials, with all their biases, valid sources of community information? What about secondary analysis — does it really get at what the researcher needs to have? These questions are never easy to answer. Efforts to verify the consistency of parts of documents with other parts of the same document and intercoder consistency help to some extent in establishing reliability. The triangulation of methods (as suggested by Denzin, 1970) is perhaps the safest route for establishing validity. The writings of Holsti (1969) and Babbie (1979) also suggest how to maximize the value of archival data. Despite their shortcomings, then, these documents are rich sources of data that virtually no other research methodology can match.

Summary and Conclusion

Historical documentation is an approach that provides social impact assessors with important background information and raw data that can be used to study at modest costs the anticipated effects of proposed policies (whether programs or projects) on given locales. These records from the distant or recent past are located in archives and libraries of federal, state, regional, and local organizations and agencies as well as in the possession of private parties. Researchers have to determine which records exist, where they are located, and from whom they can gain permission to obtain and use them. They must also assess their appropriateness for social impact study. These tasks are facilitated through personal contact with keepers of the records and the use of reference books and computerized bibliographic and data retrieval systems.

The data obtained are either narrative or statistical. The qualititative nature of the former makes it particularly useful in sensitizing researchers to the communities under study, to their populations, lifestyles, dynamics, and problems. In addition, textual materials provide a basis for systematic analysis of the impact area under investigation. They serve as raw material for delineating boundary lines, developing social profiles, and analyzing social systems and processes in relation to environmental factors.

Archival quantitative data have several advantages. They readily lend themselves to statistical analysis and computer programming. In addition (and very importantly), researcher bias is reduced because of their objective nature. The utility of both types of documents was exemplified by my usage of maps, telephone directories, newspapers and *Dun and Bradstreet* reference books in social impact research in Appalachia and in the Arkansas River area.

Researchers, while finding advantages in the use of both narrative and statistical historical documents in terms of availability and economies in time and money, face problems with biases inherent in the records, incompleteness of records, and subjectivity of interpretations. The problems of reliability and validity, problems in all social science research, can be approached through a triangulation of historical documentation with other methods of data collection and analysis.

These documents, despite shortcomings, have advantages over surveys and interviews in obtaining a longitudinal perspective of an area. Most public projects for which social impact assessment is a prerequisite involve many years of planning, constructing, and finally operating. By tracing communities over time the researcher can note patterns of change within each given community and compare the development of the communities in the impact area. This knowledge facilitates the process of forecasting potential social impacts of a project from its incipiency to its operation as an integral part of the area's life. Thus historical documents are of great value in gaining a long view.

Notes

1. Nonprint media, whether in the form of movies, videocassettes, or other pictorial records, play an increasingly important part in documenting human history. They are not discussed here, however. The reader can adapt the ensuing discussion to these records.

2. Space limitations do not permit discussion of content analysis of other data sources. The reader may wish to consult Motz (1977, 1979) for more complete explanations.

References

BABBIE, E. R. (1979) The Practice of Social Research. Belmont, CA; Wadsworth.

DENZIN, N. K. (1970) The Research Act: A Theoretical Introduction to Sociological Methods. Chicago: Aldine.

HOLSTI, O. (1969) Content Analysis for the Social Sciences and Humanities. Reading, MA: Addison-Wesley.

LIN, N. (1976) Foundations of Social Research. New York: McGraw-Hill.

MARKOFF, J. et al. (1974) "Toward the integration of content analysis and general methodology," pp. 1-58 in D. R. Heise (ed.) Sociological Methodology. San Francisco: Jossey-Bass.

MOTZ, A. B. (1979) Community Dynamics in the 100-Year Flood Plain of the Tug Fork River in West Virginia and Kentucky: A Sociological Perspective. Ft. Belvoir, VA: Institute for Water Resources, U.S. Army Corps of Engineers.

———— (1977) A Research Strategy for Social Impact Assessment: A Tale of Three Cities. Ft. Belvoir, VA: Institute for Water Resources, U.S. Army Corps of Engineers.

———— (1974) Social Science Data Banks and the Institute for Water Resources. Ft. Belvoir, VA: U.S. Army Corps of Engineers.

NACHMIAS, D. and C. NACHMIAS (1976) Research Methods in the Social Sciences. New York: St. Martin's.

SCHUTZ, A. (1975) Collected Papers I: The Problem of Social Reality (M. Natanson, ed.). Chicago: University of Chicago Press.

SELLTIZ, C. et al. (1976) Research Methods in Social Research. New York: Holt, Rinehart & Winston.

SHYNE, A. W. (1975) "Exploiting available information," in N. A. Polansky (ed.) Social Work Research. Chicago: University of Chicago Press.

WEBB, E. D., A. CAMPBELL, R. SCHWARTZ, and L. SECHREST (1966) Unobtrusive Measures: Nonreactive Research in the Social Sciences. Chicago: Rand McNally.

WILLIAMS, M. E. (1982) Computer-Readable Databases: A Directory and Data Sourcebook. Urbana: American Society for Information Science, University of Illinois.

7

Demographic
Change Assessment

○ ○ ○ ○ ○ ○ ○ ○ ○ ○ ○ ○ ○ ○ ○ ○

THOMAS DIETZ and C. MARK DUNNING

○ ○ ○ ○ ○ ○ ○ ○ ○ ○ ○ ○ ○ ○ ○ ○

● Resource development activities have produced profound socioeconomic changes in small communities. Industry and government have recognized that massive social and economic dislocations are dysfunctional not only to the communities in which they occur but to the successful completion of projects as well (see, for example, Kent, 1977). For this reason, considerable effort has been devoted to developing methods for anticipating the types and magnitude of socioeconomic changes associated with large-scale development projects. An important part of such socioeconomic impact assessments is the analysis of changes in basic demographic variables such as size, number, age, and sex composition of the population of communities near large development projects.

In this chapter we review recent work on predicting demographic changes in affected communities. Several interrelated topics are discussed. First, we review the relationship between demographic changes associated

Authors' Note: The authors thank C. Southcott for skillful typing. An earlier version of some of the material presented here appeared in Dietz (1981) and Dunning (1982).

with development activities and other socioeconomic impacts on local communities. Then a general outline of the demographic impact assessment process is presented. This outline serves to focus discussion on issues important to those performing, reviewing, or using such assessments. Finally, several computer models that perform demographic impact assessments are reviewed. The strengths and weaknesses of these systems as they are used in typical applications are emphasized.

Development, Demographic Change, and Socioeconomic Impacts

Constructing or operating large projects such as electric generating facilities, synfuel plants, or water projects requires many skilled workers. Such facilities are frequently sited in remote areas where demand for skilled labor can outstrip the local supply. In such instances, workers must be imported from other areas. Increases in population produced by the inmigration of workers and their families have a number of direct socioeconomic consequences for local communities. Demand for housing and other community services such as roads, sewers, and schools will increase. In addition, inmigrating populations may differ from the local population in age composition, education and income levels, and values. Such differences can lead to conflicts between "oldtimers" and "newcomers" (see, for example, Gold, 1974; Freudenberg, 1977; Gilmore and Duff, 1975). Development projects can also affect local economies by pumping in large sums of money. Wages provided by the projects and by local expenditures for equipment and supplies may induce expansion of local businesses. Such growth may create secondary employment and thus spur additional population increases.

This rapid expansion in the population and economy of local communities is the "boom" that can be followed by the "bust" upon completion of the development project. Once initial construction of a facility is complete, construction workers and their families move on. Precipitous declines in the population of local communities have significant consequences for the entire social system (Gilmore and Duff, 1975; Lemmerman, 1974). Businesses that expanded to service the larger population may be faced with excess capacity. Governments that financed capital improvements to provide services (schools, water, roads, and so on) may be faced with reduced tax rolls to pay off long-term obligations.

The severity of local socioeconomic impacts — whether associated with the rapid expansion or the decline of the population of local communities, or both — can be reduced by anticipating and planning for population changes. In addition, impact assessments can provide a guide for developers in providing compensation to local areas for the short-term effects of construction activity (Harnisch, 1980; Susskind and O'Hare, 1977).

Identifying the size of the population influx of a work force and dependents is of critical importance in predicting the magnitude and severity of population changes associated with development projects. Other characteristics of the work force group, such as age composition of dependents, occupational composition, and possible long-term mobility plans of inmigrants, are also important in assessing the implications of population changes on socioeconomic conditions in local communities. The process of projecting changes in population size and composition caused by development activities is demographic impact analysis.

The basis for assessing the demographic effects of development projects involves a comparison of a baseline or "without-project" development scenario with one or more "with-project" development scenarios. The steps in this process are illustrated in Figure 7.1. Differences in key variables, such as total population or age composition, between "with-project" scenarios and "without-project" scenarios constitute the demographic impacts of the project. Such demographic effects are usually translated into impacts on community infrastructure by assessing the demands on community services created by added population.

The methodology for demographic impact assessment outlined in Figure 7.1 is elaborated below. Our purpose is not to explain the process in great detail, but rather to call attention to issues that should be understood by those who intend to use the methodology, and to indicate data sources and previous research efforts that can be used in performing such analyses.

Without-Project Scenario

Building a without-project scenario involves forecasting what the local community will be like at some time in the future in the absence of the development project. Generally, such scenarios forecast without-project socioeconomic conditions at the time of peak construction or development activity, and also at some later period of time corresponding to postpeak conditions. The key tasks in developing such a scenario are forecasting the population of areas to be affected and identifying ongoing socioeconomic trends. Each of these tasks is discussed below.

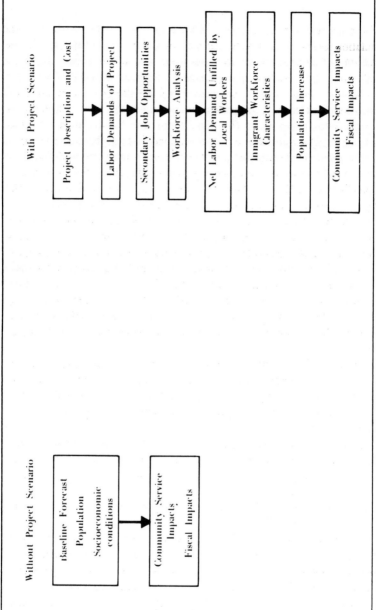

Figure 7.1 Demographic Impact Assessment Process

Demographers are well aware that the relative errors associated with population forecasts are inversely proportional to the size of the population at the start of the projection period. Since most impact assessment deal with small rural communities, the problems of small-area forecasting are especially pertinent to the impact analyst. There are two commonly used approaches to small-area population forecasting. Cohort survival methods break population change into migration, fertility, and mortality and develop separate projections for each of these components. Regression and extrapolation techniques forecast total population change on the basis of historical trends. A full treatment of the available methods is beyond the scope of this chapter; however, the topic has been extensively treated elsewhere (Oak Ridge Associated Universities, 1977; Shryock et al., 1971).

The process of describing current socioeconomic conditions in transition communities is generally known as "social profiling." Social profiles identify income and occupational distributions, social class differentiations, patterns of community influence and leadership, community issues, and dominant and competing norms and values (for examples of social profiles that incorporate analyses of such variables, see Motz, 1977; Motz and Van der Slice, 1980; Love, 1980). The social profile forms the basis for estimating future socioeconomic conditions under the without-project assumption.

Accurate and up-to-date social data on small areas are important for developing social profiles. In the United States, federal, state, and local agencies and a variety of private institutions generate large amounts of data. Many of these data can be used for social profiling. Indeed, so much information is available that the problems for the analyst are finding the germane subset of data and evaluating its quality and applicability for the impact study. Time is short in most impact studies, so there is pressure to concentrate on the analysis of data and to spend minimal time on searching for and assessing data quality.

Fortunately, the U.S. Bureau of the Census is making a serious effort to make official data easily available to the user community. Each of the twelve regional offices of the Bureau has an information specialist on the staff who can provide the impact analyst with access to, and evaluations of, available federal data. In addition, the Bureau in Washington has information specialists in dozens of topical areas of concern in impact assessments. Table 7.1 provides phone numbers for the national and regional offices. Several state governments have begun a cooperative effort with the Bureau to establish state data centers. These centers serve as repositories for all published and microform census reports dealing with the

TABLE 7.1 Census Bureau Telephone Numbers Useful for Impact Analysts

Data User Services Division	(202) 763-4100
Regional Offices	
Atlanta, Georgia	(404) 881-2274
Boston, Massachusetts	(617) 223-0226
Charlotte, North Carolina	(704) 371-6144
Chicago, Illinois	(312) 353-6631
Dallas, Texas	(214) 767-0624
Denver, Colorado	(303) 234-5825
Detroit, Michigan	(313) 226-4675
Kansas City, Kansas	(816) 374-4601
Los Angeles, California	(213) 824-7291
New York, New York	(212) 264-4730
Philadelphia, Pennsylvania	(215) 597-8313
Seattle, Washington	(206) 442-7081

state, and for publicly accessible data tapes whose sampling frame allows analysis of the state or areas within it. The centers have staff capable of conducting special analyses and consulting with users on special applications.

Banks, utilities, and the publishers of local directories can also provide information useful to the impact analyst. Even the local yellow pages can be used as a source of data on the number and type of community associations or commercial establishments in a community. Burdge and Johnson (1977) provide an inventory of the kinds of data generally available from private as well as public sources. Actual availability, data quality, and, in particular, the willingness of private institutions to share proprietary information will vary greatly. State data centers and regional census offices are usually aware of private studies and can suggest contacts at the local level. Bank officers, chamber of commerce officials, and local government staff are also useful in guiding the analyst to private data sources.

The decennial U.S. Census provides baseline data for nearly all small-area statistics in the United States. Data for time points between census dates must be based on sample surveys or extrapolated from census figures. There are a few local-area statistics, such as the number of welfare recipients, high school enrollments, or the number of felony convictions, that can be derived from local administrative procedures. Some of those indicators can be used to update census figures. Birth and death registers allow fairly precise assessment of natural increase in the population between census counts. School enrollments and driver's licenses provide indicators of youth and young adults and can be used to estimate the amount of migration for intercensus periods. These techniques are described in detail in Pittenger (1976) and Dietz (1977a).

However, data collected by local governments are subject to large errors and biases, either because such data are of little importance and thus are likely to be collected sloppily, or because they are of considerable political importance and are likely to be biased. So, whether relying on sample data, extrapolated census data, or figures derived from administrative procedures, the analyst must take account of imprecision. The degree of imprecision can be reduced somewhat by pooling alternate estimates of the same phenomena. Techniques for incorporating survey data into intercensal estimates or for combining official records and survey data are being developed and provide great promise for small-area estimation (Purcell and Kish, 1979). At present, however, intercensal estimates for small areas are very imprecise. For example, county-level estimates of welfare participation rates or unemployment may have coefficients of variation of 0.5 or larger. In addition, the confidence bands around these point estimates, when they can be calculated, are usually not symmetric. The impact analyst must therefore be careful to ensure that studies based on imprecise data convey a sense of this imprecision.

With-Project Scenario

The key problem in developing the with-project scenario is arriving at an estimate of the total number of people migrating into the local area. Once a total population estimate is derived, additional estimates of the age structure, occupational composition, housing needs, and locational patterns of inmigrants can be made. The total population impact induced by a development can be broken into two basic components: inmigration caused directly by the development project, and inmigration caused by perceived increases in job opportunities associated with providing services to an expanding population.

ESTIMATING DIRECT DEMOGRAPHIC IMPACTS

Estimating the number of workers likely to inmigrate because of a development project requires information on the labor demands of the project, and some assessment of the ability of the local area to supply the numbers and types of skills needed to meet that demand. Plans of large development projects are likely to have some breakdown of the numbers and kinds of workers needed for construction and operation. In addition, the U.S. Bureau of Labor Statistics publishes ratios of the number of man-years of construction per dollar expenditure for a variety of construction projects (Ball, 1981). These ratios can yield reasonable "ball park" estimates of numbers of workers required. More detailed estimates of worker demands by craft can be obtained from the Department of Labor's Construction Labor Demand System. This system's estimates are based on relationships between craft usage and dollar value of construction for a wide variety of construction projects (U.S. Department of Labor, 1979).

Employment generated by a development project is not constant over time. There is generally an initial phase of site preparation with gradually increasing employment, a peak phase when construction activity is most intense, and a final phase when employment drops off to the number of workers who operate and maintain the project. Figure 7.2 presents typical patterns of basic employment over time for two projects discussed in Chalmers and Anderson (1977). While the scale of projects differ by a factor of five, they exhibit similar activity patterns, though the larger project has a peak of greater duration. Policies that affect the timing and duration of labor demand can be important in determining the intensity and magnitude of demographic and other socioeconomic impacts. For example, the use of local labor or development projects is facilitated by policies that lengthen the development schedule and thus lower and broaden the "peak" observed in Figure 7.2, that emphasize labor intensive construction methods, or that disperse contract effort rather than concentrate the effort (Thompson and Sulvetta, 1975; Freudenburg, 1976).

Once an estimate of labor demand for a project has been developed, an assessment of the ability of the local area to meet the demand is performed. Usually a "laborshed" is defined around a project. It is assumed that the area so defined is likely to provide the bulk of local labor for the project. In most cases, the laborshed is defined on the basis of time and distance factors. For example, some construction work force studies have used a radius of 50 miles to define laborshed (Malhotra and Manninen, 1979; Dunning, 1981); others have based the definition on commute time (Chalmers and Anderson, 1977), or a combination of these factors (Battelle Columbus Laboratories, 1979). Still other approaches have combined labor market analyses (trade patterns) with time and/or distance factors (Henningson, Durham and Richardson, Inc., 1980).

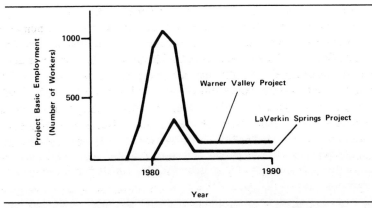

Figure 7.2   Basic Employment over Time for Two Construction Projects

SOURCE: Dietz (1981).

With a laborshed identified, the availability of workers with skills needed for the development project is estimated. It is generally assumed that workers from within the laborshed will come from three sources. First, they may come from the pool of unemployed labor having appropriate skills and qualifications. Second, already employed workers may be bid away from another job because of higher wages or better opportunities. Finally, there may be opportunities for some fully employed workers to take on a second job.

While the pool of unemployed labor in a laborshed may appear adequate to meet labor demands of a project, this unemployed labor may not have the proper skills or qualifications to meet the demands of the development project. Among the important characteristics for being hired on large construction projects are skill, education, and union membership. Only a small percentage of the workers in the local unemployed labor pool may have the necessary qualifications (Lovejoy, 1980). Even if an unemployed labor pool appears to have sufficient numbers of qualified workers, there may be other ongoing development projects in the region that will compete for this qualified segment of the unemployed work force.

When major projects are under development, workers already employed in the local economy may be drawn to the project, and leaving vacancies to be filled by others. Shifts of employment from lower-paying to higher-paying positions might occur under conditions where a federal project inflates local wages, or in a situation where a shortage of labor with particular skills bids up wages for certain crafts. Although this effect has not been well documented in the literature, it is another potential source of local employment generated by development projects.

Fully employed workers in agricultural industries sometimes possess the skills and time to pursue two occupations. Harnisch (1980), for example, found that farmers in the vicinity of the Chief Joseph Dam project possessed the necessary qualifications to be operating engineers. Many worked on the project in that capacity, while continuing to work their farms in off hours.

Studies of work forces engaged in either the construction or operation of major development projects have documented great variability in the use of local workers. A study of twelve Bureau of Reclamation projects under construction showed that an average of 47 percent of the work force was composed of local workers, but the proportion of the work force that was local varied from a low of 11 percent to a high of 88 percent (Chalmers, 1977). Other studies have shown similar variability (Old West Regional Commission, 1975; Wieland et al., 1977; Dunning, 1981). Several factors seem to determine the proportion of the work force that will be hired from the local labor pool. Singley (1980) has shown that projects located in the eastern United States have higher proportions of local workers employed than projects located in the West. Other studies have also shown that nearness of project to an SMSA, large population in laborshed, and a high unemployment rate in the laborshed are associated with increased use of local workers (Chalmers, 1977; Dunning, 1981).

The proportion of the direct labor requirement that is likely to be supplied by inmigrants can be estimated with data provided by work force surveys of similar projects and/or projects in similar geographic locations or with labor supply models. Inmigrants are also referred to in the literature as "nonlocals" or "movers." Much of demographic impact analysis focuses on identifying the number and characteristics of these inmigrants and their dependents. Here variables such as the number and age composition of dependents accompanying inmigrating workers, worker housing preferences and requirements, location preferences, and plans regarding length of stay are critical. Each of these variables has a direct relationship to the demand for community services. In addition, each variable has its own implications for project impacts in the local area.

A substantial body of information concerning the social and demographic characteristics of workers has been accumulated through the various "work force surveys" that have been conducted. Table 7.2 presents a description of several major work force surveys. While these surveys have employed different methodologies, similarities can be seen in many of the

TABLE 7.2 Characteristics of Recent Work Force Surveys

	Corps of Engineers	Bureau of Reclamation	North Dakota University	Battelle	Tennessee Valley Authority
Date of survey	Summer 1979	Summer 1977	Summer 1975	not provided	1967-1975
Number of projects surveyed	55	12	2	13	6
Response	4089	608	264	not provided	9627
Response rate (%)	65	52	26	82	75
Location of project	nationwide	West	North Dakota	Northeast, Midwest, South, Southeast	Southeast
Type of projects	water	water	electrical	electrical	electrical

TABLE 7.3 Comparison of Construction Work Force Survey Findings

	Corps of Engineers	Bureau of Reclamation	Battelle	Tennessee Valley Authority	North Dakota University
Variable					
Percentage nonlocal	29.6	52.8	17-34	28.6	50.0
Percentage of nonlocal workers accompanied	58.9	64.9	51-72	63.4	59.7
Ratio of total dependents to nonlocal workers	1.24	1.14	—	—	—
Ratio of school-age children to total nonlocal workers	0.50	—	—	0.56	—
Ratio of school-age children to accompanied nonlocal workers	0.85	—	0.7-0.9	0.88	—

measures of demand characteristics. Table 7.3 compares findings from these studies regarding percentage of inmigrant workers accompanied by family, the ratio of dependents to inmigrant workers, the ratio of school-age children to inmigrant workers. It should again be emphasized that these figures contain substantial variability. To date, very little empirical work has been done in identifying the sources of this variability, so information from these studies must be extrapolated to new situations with caution.

Another important component of the analysis of inmigration is the distribution of the inmigrant population within the local area. Methods for predicting the locational choices of inmigrant populations generally use a judgmental approach — in which communities in the local area are weighted on attractiveness criteria and inmigrants are distributed according to these weights (Harnisch, 1980) — or a gravity model approach to allocating inmigrants (Chalmers and Anderson, 1977). The use of the gravity model for demographic impact assessment has been critically discussed elsewhere (Stenehjem and Metzger, 1976; Murdock et al., 1978). Figure 7.3 presents one-way distance commuted to work by local and inmigrant workers in a survey of the Corps of Engineer construction work force. As can be seen, the distance commuted to work drops off in a manner consistent with gravity functions. In this same survey, inmigrant workers were also asked to select the most important reasons for locating where they did from among a list of common location preference factors. "Nearness to project site" was chosen much more frequently than other factors such as the presence of shopping, schools, or other community services. These results are summarized in Table 7.4.

ESTIMATING INDIRECT DEMOGRAPHIC IMPACTS

Just as a development project creates demand for labor, the earnings of the work force and expenditures for supplies and materials needed for the project spent in the local area create additional demands for labor. These latter demands are referred to as indirect or secondary employment effects or development. In general, the measurement and projection of the secondary effects of development projects have not received as much attention among researchers as have direct effects.

The most commonly used procedure first estimates the number of workers required for the development project. Next, an assessment of the ability of the local laborshed to provide labor for these jobs is made. Any surplus labor demand is assumed to be filled by inmigrants. Estimates of the total population influx associated with indirect jobs filled by inmigrants must be made, as well as assumptions about age composition and settlement patterns of this group. These topics are discussed briefly below. In general, the issues involved in the estimation of the demographic effects of indirect

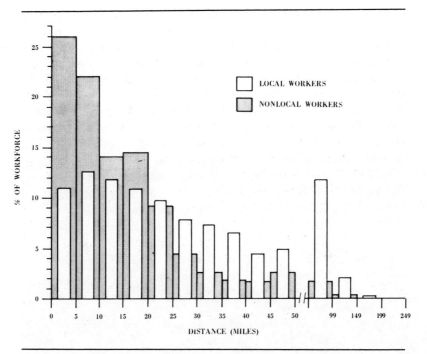

Figure 7.3 Travel Distance to Work for Local and Nonlocal Workers

SOURCE: Dunning (1981).

TABLE 7.4 Factors Influencing Choice of Residential Location of Nonlocal Workers

Factor	Workers with Dependents Present		Workers Without Dependents Present		All Nonlocal Workers	
	N	%	N	%	N	%
Close to project	334	43.3	271	52.2	605	46.9
Cost of housing	75	9.7	68	13.1	143	11.1
Availability of housing	176	22.8	92	17.7	268	20.8
Good schools	58	7.5	8	1.5	66	5.1
Friends nearby	60	7.8	44	8.5	104	8.1
Shopping	30	3.9	11	2.1	41	3.2
Community services	3	0.4	4	0.8	7	0.5
Other	35	4.5	21	4.0	56	4.3
Total	771	100.0	519	100.0	1290	100.0

SOURCE: Dunning (1981).

employment are the same as those involved in estimating the impacts of direct employment.

Increased demand translates into additional employment opportunities as businesses expand. The ability of local economics to expand is often projected using multipliers. Multipliers are a central component in macroeconomic analysis, and their derivation will not be discussed here. For detailed treatment of this concept, refer to Leistritz and Murdock (1981). The stimulus to local economies comes from the earnings of workers directly employed by the development project, and from procurement of locally available materials and supplies needed for the project. Local businesses may expand to meet the additional demand or new businesses may be formed. The estimation of the multiplier effects of additional demands from wages and procurement has been approached using export base methods (Chalmers and Anderson, 1977) and also using input-output analyses (Cartwright et al., 1981). Export base multipliers consist of the ratio of employment in secondary industries to employment in basic industries. Basic employment is the employment in a region that is determined by factors external to the region, while secondary employment is determined by forces internal to the region and by shifts in basic employment. Following the export base method, an increase in basic employment provided by a development project would generate the number of secondary jobs corresponding to the overall ratio of basic to secondary jobs. Local procurement expenses can be translated into basic jobs by applying a standard wage rate to the dollar value of goods purchased locally.

Meidinger (1977) has prepared an empirical and theoretical critique of the economic base approach to estimating induced employment. He notes that the key assumption behind the approach is that the multiplier that translates basic into secondary employment is constant over time. In examining the actual ratio of secondary to basic employment in two developments in the Great Plains, Meidinger finds substantial variation. We have plotted his data for a heavily affected county in Figure 7.4. The secondary to basic ratio varies by a factor of three, from a low of 0.5 to a high of 1.5. Secondary employment lags behind base employment in most circumstances, and it is likely that a large project will alter the structure of the local economy. But Meidinger also finds significant variation in the secondary to basic ratio in control counties that were not affected, so it seems that the structural change reflected by changes in this ratio is not restricted to affected areas.

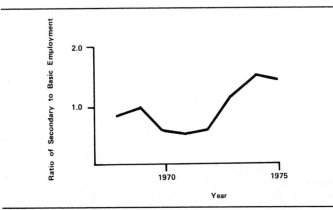

Figure 7.4   Changes in Secondary to Basic Employment Ratio over Time

SOURCE: Dietz (1981).

Input-output approaches to multiplier creation offer the advantage of greater specificity and stronger theoretical justification. However, they require more data than do economic base methods. With an input-output framework, an additional unit of demand in one industry is translated into employment in other industries. By summing over industries, the total impact on employment can be estimated.

With estimates of secondary employment created by the direct employment and the local procurement expenditures from a development project, the ability of the local laborshed to supply the additional labor must be assessed. As with estimation of the number of local workers directly employed, this procedure involves an examination of the unemployed pool of labor available locally. Since many secondary jobs do not require high skill levels, the dependents of inmigrating workers also form a potential source of labor for secondary jobs. In some analyses, the general labor force participation rates for females and teenagers have been used to derive estimates of the pool of workers potentially available from direct inmigrant work force dependents (Henningson, Durham and Richardson, Inc., 1980).

Any additional unmet demand for secondary labor is assumed to be met by inmigrants. Estimates of numbers and age composition of dependents of workers inmigrating as a result of secondary employment opportunities can then be made. Averages of family size and age composition breakdowns provided by national or regional census data have been used for these estimates (Henningson, Durham and Richardson, Inc., 1980).

An allocation of inmigrant populations associated with secondary employment opportunities must also be made. No empirical work examines the location patterns of secondary workers. Studies have generally made the assumption that secondary inmigrant populations would be distributed in the local area in the same manner as the population inmigrating because of direct employment opportunities.

TOTAL POPULATION IMPACT

The outputs of the direct and indirect employment estimation procedures are forecasts of total population attributable to the project, age breakdown of this population, and some assessment of their settlement patterns. These estimates are used to derive estimates of net fiscal impact on local communities. The net fiscal impact is computed using costs associated with providing public services for the inmigrating population and tax revenues generated by the populations. Costs for providing public services are estimated by identifying the demand for community services associated with population increases attributed to the project. Dickinson and Blackmarr (1977) and Muller (1976) describe fiscal balance and cost revenue analysis in detail.

There are two ways to estimate such demands. The most common approach is to consult existing state, federal, and professional standards. For example, the Public Library Association suggests that a community of 2,000 have a library with 10,000 volumes and that a community of 4,000 have a library with 11,500 volumes, so a population doubling would, according to the standards approach, generate a demand for 1,500 additional volumes. Chalmers and Anderson (1977) provide an inventory of service standards. The facilities in many rural communities do not meet standards before the start of construction, so some researchers feel the standards approach produces unrealistically high estimates of future service demand. Instead, they use a normative approach, which calculates the level of services supplied per capita for communities in the project area. Under the assumption that per capita service provision will remain constant, future service demand is calculated by multiplying future population by the current service to population ratio. Once demand is identified, cost estimates for providing the level of services are computed. Standards of cost per service unit are generally employed to obtain total costs for public services. Local tax revenues are estimated in steps. First, employment figures are translated into earnings based on occupational breakdowns, and resulting tax revenues are estimated. Second, new tax revenues generated as a results of changes in property values are calculated. Third, additional sales and other taxes are estimated. All these sources are added to produce an estimate of total increases in revenues (Leistritz and Murdock, 1981).

Demographic Impact Simulation Models

The process described in the preceding section is complex and requires many assumptions. A change in any major assumption will necessitate extensive recalculation. Policymakers are concerned about intervening in systems. They are interested in asking "what if" types of questions about policies that may be used to manage impacts associated with development projects. Therefore, they are likely to be interested in varying assumptions. The complexity of the assessment process, coupled with the need to make many assessments with varying assumptions, has led to the popularity of computerized demographic impact assessment models. Such computerized models are something of a growth industry. A recent report identified twelve such forecasting models (Leistritz and Murdock, 1981), and additional models are under development. Most existing demographic impact assessment models consist of several major subroutines that correspond to the logic of the impact assessment process illustrated in Figure 7.1.

The direct project employment subroutine is the starting point for impact assessment. At this point in the analysis, estimates of either the number of workers to be employed or of the payroll are input. An average wage rate or wage schedule is used to translate employees to payroll or vice versa. Since basic employment is not constant over time but has a peak phase when construction activity is most intense, demographic impact assessment models usually calculate impacts on a year-by-year basis to allow for variation in employment.

The next subroutine estimates secondary, or induced, employment from the basic, or direct, employment. Most models use export base employment multipliers. However, the Regional Impact Multiplier System of the Bureau of Economic Analysis and the Texas Assessment Modeling System use a modified input-output approach to generate multipliers (Cartwright et al., 1981; Murdock et al., 1978).

The direct and secondary employment routines provide estimates of the total employment that is likely to result from the project. A migration subroutine then estimates how many of these jobs will be filled by local workers, and how many will be filled by inmigrants. This subroutine uses information on local communities, counties, or labor market areas, as well as data on construction work force characteristics derived from work force surveys to estimate how many workers will migrate to the project site, and how many spouses and children will accompany them. Estimated migration increases are input to the demographic submodel that projects population for the local area. Most models employ a cohort-survival method to forecast population. Dietz (1977a) and Pittenger (1976) provide descriptions of the cohort-survival method.

The service demand subroutine estimates the amount of public and private services that must be supplied to meet the needs of the local population. Most models use existing state, federal, and professional standards to estimate service demands. A few use a normative approach in which the level of services supplied per capita for communities in the local area is used to calculate project-induced changes in demand.

In some models, the income subroutine translates direct and secondary employment into total income for the project area. This subroutine provides an estimate of the economic growth induced by the project in dollars, rather than an estimate of employment. The fiscal balance submodel estimates the costs required to meet the service demands estimated. Some models use national or regional figures on costs per unit service; others use typical local expenditure patterns. Revenues are estimated from aggregate income figures developed in the income submodel. A comparison of estimated costs and estimated revenues yields a cost-revenue projection for local governments.

In summary, demographic impact simulation models begin with basic employment figures derived from the project proposal, and use these to estimate secondary employment. Migration submodels use information on local communities, project employment, and typical construction worker behavior to determine how many workers will migrate to the project site and how many spouses and children will accompany them. Estimated migration increases are input to a demographic submodel that projects future population by age. Population changes are used to estimate changes in service requirements and, with project data, changes in local income. Service and income data are used in the fiscal balance subroutine to assess the fiscal impacts of the project on local communities.

Formal demographic impact simulation models can play an important role in the overall impact assessment process. Once the capital costs of model development are absorbed, such models are relatively inexpensive to use. Chalmers and Anderson (1977) were able to complete a rather detailed case study in two months, with a total time expenditure of about 60 person-days. The effort required will, of course, depend on the availability of site-specific data.

The assumptions driving an impact assessment model of this sort are explicit as well as consistent across analyses. This is an advantage if — and only if — the assumptions are understood by analysts and the consumers of model impact predictions. Pittenger (1980: 138), discussing population forecasts, makes clear the importance of explicit assumptions:

> Standards or guidelines [for population forecasts] should require information documenting and justifying the assumptions embodied in the primary planning forecast. Requiring assumption justification should eliminate excessively narrow assumptions. Assumption justification could also clarify "black box" forecasts, if a model is so complex that its workings cannot be explained to a review board of intelligent laymen, its forecasts should be treated with skepticism.

Unfortunately, impact simulation models are complex, so great care is needed in making the explicit assumptions buried in them clear to potential users and to decision makers.

Demographic impact assessment models produce a large amount of output. Readers are likely to be overwhelmed by point estimates, even without error bands. Extensive and creative use of graphics seems to be the only way to communicate with a diverse audience. Indeed, graphics can be a powerful analytical tool as well as a means of communication. For example, in an analysis of water- related local growth impacts, maps of vacancy rates, commuting times, public lands, water supply restrictions, and agricultural preserve land were overlaid. The resulting map identified specific localities where water supply will strongly influence growth. It allowed the research team to focus its limited resources on high-priority areas and heightened awareness of the issues in those communities (Dietz, 1977b; Dietz and Ray, 1977).

Happily, the need for improved graphics in impact assessment work comes at a time when statisticians and others are devoting their efforts to developing better graphic tools. Tukey (1977) and his followers have proposed a number of simple displays that emphasize pattern and deviation from pattern in batches of data. A number of researchers are investigating the clarity of alternative mapping and graphic techniques (Wainer and Francolini, 1980; MacDonald-Ross, 1977; Fienberg, 1979). And most major social science statistical packages are incorporating extensive graphics capabilities and interface with mapping programs. These developments make it easier and cheaper to incorporate effective graphics into impact reports.

Existing demographic impact assessment models are designed to make predictions for small areas. Some of them allow analyses for single towns and incorporate factors that allocate migration and employment across towns, as noted above. Such geographic disaggregation is important because it provides information on "spillover" effects in communities not in the immediate vicinity of the project, and permits identification of local impacts that might average out, or be lost as a result of model imprecision, at a higher level of aggregation.

Incorporation of a finer degree of social disaggregation in models could enhance their ability to identify politically salient impacts. Schnaiberg and Meidinger (1978) have argued that the most important impacts of most resource development projects are distributional. The geographical disaggregation in current models allows analysis of the distribution of costs and benefits across communities. But most costs and benefits occur differentially to social classes and ethnic groups. It will be difficult to build a model that disaggregates by class or ethnicity, but the distributional effects it reveals may be substantial and will certainly be salient to those affected.

Of course, no demographic impact simulation model can be expected to identify and estimate all important impacts. Indeed, there is a real danger that the use of sophisticated models will divert attention away from impacts that are difficult to predict, or even measure, quantitatively. It has been argued elsewhere that social impact assessment must emphasize the identification of politically important impacts (Cramer et al., 1980). Formal demographic models can make an important contribution to the impact assessment process by providing information on key social changes induced by a project. But the use of these models must be tempered with an understanding of the imprecision inherent in them and with concern for impacts that fall outside of their domain.

Conclusion

The demographic impact assessment process has been described. The information provided by such assessment forms a foundation for subsequent steps in the socioeconomic assessment process. When there are large numbers of inmigrants relative to the ability of community infrastructure to provide support, the social and psychological dimensions of community life become increasingly problematic. As Freudenburg (1976) has noted:

One does not need to be a sociologist to know that people rarely attempt or commit suicide because of inadequate sewage facilities. What sociologists can and should offer is a more complete explication of the factors that are important for human well-being in a boom situation. It would be unwise to pretend that logistical considerations are not among those factors, but it would be at least equally unwise to pretend that nothing else is needed to keep the human organism running properly.

While the techniques discussed in this chapter provide a means of anticipating some of the socioeconomic changes produced by development activities, other important issues still need to be addressed if we are to assess the impacts of development adequately.

References

BALL, R. (1981) "Employment created by construction expenditures." Monthly Labor Review: 38-44.

Battelle Columbus Laboratories (1979) Socio-Economic Effects of the DOE Gas Centrifuge Enrichment Plant. Columbus, OH: Author.

BURDGE, R. and S. JOHNSON (1977) "Sociocultural aspects of the effects of resource development," pp. 241-278 in J. McEvoy III and T. Dietz (eds.) Handbook for Environmental Planning. New York: John Wiley.

CARTWRIGHT, J., R. BEEMILLER, and R. GUSTELY (1981) Regional Input-Output Modeling System: Estimation, Evaluation and Application of a Dissaggregated Regional Impact Model. Washington, DC: Bureau of Economic Analysis, U.S. Department of Commerce.

CHALMERS, J. (1977) Construction Worker Survey. Tempe, AZ: Mountain West Research, Inc.

——— and E. ANDERSON (1977) Economic Demographic Assessment Manual. Tempe, AZ: Mountain West Research, Inc.

CRAMER, J., T. DIETZ, and R. JOHNSTON (1980) "Social impact assessment of regional plans." Policy Sciences 12: 61-82.

DICKINSON, T. and J. BLACKMARR (1977) "Evaluation of private and public economic impacts caused by private developments," pp. 163-199 in J. McEvoy III and T. Dietz (eds.) Handbook for Environmental Planning. New York: John Wiley.

DIETZ, T. (1981) "The use of demographic information in social impact assessment," pp. 196-206 in K. Finsterbusch and C. P. Wolf (eds.) Methodology of Social Impact Assessment. Stroudsburg, PA: Hutchinson Ross.

——— (1977a) "Demographic perspectives on impact assessment," pp. 65-105 in J. McEvoy III and T. Dietz (eds.) Handbook for Environmental Planning. New York: John Wiley.

——— (1977b) "The role of demography in social impact assessment." Social Impact Assessment 21/22.

———— and D. Ray (1977) "The social impacts of growth in Santa Barbara and San Luis Obispo Counties." Social Impact Assessment 21/22: 3-8.

DUNNING, C. (1982) "Construction work force characteristics and community service impact assesment." Water Resources Bulletin 18, 2: 239-244.

———— (1981) Report of Survey of Corps of Engineers Construction Workforce. Ft. Belvoir, VA: Institute for Water Resources, U.S. Army Corps of Engineers.

FIENBERG, S. (1979) "Graphical methods in statistics." American Statistician 33: 165-178.

FREUDENBURG, W. (1977) "A *social* social impact analysis of a Rocky Mountain energy boomtown." Department of Sociology, Washington State University.

———— (1976) "The social impact of energy boomtown development of rural communities." Department of Sociology, Yale University.

GILMORE, J. and M. DUFF (1975) Boomtown Growth Management. Boulder, CO: Westview.

GOLD, R. (1974) "Social impacts of strip mining and other industrializations of coal resources," in C. P. Wolf (ed.) Social Impact Assessment. Milwaukee: Environmental Design Research Association.

HARNISCH, A. (1980) Community Impact Reports: Chief Joseph Dam. Ft. Belvoir, VA: Institute for Water Resources, U.S. Army Corps of Engineers.

Henningson, Durham and Richardson, Inc. (1980) Environmental Impact Statements for MX Development. Santa Barbara, CA: Author.

KENT, J. (1977) "Social impacts: a new era for industry and citizen participation," in Colorado Mining Association Yearbook. Denver: Colorado Mining Association.

LEISTRITZ, F. and S. MURDOCK (1981) The Socioeconomic Impact of Resource Development: Methods for Assessment. Boulder, CO: Westview.

LEMMERMAN, K. (1974) Columbus/Noonan Study. Denver: Northern Great Plains Resource Program.

LOVE, R. (1980) "Social effects assessment for multiple use of water resources," in Electric Power Research Institute (ed.) Proceedings of the Workshop on Water Supply for Electrical Energy. Palo Alto, CA: Electric Power Research Institute.

LOVEJOY, S. (1980) "Predictions of local employment from western energy development." Presented at the annual meeting of the Rural Sociological Society, Ithaca, NY.

MacDONALD-ROSS, M. (1977) "How numbers are shown." Audio-Visual Communication 25: 359-409.

MALHOTRA, S. and D. MANNINEN (1979) Socio-Economic Impact Assessments: Profile Analysis of Worker Surveys Conducted at Nuclear Power Plant Construction Sites. Seattle: Battelle Memorial Institute.

MEIDINGER, E. (1977) "Projecting secondary jobs: an empirical examination and epistemological critique." Presented at the annual meeting of the American Sociological Association, Chicago.

MOTZ, A. B. (1977) A Research Strategy for Social Impact Assessment: A Tale of Three Cities. Ft. Belvoir, VA: Institute for Water Resources, U.S. Army Corps of Engineers.

———— and A. VAN DER SLICE (1980) The Tug Fork Valley Community Study. Ft. Belvoir, VA: Institute for Water Resources, U.S. Army Corps of Engineers.

MULLER, T. (1976) Fiscal Impacts of Land Development. Washington, DC: Urban Institute.

MURDOCK, S., J. WIELAND, and F. LEISTRITZ (1978) "An assessment of the validity of the gravity model for predicting community settlement patterns in rural energy-impacted areas in the West." Land Economics 54: 461-471.

Oak Ridge Associated Universities (1977) Population Forecasting for Small Areas. Oak Ridge, TN: Author.

Old West Regional Commission (1975) Construction Worker Profile. Washington, DC: Author.

PITTENGER, D. (1980) "Some problems in forecasting population for government planning purposes." American Statistician 34: 135-139.

——— (1976) Projecting State and Local Populations. Cambridge, MA: Ballinger.

PURCELL, N. and L. KISH (1979) "Estimation for small domains." Biometrics 35: 365-384.

SCHNAIBERG, A. and E. MEIDINGER (1978) "Social reality and analytic methodology: social impact assessment of natural resource utilization." Presented at the annual meeting of the American Sociological Association, San Francisco.

SHRYOCK, H., J. SIEGEL, et al. (1971) The Materials and Methods of Demography. Washington, DC: Government Printing Office.

SINGLEY, J. (1980) "Socioeconomic impacts of energy development for eastern and western projects." Presented at the annual meeting of the Society for the Study of Social Problems, New York.

STENEHJEM, E. and J. METZGER (1976) A Framework for Projecting Employment and Population Changes Accompanying Energy Development. Chicago: Argonne National Laboratory.

SUSSKIND, L. and M. O'HARE (1977) Managing the Social and Economic Impacts of Energy Development. Cambridge: Energy Impacts Program, Massachusetts Institute of Technology.

THOMPSON, N. and A. SULVETTA (1975) An Evaluation of the Public Works Impact Program. Washington, DC: Economic Development Administration, U.S. Department of Commerce.

TUKEY, J. (1977) Exploratory Data Analysis. Reading, MA: Addison-Wesley.

U.S. Department of Labor (1979) Construction Labor Demand System. Washington, DC: Employment Standards Administration, U.S. Department of Labor.

WAINER, H. and C. FRANCOLINI (1980) "An empirical inquiry concerning human understanding of two-variable color maps." American Statistician 34: 81-93.

WIELAND, J., F. LEISTRITZ, and S. MURDOCK (1977) Characteristics and Settlement Patterns of Energy Related Operating Workers in the Northern Great Plains. Fargo: North Dakota Agricultural Experiment Station.

8

Social Indicators Research

○ ○ ○ ○ ○ ○ ○ ○ ○ ○ ○ ○ ○ ○ ○ ○

MICHAEL J. CARLEY

○ ○ ○ ○ ○ ○ ○ ○ ○ ○ ○ ○ ○ ○ ○ ○

● In the mid-1960s a growing dissatisfaction with the amount and quality of social information available to government decision makers spawned what came to be known as the "social indicators movement." Initially this was a reaction against an overemphasis on measures of economic performance as indicative of social well-being. These economic indicators had obvious limitations in evaluating wider social welfare considerations, such as qualitative aspects of life, equity, and the side effects or externalities of economic prosperity, such as environmental pollution. The following are some of the more specific criticisms of economic indicators, or the GNP approach:

(1) Such measures cannot be equated with psychological satisfaction, happiness, or life fulfillment.

(2) The market valuations of goods and services are not necessarily related to their welfare content.

(3) Economic measures often obscure important income distributional effects by averaging (Encel et al., 1975).

Although there has been some cross-fertilization between the social indicators field and the social impact assessment (SIA) field, it has not been extensive. While this may seem surprising at first, it is probably due to two factors. First, there is a lack of interdisciplinary integration in the social sciences generally. Second, although social indicators and SIA both involve the practical application of social measurement to decision making, they have tended to focus on different things. SIAs have concentrated on predicting the impacts of particular developments, and have been project specific and of a limited preproject duration. Social indicators research, on the other hand, has concentrated on attempts to develop measures of the *quality of life*, on indicator systems for *monitoring* an existing situation in society at a particular administrative or geographic level, and on the development of *performance measures* of public service delivery.

The rest of this chapter defines some important aspects of social indicators; explores quality of life studies, community monitoring systems, and public service delivery measurement; and concludes with a discussion of some methodological issues in social indicators research.

SIA and Social Indicators: A Common Basis

Although the phrase "social indicators," as opposed to economic indicators, was not coined until the 1960s, there is general agreement that the historical basis for this activity goes back to the work of the British economist A. C. Pigou (1924), who argued in *The Economics of Welfare* that neoclassical economics could no longer ignore the concept of social costs that might cause public welfare to differ from private welfare. This difference reflected an imperfect working of the market economy and a role for intervention in the workings of that economy.

Pigou went on to point out that overall public welfare could be lessened by those social costs, or disservices, that exceed the private costs of production. He gave examples: the lessening of the amenity of residential neighborhoods by factory construction, or the cost of police services related to liquor sales, neither of which would be the concern of factory owners or distillers in their corporate balance sheets. He argued that these types of social costs had to be quantified to determine their effect on the net social product. Today we sometimes call these social costs "impacts."

Pigou's arguments on social cost had little effect until the 1950s, when the concept was incorporated into welfare economics, and especially cost-benefit analysis, as what the economists now call externalities. The social cost concept explicitly argued that a consideration of these externalities was essential to good decision making, and this suggested a whole variety of social factors that needed to be measured. This concept of social cost is an important dimension not only of social indicators research, but also of related fields, such as SIA. The common basis of social indicators research, SIA, and modern welfare economics also suggests one reason it turned out to be almost impossible to draw a fine distinction between economic and social indicators of well-being.

Social Indicators: What Are They?

It is perhaps worthwhile to begin in the simplest terms. In everyday life we use certain kinds of symptoms or tokens as indications of less visible yet important states of being or situation. For example, the color of a man's face or the temperature of his forehead tells us something about his health, based on our experience. Color or temperature, therefore, may be crude indicators of health. In the field of socioeconomic policy we can assume that action of government (usually) exists to maintain or improve the well-being of individuals or society as a whole. If we accept this, then for either policy development or program evaluation the government needs some way to ascertain that maintenance of or improvement in well-being is taking place. That is, measurements are needed, unless intuitive assessments are to be relied on. Unfortunately, we are unable to measure well-being directly, since neither individuals nor countries carry convenient gauges of well-being. So surrogates for more direct measures of well-being are required. These surrogates may be termed social indicators, which are measures of an observable trait of a social phenomenon that establish the value of a different unobservable trait of the phenomenon.

This points up two important characteristics of social indicators: They are "surrogates" and they are "measures." As surrogates, social indicators translate abstract or unmeasurable social concepts (such as "safe streets") into operational terms (such as "number of crimeless days") that allow consideration and analysis of the concept. A social indicator must always be related back to the unmeasurable concept for which it is a proxy. As "measures," social indicators are concerned with information that is conceptually quantifiable, and must avoid dealing with information that cannot be expressed on some ordered scale.

A Definition of Social Indicators

There are numerous definitions of social indicators, many not very rigorous. A complete definition, however, is Carlisle's (1972: 25), in which a social indicator is described as "the operational definition of any one of the concepts central to the generation of an information system descriptive of the social system." The two most important elements in this definition are, first, that social indicators are the result of "operationalizing" abstract concepts, such as health, by translating them into measurable terms in the form of proxies such as "number of days without sickness." Second, social indicators are part of an "information system" that is used by policymakers in understanding and evaluating those parts of the social system over which they exert some power. This information system must satisfy, therefore, not only analytic requirements for making resource-maximizing decisions, but equally important political and bureaucratic needs.

Input, Throughput, and Output Measures

Social indicators may be measures of input, throughput, or output. Input measures are the resources available to some process affecting well-being in the social environment, for example, number of doctors per unit of population. Second, "throughput" indicators are usually based on workload or caseload measures — number of doctor visits for work-related injuries, for example. Third, there are intermediate output indicators, which are measures of the results of specific activities performed, for example, extension of life expectancy, reduction in morbidity, or infant mortality. These constitute some of the most policy-useful social indicators. However, they represent quantity, not quality, of life and so there are final output measures of such concepts as a "healthy" population or a "better" environment. Final output measures are often measured by subjective social indicators, and most objective social indicators are of the input, through-put, or intermediate output variety.

Subjective Social Indicators
and the Quality of Life

For most researchers, quality of life research means attention to subjective social indicators. Objective indicators are measured by counting the occurrences of a given phenomenon, and subjective indicators are based on reports from individuals about their own perceptions, feelings, and responses. Objective indicators are familiar as variations of time-series social statistics. Subjective indicators are usually based on questionnaires composed of a series of rating scales that ask respondents to codify their satisfactions with, or evaluations of, a large variety of the aspects and circumstances of their lives (Cullen, 1978). This is often done by using a five- or seven-point Likert scale that involves statements such as "My housing meets all my family's housing needs" presented in conjunction with a scale listing possible responses, such as (1) agree strongly, (2) agree, (3) indifferent, (4) disagree, and (5) strongly disagree. These Likert scales give a relative intensity of respondent feelings if not interval values. A complete set of such statements with attendant scales are used to elicit feelings as a basis for developing social indicators. Techniques of even more sophistication have been proposed that yield interval data and force the respondent to consider positive and negative aspects of particular feelings simultaneously. Such techniques — for example, Clark's (1974) "budget pies" for assessing citizen feelings about urban expenditure, or the use of priority evaluation games for evaluating preferences in environmental and transport planning (Hoinville and Courtenay, 1979) — may be applied more generally to subjective social indicators in the future.

Activity in the subjective indicator field has its roots in the work of both Hadley Cantril and Abraham Maslow in the 1950s and early 1960s. Cantril and his associates interviewed a cross section of people from various countries to determine what aspects of life they found important from positive and negative points of view, and where they scaled their personal standing in the present and future. This was done by presenting the respondents with a "ladder of life" device, or the Cantril Self-Anchoring Striving Scale (Cantril, 1965: 22), on which a person expressed perceived variations between his or her ideal situation and his or her actual condition. These variations were assessed on a scale ranging from 0 for the worst to 10 for the best possible situation in any one of a number of life areas, and are reported in *The Pattern of Human Concerns* (Cantril, 1965).

Similar to Cantril's work, and frequently cited, is the work of Maslow (1970), who proposed a hierarchical classification of five levels of human needs. On the lowest level are the physiological needs, for food, water, sleep, shelter, sex, and so on. On the second level is the need for security and safety for self and family. The third level is made up of various facets of the needs for "belongingness" and love, and the fourth level includes the needs for independence and freedom. On the highest level in this hierarchy are the needs for aesthetic beauty and knowledge as ends in themselves.

There are two important points to this hierarchy. First, Maslow argues that needs must be met in some semblance of ascending order, that is, physiological needs must be met before any higher-order needs can be met. Second, Maslow argues that man is "self-actualizing," that is, "what he can be, he must be." Humankind's self-actualization process (quality of life) can be helped or hindered by the nature of society. This concept of self-actualization implies a strong relationship between the more general nature of society and the environment, as often measured by objective indicators. Further, the concept of hierarchical human needs implies that relationships among areas of life satisfaction are as important as expressions of satisfaction with any one area. This means that careful attention must be paid to both the structuring and the interpretation of surveys from which social indicators are developed. This lesson is important for SIA. For example, the inherent value of proximity to recreational facilities may be quite different for people whose housing situations vary from adequate to inadequate.

Beyond these early research efforts, interest in subjective indicators was renewed in the 1970s, at least in part, by a lack of confidence in the correlation between objective indicators and life quality. For example, Schneider (1974: 508) warns, "The use of objective measures alone as quality of life indicators is . . . highly suspect." His research into over thirty objective indicators used in U.S. urban areas showed poor correlation between these common indicators and individuals' satisfaction with various aspects of their lives. Other research into work satisfaction shows strong socioeconomic strata differences in the correlations between socioeconomic indicators and life satisfaction.

Recent research in Canada points to similar conclusions. Kuz (1978) undertook a study in Manitoba based on 21 objective indicators and 13 subjective measures. He concluded that quality of life research using only objective variables is highly suspect in that it examines only one aspect of a multidimensional problem and that the subjective realities are equally important to overall quality of life. Kennedy et al. (1978: 464), in a study of social indicators for Edmonton, Alberta, found similar results and suggested that "the reasons for this low or lacking relationship between objective states and subjective perceptions lie in the fact that different individuals can be satisfied or dissatisfied by the same objective conditions."

In other words, two important social processes are at work in human society. First is the fact that one objective condition (such as poor accessibility to public open space) can quite easily elicit very different subjective responses from different individuals (for example, strong dissatisfaction versus complete indifference). Second, to compound the situation, similar subjective responses can result from widely differing objective situations. For example, people may experience as complete satisfaction with life in a mobile home as with life on a large country estate. Given that both these processes will be simultaneously existing in society, and will vary according to population subgroups and even from individual to individual, it is not surprising that researchers find a poor correlation between objective indicators and subjective responses. Attention to subjective social indicators is seen as a means of increasing this correlation between indicator sets and the reality of well-being. SIA methodology is now beginning to recognize this, with an increasing stress on the importance of integrating objective data with subjective responses (for example, see Flynn et al., 1982).

The broadest study in the quality of life (QOL) field, and one very much in the spirit of Cantril, if not in the methodology, is that of Andrews and Withey (1976) on Americans' perceptions of their quality of life. Their research involved interviews with over 5000 respondents and addressed the following issues:

the significant general concerns of Americans

the relative strengths of each concern vis-à-vis well-being

the relationship of the concerns to one another in terms of covariation and distinction

the relationship of the perception of general well-being to particular concerns

the stability of evaluations of concerns

comparability between population subgroups

The benefits of this type of research are that it provides a data base against which subsequent measures can be compared and that it gives information on the distribution of perceptions across society and on the structure and interdependence of these perceptions. Further, it helps in understanding how people evaluate and feel about such areas of life as family, job, housing, and neighborhood and how they combine various feelings into an overall evaluation of the value of life. The basic concepts in the Andrews and Withey model concern well-being at several levels of specificity. The most general are global indicators, which refer to life as a whole. The next level is of "concerns," which are aspects of life about which people have feelings. These are divided into "domains" and "criteria." Domains are subject areas (house, marriage, and so on) that can be evaluated in terms of the criteria (privacy, comfort, security, and so on).

Similar research is that of Knox (1976, 1978), who attempted to gauge whether there exists a clear order of priority preferences for different aspects (domains) of social well-being, and whether this varies by social class, age, region, or neighborhood. Knox used an eleven-point self-anchoring scale to establish priority rankings. He found that overall (for

Britain) the rankings are health (most important), then family life, social stability, housing, job satisfaction, neighborhood, financial situation, educational opportunity, and recreation. The ranking of health first corroborates similar findings of an earlier study (Hall and Perry, 1974). Beyond an overall consensus on the importance of health, however, Knox found considerable variations in preferences expressed by social, economic, demographic, and geographic population subgroups. Especially noteworthy are the strong regional variations for the domains of educational attainment, leisure, and social status. This type of research could be of considerable value to SIA analysts who are attempting to determine the significance of impacts or establish priorities for mitigation and compensation schemes. Knox's research demonstrates, however, that regional variations must be taken into account.

Quality of Life in Cities in the United States

A relatively common use of social indicators is to compare and contrast cities and counties on a variety of measures. This is especially true in the United States, where Flax (1978) has identified 25 such studies. The apparent aim of such exercises seems to be to point out which cities or jurisdictions are deficient on certain indicators as a way of stimulating decision makers to improve performance on the deficient indicators as a means of improving quality of life. Sometimes the indicators are aggregated, usually by an explicit value-weighting scheme, and then the areas are ranked as to their performance on the overall quality of life measure.

One very large study of this type was undertaken by Liu and his associates and is reported in *Quality of Life Indicators in U.S. Metropolitan Areas* and in numerous academic journal articles (Liu, 1976a, 1976b, 1977, 1978a, 1978b). This study has serious theoretical and methodological flaws. It hypothesizes that the quality of life, or satisfaction of wants, is an output that is the function of two factor inputs, the physical and psychological. The physical inputs are seen as consisting of quantifiable material goods and services that satisfy most of the basic needs of human beings. The psychological inputs include subjective spiritual factors, reminiscent of Maslow, such as love, affection, esteem, self-actualization, and community belongingness (Liu, 1977).

The statistical analysis was done by way of approximately 150 indicators selected by the researchers and drawn from five goal areas: economic, political, environmental, health and education, and social. The researchers chose those goal areas and subsequent indicators that they felt represented the major concerns of most people, with the objective of developing as common as possible a concept of well-being. Unfortunately, the researchers (Liu, 1977: 229) took the line that psychological factors are not quantifiable and thus may be held constant, so QOL becomes a funtion of those economic, political and welfare, health and education, and social inputs that are quantifiable. Furthermore, many of their indicators have very ambiguous associations with quality of life and reflect only the researchers' value judgments. To suggest, for example, that "motorcycle registrations per 1000 population" is positively related to quality of life is an arbitrary assumption. Such vehicle registration figures may in fact reflect a lack of public transportation, which expecially hits the poor and the elderly. Similarly, the argument that "population density" is negatively related to QOL will be refuted by many people living happily in Manhattan or in downtown Chicago or San Francisco.

Social Well-Being in U.S. Counties

Similar to the previous study but far less aggregated is research carried out by the U.S. Department of Agriculture (USDA) and directed at "policy makers and scientists working in the social indicators field" (Ross et al., 1979: i). This study developed four separate composite indicators of well-being: socioeconomic status, health, family status, and a measure of alienation. These were analyzed for geographical variations, but no attempt was made to produce any overall QOL measure. There are 3097 counties in the United States, and the analysis was carried out at this level because many public services are provided by county governments and because the researchers felt that aggregation to the state level would have masked considerable substate variations in well-being. They suggest that state-level indicators may be misleading and may have limited usefulness to policy-makers, and they argue that national development policies are best conceived at a county level. SIA is often carried out at this county level.

The Ross et al. study used 1970 U.S. Census county data on a wide array of socioeconomic characteristics, and 1965-1969 *U.S. Vital Statistics* on mortality. No subjective indicators were included. An initial pool of indicators was selected reflecting conditions of income, employment, labor force participation, education, health, family life, and social disorganization. From this pool an initial set of 35 indicators was chosen for further study on the basis of redundancy, simplicity, stability, and independence.

A principal components analysis was then used to identify patterns of relationships among the 35 indicators. This suggested 12 indicators, which were grouped into the 4 composite measures:

> *socioeconomic status:* median family income, employed male heads not in poverty, school attainment level, and dwelling units with complete plumbing
>
> *health:* overall mortality, infant mortality, and mortality from influenza and pneumonia
>
> *family status:* proportion of children living with both parents, ratio of males to females in the labor force, and percentage of families with female heads
>
> *alienation:* suicide rate and mortality from cirrhosis of the liver

The composite indicators were then constructed based on the numerical scores for each indicator standardized to a common scale.

The authors of this report urge us to be careful in the interpretation of their results. They warn us that they have not tapped many important dimensions of well-being and that the composite scores of individual counties are to be "interpreted with caution' (Ross et al., 1979: 14). The indicators were designed to monitor some areas of well-being and to expose geographical variation, for example, in the different scores on health indicators between urban and rural areas.

Community Monitoring Systems

One of the most common uses of social indicators is for the identification and description of particular geographical areas for planning and policy purposes. This type of activity is common in North America. Flax (1978), for example, identified 57 such studies in the United States with such names as "needs assessments," "community profiles," and "neighborhood surveys." Most of these have been designed to suit particular research needs and as such are "snapshots" of one community at one or more points in time. Of more interest to the SIA analyst are those social indicators systems that are applicable across a range of situations. These are useful as classification schemes that seek to identify and separate geographic areas according to how alike and different they are in terms of some social characteristics, and they may have potential for use in monitoring community impacts over time.

Social Economic Accounts System

An extensive system of indicators, developed in the United States by Fitzsimmons and Lavey (1976, 1977), is the Social Economic Accounts System (SEAS), which presents 477 community-level indicators organized into 15 programmatic categories. SEAS is designed to enable public officials, developers, and social scientists to monitor the effects of various types of public investment upon a variety of indicators. These indicators are taken to reflect the quality of life of individuals in various domains, and the relative social position of groups of people in the community.

The indicators within each of the programmatic areas or sectors (education, health, welfare, and so on) are organized into state variables, which describe people's lives at one point in time; system variables, which describe the institutional arrangments affecting people's lives; and relevant condition variables, which are state and system variables from other sectors affecting the sector under consideration. Within the state and system variables, some are subjective social indicators obtained by resident survey. For example, there are 44 health sector variables in the SEAS system. Within the health sector, for example, a state variable is "number of deaths per 1,000 live births," a system variable is "number of full-time physicians per 1000 population," a relevant condition variable is "mean age of population," and within the state variables an attitudinal variable is "personal satisfaction of residents with health services." Notice that the state variables tend to be ouput measures, while the system variables are measures of input and throughput.

The authors of SEAS have also developed a paradigm for the analysis of communities that conceptualizes community as a systematic, interactive, and dynamic entity. The purpose of this paradigm is to provide the researcher with a common framework for using the community, with its subsystems, as a unit of analysis. An operational definition is proposed in which linkages are established among the fifteen programmatic indicator categories, five "concept" categories (interaction, changes, and so on), and eight potential research objectives (for example, to identify types of interaction). In this manner it is suggested that a common framework is provided whereby various research activities relating to a specific community, or the concept of community, can be integrated to improve the practical understanding of communities. Given this necessary attention to causal relationships in communities, SEAS could be adapted to the requirements of the SIA analyst who needs to monitor community-based social change.

CIPFA Community Indicators

Another indicator system is the Community Indicators Programme of the United Kingdom's Chartered Institute of Public Finance and Accountancy (CIPFA). Similar to SEAS, with an emphasis on community as a unit of analysis, it is less comprehensive, but it actually publishes social indicator data for U.K. communities and attempts to aid decision making by local governments. The system relies on existing data sources. Wherever possible, indicators of individual "need" are used in preference to input or throughput measures. The criteria for structuring the indicators are that they be readily comprehensible, disaggregated to the local government level, and as up-to-date as possible. The need indicators are further classified into normative need, that is, target standards laid down by various levels of government, and perceived need, which is felt by individuals or expressed institutionally, for example, in the form of a waiting list for public housing.

An interesting aspect of the CIPFA system not generally found in other social indicator systems is the identification of principal client groups for the range of services that the local government might offer. This makes the indicators themselves more readily relevant. Client groups are of three types: those directly identifiable (such as school pupils), who impose a mandatory obligation for service: those indirectly identifiable (such as the elderly), whose needs may or may not be met by local agencies; and the population generally, for such services as public transport. For example, a service need for the population group "under 5" is "preschool education" and indicators of service provision include "places per 1,000 population" and "pupils per preschool assistant." For the client group "total population," one service is libraries and an indicator of service provision is book stock per 1,000 population.

This community indicator system is useful for two reasons. First, it is designed to facilitate the setting of priorities for resource allocation among various services in a local area, both for policy and budget planning. Second, it assists in performance measurement — the study of efficiency or the ratio of input to outputs, and the study of effectiveness, which is the extent to which goals or objectives are met by service provision. CIPFA is especially noteworthy for its efforts to be relevant to community-level decisions and for disaggregating data for various client groups. Such community service indicators would be ideal measures of service impact in SIA monitoring programs, as would many of the indicators developed for measuring changes in public service delivery.

Measuring Improvements in Public Service Delivery

Both the dramatic growth of pubic expenditure over the past few decades and the need to get "value for money" in that expenditure have given rise to attempts to use objective and subjective indicators to measure tangible improvements and cost effectiveness in public service delivery. Sometimes termed "productivity measurement" or "performance auditing," at the extreme these various terms define anything from detailed time-budget studies of the activities of individuals or small groups to overall measures of the effectiveness of public policy. In many ways these efforts can be termed "program impact assessments," and in practice performance measurement most often makes use of objective indicators of efficiency in terms of the conversion of organizational inputs to outputs. Effectiveness measures (as opposed to efficiency) are usually citizen assessments, using subjective indicators, of the perceived quality of service delivery.

Areas subject to study include recreational services, library services, police and fire services, public transport, and educational and other social services. Proponents of performance measurement studies argue that at any governmental level such studies can (1) help determine progress toward targets or goals set by public administrators; (2) identify problem areas and help set priorities for efforts at improving productivity; and (3) help implement worker incentive schemes. Comparison between local governments or operational units may also help set priorities for allocating resources. Such performance measurements are very similar to measures that have been used in some impact mitigation agreements (for example, see Western Fuels Utah et al., 1981) between industry and local government, and have direct applicability to many formal impact management, mitigation, and compensation schemes.

The Urban Institute suggests the following criteria for selection of performance indicators:

(1) *Appropriateness and validity:* Indicators must be quantifiable, in line with goals and objectives for that service, and oriented toward the meeting of citizen needs and minimizing detrimental effects.

(2)   *Uniqueness, accuracy, and reliability:* Indicators need not overlap, double counting should be avoided, but some redundancy may be useful for testing the measures themselves.

(3)   *Completeness and comprehensibility:* Any list of indicators should cover the desired objectives and should be understandable.

(4)   *Controllability:* The conditions measured must be at least partially under government control.

(5)   *Cost:* Staff and data collection costs must be reasonable.

(6)   *Feedback time:* Information should become available within the time frame necessary for decision making (Hatry et al., 1977).

Measures of performance take a number of forms. A common indicator is the ratio of input to output, with the amount or level of service delivery as the output measure, and the employee hours or unit cost of service provision as the input measure. Examples of such measures in the crime control and recreation fields are speed and apprehension of criminals after crime per employee hour, percentage of crimes cleared after X days, number of hours of recreational facility operation per monetary unit, and number of hours of citizen recreational participation per employee hour. The assumption in each of these type of measures is that the *quality* of the output is held constant or improves as more efficient ratios are achieved. The output measures most easy to develop are those that cover services with the most tangible outputs. For example, garbage collection measures are much easier to obtain than measures of police efficiency or social service effectiveness. In the police case a measure such as "number of arrests per employee hour" may encourage such perverse effects as inadequate investigation. This type of problem, however, may reflect not so much an inadequacy in the approach as the primitive methodology for measuring some service outputs.

Another common supplement to these measures are citizen evaluations of the quality of service provision. This generally takes the form of interviews of actual or past clients to ascertain the number satisfied with a service per monetary unit or employee hour expended. Such measures thus combine the traditional and somewhat suspect number of clients served with satisfaction levels. The Urban Institute suggests that this form of measure will be particularly important to those who believe that citizen, or client, satisfaction with services is a major product of government services.

Conclusion:
Reviewing Some Methodological Issues

Aside from difficulties associated with the relatively primitive state of social theory, there are obviously a number of problems associated with using social indicators. One is simply the sheer difficulty of establishing the *significance* of responses and findings. The meaning and values represented by responses may vary greatly. Beyond that, a number of researchers have noted a "happiness barrier," or a tendency for people to respond in an overly positive manner at a general or global level (Campbell et al., 1976; Allardt, 1977). At the same time, at specific domain levels, people are quite willing to be critical of their life situation and express considerable dissatisfaction about specific matters. This casts doubt on the efficacy of attempting to develop global measures of life quality, and it may be that domain-specific research (housing, health, recreation, and so on) has the best chance of capturing the rather elusive reality of well-being and is the most practical application in SIA.

For community monitoring programs, one difficulty can be the sheer volume of the statistics produced, and such reports may contain pages of data irrelevant to community problems. Researchers seldom wish to camouflage critical issues but sometimes do just that by refusing judiciously to select and highlight data critical to the issues and putting out reports that are too broad and vague and have not concentrated on policy-manipulable variables. Such unaggregated quantitative data strain decision makers' limited time resources.

Misguided attempts at comprehensiveness that result in "information overload" must be dealt with by attention to synthesis and communication. Overaggregated data, on the other hand, will be accused of hiding information vital to the decision process and of offering vague generalities. This is a classic dilemma of analysis, to which the only solution is the judicious presentation of information geared to the particular SIA problem at hand. It would also help if selected social indicators were accompanied by a written "measurement rationale" justifying why a statistic should be regarded as a measure of the social variable under consideration. Such a rationale makes explicit researchers' logic that substantiates the selection of one indicator over another. This would also reduce the dangers of "cultural imperialism," in which the researcher's own values implicitly substitute for those values of the individuals in the community under study. For a contentious impact mitigation program such a measurement rationale could increase the political feasibility of the program.

Finally, there is the question of the usefulness of social indicators research. Efforts at global measures of quality of life remain vague and general, and it is difficult to imagine their value to policy beyond that of the average Gallup poll. Domain-specific research, on the other hand, may have considerable usefulness — especially when disaggregated by demographic variables. User satisfaction surveys in the housing field, for example, can be very helpful in the design of new housing. Social indicator research, crosscut by specific demographic variables, could also be well utilized in social impact assessments. Knox (1976b), for example, has conducted extensive research into the relationship between social well-being and oil and gas developments in Scotland. Other social indicators research has similar potential for incorporation into the SIA field. A more detailed look at social indicators research can be found in Rossi and Gilmartin (1979) and Carley (1981), and in the journal *Social Indicators Research*.

References

ALLARDT, E. (1977) On the Relationship Between Objective and Subjective Predicaments. Research Report 16. Helsinki: Research Group for Comparative Sociology, University of Helsinki.

ANDREWS, F. M. and S. B. WITHEY (1976) Social Indicators of Well-Being. New York: Plenum.

CAMPBELL, A., P. E. CONVERSE, and W. L. ROGERS (1976) The Quality of American Life: Perceptions, Evaluations, and Satisfactions. New York: Russell Sage.

CANTRIL, H. (1965) The Pattern of Human Concerns. New Brunswick, NJ: Rutgers University Press.

CARLEY, M. J. (1981) Social Measurement and Social Indicators: Issues of Policy and Theory. London: Allen & Unwin.

CARLISLE, E. (1972) "The conceptual structure of social indicators," in A. Shonfield and S. Shaw (eds.) Social Indicators and Social Policy. London: Heinemann.

CLARK, T. N. (1974) "Can you cut a budget pie?" Policy and Politics 3: 3-31.

CULLEN, I. G. (1978) "Measuring the impacts of urban social policies." Presented to the Ninth World Congress of Sociology, Bartlett School of Architecture and Planning, University College, London.

ENCEL, S., P. K. MARSTRAND, and W. PAGE [eds.] (1975) The Art of Anticipation. London: Martin Robertson.

FITZSIMMONS, S. J. and W. G. LAVEY (1977) "Community: towards an integration of research, theory, evaluation and public policy considerations." Social Indicators Research 4: 25-66.

——— (1976) "Social Economic Accounts System (SEAS): toward comprehensive community-level assessment procedures." Social Indicators Research 2: 389-452.

FLAX, M. J. (1978) Survey of Urban Social Indicator Data 1970-1977. Washington, DC: Urban Institute.

FLYNN, C. et al. (1982) An Integrated Methodology for Socioeconomic Impact Assessment and Planning. Seattle: Social Impact Research, Inc.

GEHRMANN, F. (1978) "Valid empirical measurement of quality of life?" Social Indicators Research 5: 73-110.

HALL, J. and N. PERRY (1974) Aspects of Leisure in Two Industrial Cities. London: SSRC Survey Unit.

HATRY, H. P. et al. (1977) How Effective Are Your Community Services? Procedures for Monitoring the Effectiveness of Municipal Services. Washington, DC: Urban Institute.

HOINVILLE, R. and G. COURTENAY (1979) "Measuring consumer priorities," in T. O'Riordan and R. D'Arge (eds.) Progress in Resource Management and Environmental Planning. New York: John Wiley.

KENNEDY, L. W., H. C. NORTHCOTT, and C. KENZEL (1978) "Subjective evaluation of well-being: problems and prospects." Social Indicators Research 5: 457-474.

KNOX, P. L. (1978) "Territorial social indicators and area profiles." Town Planning Review 49: 75-83.

——— (1976a) Social Priorities for Social Indicators. Occasional Paper 4. Dundee, Scotland: Department of Geography, University of Dundee.

——— (1976b) "Social well-being and North Sea oil: an application of subjective social indicators." Regional Studies 10: 423-432.

KUZ, T. J. (1978) "Quality of life and objective and subjective variable analysis." Regional Studies 12: 409-417.

LIU, B.-C. (1978a) "Variations in social quality of life indicators in medium metropolitan areas." American Journal of Economics and Sociology 37: 241-260.

——— (1978b) "Technological change and environmental quality: a preliminary survey of environmental indicators in medium metropolitan areas." Technological Forecasting and Social Change 12: 325-336.

——— (1977) "Economic and non-economic quality of life." American Journal of Economics and Sociology 36: 226-240.

——— (1976a) Quality of Life Indicators in U.S. Metropolitan Areas: A Statistical Analysis. New York: Praeger.

——— (1976b) "Social quality of life indicators for small metropolitan areas in America." International Journal of Social Economics 3: 198-213.

MASLOW, A. (1970) Motivation and Personality. New York: Harper & Row.

PIGOU, A. C. (1924) The Economics of Welfare. London: Macmillan.

ROSS, P. J., H. BLUESTONE, and F. K. HINES (1979) Indicators of Social Well-Being for U.S. Counties. Rural Development Research Report 10. Washington, DC: Economics, Statistics and Cooperatives Service, U.S. Department of Agriculture.

ROSSI, R. J. and K. J. GILMARTIN (1979) Handbook of Social Indicators. New York: Garland.

SCHNEIDER, M. (1974) "The quality of life in large American cities: objective and subjective social indicators." Social Indicators Research 1: 495-509.

Western Fuels Utah et al. (1981) Socioeconomic Impact Mitigation Agreement for the Desarado Mine, Bonanza Station, and Associated Facilities. Provo: Author.

IV
SPECIAL
METHODOLOGIES

9

Computerized Socioeconomic Assessment Models

O O O O O O O O O O O O O O O O O

STEVE H. MURDOCK
and F. LARRY LEISTRITZ

O O O O O O O O O O O O O O O O O

● The socioeconomic impacts of large-scale industrial and resource development projects are of increasing concern to public and private managers and decision makers. Such impacts are of major concern to residents in affected areas, and, increasingly, litigation concerning such impacts is a cause for delays in project completion (Murdock and Leistritz, 1979). Thus project-related population growth, increased levels of economic activity, increased demands for public services, changes in public costs and revenues, and changes in the social characteristics of an area are among the most evident impacts of resource development. These impacts must be assessed accurately if residents in affected areas are to take advantage of the benefits of such development, if steps must be taken to mitigate the negative impacts, and if costly delays in project completion are to be avoided.

The nature of socioeconomic impacts and the context in which socioeconomic assessments take place, however, often make the accurate projections of such impacts difficult. Socioeconomic analysts are often

Authors' Note: Parts of this chapter are derived from Murdock and Leistritz (1980) and Leistritz and Murdock (1981).

required to project too wide a range of phenomena that includes nearly all factors not analyzed by their physical or biological science counterparts, including levels of public acceptance of the project, to do so in extremely short time frames, and to complete assessments with minimum resources. As a result, socioeconomic assessments often require social science analysts to use readily available methodologies and provide little time for the refinement of such methodologies. Despite the increasing availability of socioeconomic assessment techniques, social scientists and decision makers alike require more cost- and time-effective projection methodologies.

One response to this need has been the development of a substantial number of computerized socioeconomic impact assessment models. These models all provide a relatively wide range of outputs and do so in an extremely flexible and timely manner. At the same time, such models differ widely in their input structures, computational procedures, and outputs, and, in nearly all cases, their adaptation and use can be quite expensive. Thus, for the impact researcher or for the sponsor of impact assessments, such models are both appealing and foreboding.

Thus such models may appear to provide a substantial number of the data items required for an impact assessment, but, at the same time, their use may require the examination of technical criteria that few researchers or administrators have the background to evaluate. For such potential users, it is critical that the answers be available to such questions as the following:

> When is it and when is it not cost effective to use such models?
>
> What are the characteristics (outputs, data requirements, and so on) that should be considered in selecting such a model for use?
>
> How do existing models compare in terms of their methodological, design, use, and similar characteristics?

Unless potential users of such models have access to information that can assist them in answering such questions, socioeconomic assessment models are unlikely to be used appropriately in the assessment process and their potential utility for meeting the information needs of decision makers will remain unfulfilled.

This chapter attempts to provide general guidance for the selection and use of computerized socioeconomic impact assessment models. Specifically, the chapter (1) examines factors that should be considered in the selection and use of socioeconomic assessment models and (2) compares the characteristics of several of the most widely used models. Thus the intent of the chapter is to provide an introduction to such models and to the factors that should be considered in decisions concerning whether or not to use such models, how they should be used, and how the use, design, methodological, and other characteristics of several widely used models differ.

Criteria for the Selection and
Use of Socioeconomic Assessment Models

The decisions concerning whether or not a computerized socioeconomic impact assessment model should be used and in what manner require consideration of numerous factors related to both the characteristics of the assessment process and the characteristics of such models. Among the factors that should be considered are the following:

(1)   the characteristics of the assessment(s) to be completed
(2)   the range of socioeconomic data and the characteristics of the data required by the assessment process
(3)   the data input requirements for use of an assessment model
(4)   the system design and use characteristics of the model
(5)   the conceptual design and structure of the model
(6)   the extent to which a model has been validated

In large part, evaluation of the first of these considerations will determine whether or not a computerized assessment model should be used, while the nature of the information obtained on criteria 2-6 will indicate the characteristics of the model one should select if the use of a computerized model is appropriate. Each of the six criteria is discussed below.

The Characteristics of the Assessment and the Assessment Process

Socioeconomic assessment models should not be used in all assessments. Development costs of $200,000-$300,000 are not unusual for such a model (Leistritz et al., 1978), and the cost of a complex adaptation of an existing model may exceed $100,000 (Murdock et al., 1980). Thus, if a single set of projections are to be made for a single project, the development or the adaptation of such a model is seldom feasible.

The development or adaptation of such a model may be feasible, however, if the project to be evaluated is large or controversial and thus likely to require the preparer of the Environmental Impact Statement (EIS) to complete multiple scenarios to address the concerns of potential litigants.

Model developments or adaptations may also be feasible if numerous projections are likely to occur in the same general region. For example, areas such as eastern Texas, western North Dakota, eastern Montana, and eastern Colorado have had numerous models developed to address potential projects in these areas. Also, a federal or state agency or a private firm whose efforts are likely to be concentrated in specific areas may find model developments for such areas to be cost effective.

At the same time, because of the numerous modeling efforts that have been completed, many areas of the nation are encompassed by existing models; when models do exist for a geographic region, they can usually be used to complete assessments for a fraction of the cost of a noncomputerized assessment. Thus an expenditure of $10,000 for the use of such a model can often provide the same quantity and quality of data as a $50,000-$80,000 assessment made without the use of such a model, particularly if the model is in the public sector and the costs for its development have been absorbed by a previous sponsor.

Data and Information Requirements

Given that the decision has been made to use such a model, the starting point in selecting a specific modeling system involves assessment of the information needs of the user — what information is needed, for where, and for what periods of time. For many types of projects, environmental impact assessments are requiring an increasingly larger volume of socioeconomic data. The data usually include, at a minimum, information on the economic, demographic, public service and fiscal, and social changes likely to occur under both baseline and impact conditions and for both construction and operational phases during impact periods (Council on Environmental Quality, 1978).

The economic data usually include information on changes in income, employment and business activity, and changes by type of industry. Information on demographic changes usually includes data on population increases and, increasingly, information for particular age, ethnic, and other groups, and for small geographic units, such as municipalities, as well as total impact areas. Public service and fiscal data tend to concentrate on the number of new service facilities and personnel required to serve new inmigrating populations, on the costs of such increased services, and on the public revenues likely to be generated by new populations. Social changes are usually measured by data on a population's perceptions of development, residents' goals for their community, community satisfaction, and expected changes in social structures. Because the costs of acquisition of single data sets (social, economic, and so on) are likely to require investments that may exceed those for an entire modeling effort, the inclusiveness or lack of inclusiveness of a model may be particularly significant. Those models that provide larger proportions of the necessary data items are thus clearly of greater utility.

Equally important is the need to ascertain both the levels of geographic output provided by the model and its ability to provide outputs for alternative time periods. Many of the available models provide outputs only at the total impact area level or for counties, and not for individual cities or other jurisdictions. As a result, such models, though useful for those involved in regional planning and decision making, are likely to be of little use to the decision maker charged with allocating resources or assessing impacts for school districts or other local units of government.

At the same time, it is essential to ensure that results are provided for the necessary time periods. That is, impact periods, particularly construction periods, often show rapid changes from year to year, and these changes often require careful planning and resource allocations. However, if such models provide results for only five-year periods rather than for yearly periods, year-to-year changes will not be detected.

Finally, it is essential that the model provide separate outputs for baseline, construction impact, and operational impact periods. Since impact assessment involves comparing impact-induced changes to a projection of baseline changes over time, data for both baseline and impact conditions are essential. Also, since construction and operational phases are separate in impact assessments and have distinct types of impacts, the production of separate results for each impact phase is essential. In sum, then, the temporal as well as geographical specificity of model outputs should be analyzed.

Data Input Requirements

Another factor of critical concern in model selection relates to the availability and costs of obtaining the input data required for a model's implementation. The complexity and amount of input data required for a model are, in general, directly related to the level of geographic and temporal detail obtained in model outputs. For example, if outputs are desired for school districts and municipalities as well as counties, data inputs for these units will also unusually be required. The source to be used in obtaining data is also important. Models that use data specific to the study area are usually more expensive to implement than those that assume that the standards or patterns of larger areas, for which secondary data are more readily available, apply to the area of interest. However, they are also likely to produce somewhat less accurate projections for the study areas. The trade-off between the need for locally oriented data inputs and the costs of collecting local data must be evaluated carefully.

In addition, it is essential to understand that in most cases the amount and detail required in data inputs for model development and implementation is inversely related to the amount of data required to complete a given run of a model in the model execution phase. Those models that require extensive front-end costs to develop input data such as the characteristics of migrating workers or of the project work force usually require few data inputs to produce the outputs for a given scenario during the execution phase, while those that leave data gaps during model development usually require the user to input such data at the time the model is run.

The data input requirements of a model are thus important factors to be considered in model selection. They are most important if one is considering either developing a new model or adapting an existing model for use in the project area. If such a development or adaptation is being contemplated, then the resource requirements for data collection should be a major consideration. If an existing model has already been developed for an area, then the data collection effort necessary to use such a model is likely to be less than that for completing a noncomputerized assessment (since many of the necessary data have been collected as part of the model implementation process by the model's developers). Data requirements are thus essential factors requiring careful consideration in model selection.

System and Use Characteristics

The flexibility of use of the model should also be considered. Impact assessments and impact events involve numerous factors that are difficult to evaluate and predict. Thus it becomes essential to examine the range of potential impacts under widely varying assumptions for such factors. Models that provide easy alterations of such factors and rapid outputs for alternative development scenarios are desirable. In evaluating models, the options provided for altering key assumptions such as the number of projects, the size of the project, the location of the project, inflation rates, birthrates, per capita service usage rates, and other factors should be examined closely.

An additional criterion to be considered is the availability and adaptability of the computerized form of such models. Some models can be accessed only through the agency that implemented the model, while, in other cases, cooperative agreements can be established that provide the model code to a user agency. In general, efficient use of the model is facilitated by the ability to acquire the model code.

In addition, however, it is essential to ensure that appropriate computer facilities and computer compilers are available if the computer code is to be obtained. The incompatibility of different types of hardware and the lack of appropriate language compilers can make adaptability very costly.

Conceptual Design and Structure

Although the methodologies employed in various models involve numerous technical distinctions that are not appropriate to our discussion here, several aspects of model methodology should enter into evaluations of alternative models.

First, some methodologies are more adequate than others. Although, under any set of circumstances, several alternative methodologies may be of equal utility, general assumptions can be made about such methodologies. Thus even a brief examination of information on demographic projection techniques will suggest that techniques using age cohorts are generally superior to those with less detail (Shryock and Siegel, 1973). A short consultation with appropriate experts will generally provide similar information in regard to other model dimensions.

Second, it is essential to evaluate the extent of submodule integration in such models. Most of the existing models involve a major premise that economic and demographic aspects of developments require careful integration. Some, however, make no attempt to integrate key model components effectively, but rather simply apply separate methodologies (that is, for economic and demographic projections) to a common set of project characteristics. Socioeconomic models must attempt to interface submodules formally such that economic outputs are designed to affect demographic projections, and the results of demographic projections in turn are programmed to affect economic demand, service demands, and fiscal conditions. If such interfaces are not employed, much of the utility and strength of such models is lost. Thus the greater the degree of integration of model components, the more likely the model is to simulate reality effectively.

Finally, the assumptions underlying the methodologies employed in such models must be evaluated carefully in terms of the following dynamic modeling capabilities:

(1) ability to incorporate changes in the structure of model relationships over time
(2) inclusion of the key structural dimensions of the phenomena of interest
(3) incorporation of feedback loops for updating baseline figures

In general, models that use multiple rates for different factors (such as changes in labor force participation rates or fertility rates) during different phases of the projection period, that differentiate between key dimensions (such as industries or age cohorts), and that incorporate feedback procedures are superior to those lacking such features.

Model Validation

It is, of course, evident that an overriding factor in model selection must be an evaluation of a model's accuracy in predicting impact and baseline conditions. Although most of the existing models have been developed recently and relatively little evidence has accumulated for evaluating their validity, evidence concerning the validity of some models has been accumulated or can be derived by using available data sources. In addition, given samples of the outputs of model projections for various areas, several types of evaluations can be made quite easily. For example, estimates of economic factors (such as income) and population for counties and incorporated areas are published periodically by the Bureau of Economic Analysis and the Bureau of the Census in the U.S. Department of Commerce. These estimates can be compared to those for the various models, and some idea of their accuracy can thus be gained. This approach, which involves a comparison of data from past periods to those projected by a model for such periods, is often termed historical simulation (Pindyck and Rubinfeld, 1976). In addition, it is possible to use dynamic simulation techniques and sensitivity analysis (Pindyck and Rubinfeld, 1976) to analyze such models. The use of these techniques involves comparisons of the trends shown in the model output for the projected future periods to those noted in affected areas in the past. Such comparisons provide a valuable and clearly essential step in model analysis and model selection.

The criteria described above are thus essential for determining if a computerized model should be used and which characteristics should be sought in the structure of a model to be selected for use. Although this discussion can provide general guidance for examining computerized socioeconomic assessment models, in many cases the services of the professional modeler will be essential to evaluate data assessment needs and the feasibility of using a computerized model. Although some costs will be incurred in obtaining the services of such a professional, these costs are likely to be small in comparison to the costs of (1) attempting to develop or adapt a model, the structure of which may be inappropriate for use in a particular assessment effort; (2) failing to employ a useful model that could have largely eliminated the need for a more expensive noncomputerized assessment effort; or (3) attempting to adapt or develop a computerized model when a noncomputerized assessment would have been more efficient. For the potential user of a model, the assistance of a modeling professional is thus usually a good investment.

Comparison of Existing Models

As noted above, the number of socioeconomic assessment models is growing rapidly. Initial modeling efforts in one area often form the basis for the development of other modeling efforts in other areas, and as a result there is considerable similarity in the structure of many models. On the other hand, there are also important differences that have cost and use implications. In this part of the chapter, we compare several of the most widely used assessment models in terms of the criteria discussed above. The purpose of this section is to further familiarize the reader with socioeconomic assessment models by describing and comparing the characteristics of some of the most widely used models. These comparisons are used both to point out the potential value of certain characteristics in such models and to demonstrate areas of commonality in such models against which the characteristics of a given model and the claims of modelers can be evaluated. Finally, because of the frequency with which the structures of the models described in this section are being used as the bases for other model development and adaptation efforts, the potential model user is increasingly likely to be considering either the direct use of one of these models or an adaptation of a new model derived from one of them to complete an assessment effort. This section will thus serve both as a general source of basic knowledge on socioeconomic modeling and as a useful source of information on specific models' characteristics.

The criteria noted above for model selection and use (criteria 2-6) are discussed in this section in terms of three general categories referred to as the informational (criterion 2), use (criteria 3 and 4), and methodological characteristics (criteria 5 and 6), respectively, of such models. The use of such general criteria categories allows differences between models to be more readily displayed in table form and simplifies the textual comparison of the models. In the comparison presented below, we have attempted to include a wide set of models currently employed in socioeconomic impact assessment projects in various parts of the United States. The models evaluated include the following:

(1) ATOM 3 (Beckhelm et al., 1975)
(2) BOOM1 (Ford, 1976)
(3) BREAM (Mountain West Research, 1978)
(4) CLIPS (Monts and Bareiss, 1979)
(5) CPEIO (Monarchi and Taylor, 1977)
(6) HARC (Cluett et al., 1977)
(7) MULTIREGION (Olsen et al., 1977)
(8) NAVAHO (Reeve et al., 1976)
(9) NEW MEXICO (Brown and Zink, 1977)
(10) RED (Hertsgaard et al., 1978; Leistritz et al., 1978)
(11) SEAM (Stenehjem, 1978)
(12) SIMPACT (Huston, 1979)
(13) WEST (Denver Research Institute, 1979)

Although numerous other models are available, this set includes a majority of those that attempt to project the impacts of large-scale resource developments, have published descriptions, and have been widely used by national, regional, and local decision makers (Denver Research Institute, 1979; Markusen, 1978).

The comparison of these models is presented in three tables: Table 9.1 addresses criterion 2 and describes the information characteristics of the models. In this table, the dimensions examined by the model, the project phases, the geographical units, and the time periods for which projections are made are shown. Dimensions considered as possible components of such models are the economic, demographic, interface, distributional, public service, fiscal, and social components.

Table 9.2 addresses criteria 3 and 4 and provides information on the use characteristics of such models. In particular, it compares the data inputs and the computerization requirements of such models, and the extent to which such models allow user input though parameter alteration and the use of interactive programming.

TABLE 9.1 Informational Characteristics of Selected Socioeconomic Impact Assessment Models

Model	Economic	Demographic	Interface	Distribution	Public Services	Fiscal	Social	Baseline	Construction	Operational	Geographic Areas Included	Time Increments and Total Projection Periods	Total Number of Areal Units
			Dimensions Included						Project Phases Analyzed				
ATOM 3	X	X^a	X	X			X	X	X	X	state and county	yearly; NLS	14 counties in Arizona
BOOM1	X	X	X	X	X	X^b		X	X	X	city only	yearly; NLS	any given city
BREAM	X	X	X	X				X	X	X	region, county, cities	yearly; NLS	2 counties maximum
CLIPS	X	X	X	X		X^c		X	X	X	region, county, cities	yearly; 20 years	INP
CPHO	X	X	X		X^d			X	X	X	restricted to one area, any level	yearly OAD; NLS	1 areal unit
HARC	X	X^a	X	X	X	X		X	X	X	project, county	5 years; 30 years	INP
MULTIREGION	X	X	X	X				X	X	X	BLA region	5 years; NLS	all BLA regions
NAVAHO	X	X	X	X				X	X	X	reservation districts	5 years; NLS	9 reservation districts
NEW MEXICO	X	X	X	X				X	X	X	state planning regions	5 years; 20 years	7 state planning regions
RED	X	X	X	X	X	X		X	X	X	state, region, county, cities	yearly OAD; 25 years	8 regions, 53 counties, 350 cities
SIAM	X	X	X	X	X	X^c		X	X	X	county, cities	yearly; 30 years	INP
SIMPACT	X	X	X	X	X	X		X	X	X	region, county, cities	yearly; construction, 10 years operation	region and 11 subareas
WIST	X	X	X	X	X^d	X		X	X	X	region, county, cities	yearly; NLS	INP

SOURCE: Derived from Leistritz and Murdock (1981).

NOTE: NLS = no limit specified; OAD = or as desired; INP = information not provided.

a. Demographic model includes special population submodules.
b. Costs are aggregated.
c. Revenues are not calculated.
d. Only two services projected.

TABLE 9.2 Methodological Characteristics of Selected Socioeconomic Impact Assessment Models

| | Methodological and Integrative Forms by Component | | | | | | Dynamic Capabilities by Component | | | | | | |
Model	Economic	Demographic	Interface	Subarea Distribution	Service	Fiscal	Economic	Demographic	Interface	Subarea Distribution	Service	Fiscal	Validation
ATOM 3	I-O	CC-S	E-M-1	% share	NA	NA	yes	yes	yes	yes	NA	NA	historical
BOOM1	E-B	E-P	E-P-1	NA	P-B	per capita	yes	yes	yes	NA	NA	NA	sensitivity
BREAM	E-B	CC-S	E-M-1	% share & gravity	P-B	NA	yes	yes	yes	yes	NA	NA	INP
CLIPS	E-B	CC-S[a]	E-M-1	% share & gravity	NA	per capita	yes	yes	yes	yes	NA	yes	INP
CPEIO	I-O	CC-S	E-M-1	NA	NA	NA	yes	yes	yes	NA	NA	NA	some forms unspecified
HARC	E-B	CC-S	E-M-1	gravity	P-B	NA	yes	yes	yes	yes	yes	NA	sensitivity
MULTIREGION	E-B	CC-S	E-M-1	NA	NA	NA	yes	yes	yes	NA	NA	NA	historical
NAVAHO	E-B	CC-S	E-M-M	gravity	NA	NA	yes	yes	yes	yes	NA	NA	INP
NEW MEXICO	I-O	CC-S	E-M-M	NA	NA	NA	yes	yes	yes	NA	NA	NA	INP
RED	I-O	CC-S	E-M-M	% share & gravity	P-B	per capita	yes	yes	yes	yes	yes	yes	sensitivity/historical
SEAM	E-B	CC-S	E-M-M	LP	P-B	per capita facility	yes	yes	yes	yes	yes	yes	sensitivity/historical
SIMPACT	I-O	E-P	E-P-1	% share	P-B	per capita facility	yes	yes	yes	yes	yes	yes	INP
WEST	E-B	E-P	E-P-1	% share	P-B	per capita	yes	yes	no	yes	yes	yes	sensitivity

SOURCE: Derived from Leistritz and Murdock (1981).

NOTE: Explanation of abbreviations: *Economic:* I-O = input-output; E-B = export base. *Demographic:* CC-S = cohort component survival; E-P = employment-population ratio. *Interface:* E-M-1 = employment-migration-one phase; E-P-1 = employment-population-one phase; E-M-M = employment-migration-multiphase procedure. *Subarea Distribution:* % share = distribution to subareas on basis of employment or population ratio; gravity = gravity allocation model; LP = linear programming model. *Service:* P-B = population-based projections. *Fiscal:* per capita = per capita costs and revenues; facility = projections of facility requirements also completed. INP = information not provided; NA = not applicable.

a. Cohort component survival method used at the regional level only.

Table 9.3 compares the methodological characteristics (criteria 5 and 6) of the models. These characteristics include the form of methodology used in each of several possible major components of such models, the form of model integration, the dynamic capabilities of each model component, and the extent of validation of each model. In this table, characteristics for the economic, demographic, interface, distributional, service, and fiscal components of each model are described.

In comparing the models, we have been limited to the information provided in the reports available for each model. In cases where such reports do not discuss a particular item, the designation INP (information not provided) is used. Given these limitations, it is essential to stress the need for users to conduct careful analyses of models that appear appropriate for their particular information needs.

Although it is impossible to discuss the data in Tables 9.1-9.3 in detail, even a brief review of the items in these tables indicates how diverse the models are in overall capabilities and characteristics. As is evident from Table 9.1, only three models (RED, SEAM, and SIMPACT) contain as many as six dimensions. None covers the social dimension. All cover the three vital project phases, but coverage varies widely. Only six models project both county and city impacts. Most do provide yearly outputs, but many are limited in the total number of units that can be included in the model.

The use characteristics (Table 9.2) show great diversity from one model to another. The RED model requires the greatest amount of primary data, while the SEAM model requires virtually no local data (except for the interface procedure where local data are necessary for nonwestern areas). All other models tend to be intermediate between these two in data requirements. Only four of the models are interactive, allowing users to alter various parameters, and, of these, the RED model appears to allow the alteration of more parameters than other models. Nearly all the models are programmed in languages likely to be available at major computer installations. The use of interactive languages (GASP IV, SIMSCRIPT, and APL) is likely to decrease the core storage necessary for the use of such models, and thus models using these languages are likely to be more adaptable to smaller computer systems. On the other hand, at small and medium-sized installations, compilers for such languages may not be readily available. Finally, in almost all cases, the adaptability of such models is untested. Although several models (including BREAM) incorporate aspects of the ATOM 3 model and the BOOM1 and RED models have been adapted by researchers in Texas (Monts and Bareiss, 1979; Murdock et al.,

TABLE 9.3 Use Characteristics of Selected Socioeconomic Impact Assessment Models

| Model | Input Data Requirements | | | Flexibility | | Computerization | |
	Source	Geographical Level	Form	User-Alterable Parameters	Degree of User Interactivity	Model Language	Transferability
ATOM 3	state, local	state, county	primary I-O and other secondary	none	none	FORTRAN	other models closely related (BREAM)
BOOM1	state, local	county, city	secondary and judgmental	none	none	GASP IV	yes–Texas
BREAM	state, local	region, county	all secondary	none	none	FORTRAN	untested
CLIPS	state, local western U.S.	region, county, city	all secondary	SD, PC, INP	interactive	FORTRAN	untested
CPEIO	state, local	the given level of analysis	primary I-O and other secondary	SD, PC, AE, UNEMP, OUTPUT	interactive (knowledgeable user)	SIMSCRIPT	untested
HARC	national, state, western U.S. judgmental	county	all secondary	none	none	INP	untested
MULTIREGION	national, regional	national, regional	all secondary	none	none	FORTRAN	untested

NAVAHO	national reservation	reservation, district	all secondary	none	none	FORTRAN	untested
NEW MEXICO	state, regional	state, region, county	primary I-O and other secondary	none	none	INP	untested
RED	state, regional, local	state, region, local	primary I-O, primary labor force, other secondary	SD, PC, BR, IR, TR, GM, OUTPUT	interactive	APL	yes–Texas
SEAM	national, regional	national, regional	all secondary	SD, PC, IMP AREA	interactive	INP	untested
SIMPACT	regional, state, local	region, county, local	INP	INP	interactive	FORTRAN	untested
WEST	state, local	state, local	all secondary	none	none	FORTRAN	untested

SOURCE: Derived from Leistritz and Murdock (1981).

NOTE: SD = starting date; PC = project characteristics; AE = available employment; UNEM = unemployment; OUTPUT = type or form of output; BR = birthrate; IR = inflation rate; TR = tax rate; GM = gravity model coefficients; INP = information not provided; IMP AREA = selection of impact area.

185

1979), the adaptability and transferability of such models remain largely untested.

In terms of methodological characteristics (Table 9.3), the differences are less pronounced. Only four systems utilize an input-output model, and all but two use a cohort-component demographic projection technique. Almost all use an interface procedure that involves the matching of available and required employment to determine migration levels. Nearly all are dynamically programmed. None has received adequate validation, but some have been subjected to sensitivity and historical simulation analysis.

Overall, then, the comparisons in Tables 9.1-9.3 suggest that available socioeconomic assessment models are least different in the methodologies employed and most different in the extent of information provided and in use characteristics, and it is thus on these latter characteristics that models must be differentiated. For any given use, of course, any of the models described above might be appropriate, but many of their characteristics suggest the situations under which the various models may be most appropriately used. Thus if only regional data are desired, the MULTIRE-GION model may be quite efficient, but if details for additional geographic units are necessary, then another model must be employed. On the other hand, if data for only one individual city are required, the BOOM1 model might prove useful, while if county data or data for other units are required, then some other model must be used. If public service projections are required, ATOM 3, BREAM, CLIPS, MULTIREGION, NAVAHO, and the NEW MEXICO models are not appropriate.

If input data requirements are of concern, those models using export-base methods and population-to-employment ratios are likely to be less costly and require less time to implement than other models but will also not provide the detailed outputs by economic sector that are available from input-output models or the age and sex detail provided by cohort survival models. In terms of ease of data acquisition, the SEAM model that uses national data is perhaps the most readily adaptable, while the RED model requires the greatest expenditure of resources for data acquisition. If user interactivity (that is, the ability to ascertain the effects of changes in the values of key variables) is essential, then the CLIPS, RED, or SEAM model must be employed. In sum, the applicability of a given model depends on a number of factors, and the characteristics of the models shown in Tables 9.1-9.3 must be matched carefully with available resources (funds and time) and with individual users' data needs. A thorough review of one's information needs in regard to each of the criteria and the individual model's characteristics as described above and the assistance of a professional modeler for the evaluation of modeling methodologies are thus likely to be required for the selection of a specific model. Given such a review, however, and the increasing number of models available for impact analysis, the likelihood of locating an appropriate model for use in addressing assessment needs is excellent.

Summary and Conclusions

Socioeconomic impact assessment models are receiving increasing use for projecting the economic, demographic, public service, and fiscal impacts of resource and other large-scale development projects. They are receiving widespread use because of the rapidity with which such models can produce impact projections (once they have been developed) and the flexibility they provide for examining the implications of multiple impact scenarios. The development and adaptation of these models can be expensive and time consuming, however, and their use is not to be recommended for all assessment efforts. As the discussion in this chapter indicates, the decisions concerning whether or not such a model should be used and what type of model should be employed require careful consideration of the characteristics of the assessment to be completed and of the key characteristics of modeling systems. Given such considerations, it is evident that numerous models exist that can be implemented to address specific information needs.

It is important to recognize, however, that such models are still evolving and require elaboration and refinement. Thus none of the existing models provides outputs that directly describe the social impacts of large-scale projects. This is largely because many of the aspects and findings from social assessments cannot be sufficiently quantified to interface with the other components of such models. Socioeconomic models thus require expansion to include additional dimensions. In addition, although one of the strengths of computerized models lies in their dynamic capabilities to provide feedback from one dimension to another, the feedback loops in such models are relatively primitive. Thus few models possess mechanisms to assess the feedback effects of differences in the characteristics of inmigrants on economic demand and few have algorithms that show the effects of service and fiscal impacts on economic or population dimensions. Further integration of the components of such models is thus essential.

Such models also clearly require further validation. At present, as with nearly all other socioeconomic assessment techniques, few of the computerized assessment models have been validated adequately. As a result, it is unclear which of the models or which of the modeling methodologies provides the most accurate projections under different sets of circumstances and for different areas. It is also not clear that such models provide more accurate assessments than noncomputerized methods. There is thus a clear need for the completion of additional historical, sensitivity, and other forms of validation for both computerized and noncomputerized assessment methods.

In sum, then, computerized socioeconomic impact assessment models are a useful tool for obtaining the increasingly broad range of data required to complete impact assessments. They are, however, tools that must be evaluated carefully and used with full realization of their weaknesses as well as their strengths. If so used, they can be of considerable assistance in providing the information critical to effective impact assessments and to meeting many of the information needs of residents in impact areas.

References

BECKHELM, T. L., J. A. CHALMERS, and W. M. HANNIGAN (1975) A Description of the ATOM 3 and of the Research Related to Its Development. Washington, DC: Four Corners Regional Commission.

BROWN, F. L. and L. B. ZINK (1977) New Mexico Economic and Demographic Model, Final Report. Alburquerque: Institute for Applied Research Services, University of New Mexico.

CLUETT, C., M. T. MERTAUGH, and M. MICKLIN (1977) "A demographic model for assessing the socioeconomic impacts of large-scale industrial development projects." Presented at the annual meeting of the Southern Regional Demographic Group, Virginia Beach, VA, October 21-22.

Council on Environmental Quality (1978) "National Environmental Policy Act." Federal Register 43 (June 9): 112.

Denver Research Institute (1979) Socioeconomic Impact of Western Energy Resource Development. Washington, DC: Council on Environmental Quality.

FINSTERBUSCH, K. and C. P. WOLF [eds.] (1981) Methodology of Social Impact Assessment. Stroudsburg, PA: Hutchinson Ross.

FITZSIMMONS, S. J., L. I. STUART, and P. C. WOLFF (1975) Social Assessment Manual: A Guide to the Preparation of the Social Well-Being Account. Washington, DC: U.S. Bureau of Reclamation.

FORD, A. (1976) User's Guide to the BOOM1 Model. LA-6396-MS. Los Alamos, NM: Los Alamos Scientific Laboratory.

GILMORE, J. S. (1976) "Boom towns may hinder energy resource development." Science 191: 535-540.

HERTSGAARD, T., S. MURDOCK, N. TOMAN, M. HENRY, and R. LUDTKE (1978) REAP Economic-Demographic Model: Technical Description. Bismarck: North Dakota Regional Environmental Assessment Program.

HUSTON, M. (1979) "The United States steel project — a comprehensive approach to socioeconomic analysis," in Boom Towns: Managing Growth. Proceedings of Mini Symposium, SME-AIME Annual Meeting, New Orleans, February.

LEISTRITZ, F. L. and S. H. MURDOCK (1981) The Socioeconomic Impact of Resource Development: Methods for Assessment. Boulder, CO: Westview.

LEISTRITZ, F. L., T. A. HERTSGAARD, D. M. SENECHAL, S. H. MURDOCK, N. E. TOMAN, K. WIIG, and G. SCHAIBLE (1978) The REAP Economic-Demographic Model: Background, Structure and Applications. Bismarck: North Dakota Regional Environmental Assessment Program.

MARKUSEN, A. R. (1978) "Socioeconomic impact models for boom town planning and policy evaluation." Presented at the annual meeting of the Western Regional Scientific Association, Sacramento, February 25.

MONARCHI, D. E. and R. H. TAYLOR (1977) An Introduction to Socioeconomic Model Building and the Colorado Population and Employment Model (CPEIO). Boulder: Business Research Division, University of Colorado.

MONTS, J. K. and E. R. BAREISS (1979) Community Level Impacts Projection System (CLIPS). Austin: Center for Energy Studies, University of Texas.

Mountain West Research (1978) Bureau of Reclamation Economic Assessment Model (BREAM) Technical Description. Denver: U.S. Bureau of Reclamation.

MURDOCK, S. H. and F. L. LEISTRITZ (1980) "Selecting socioeconomic assessment models: a discussion of criteria and selected models." Journal of Environmental Management 10, 1: 1-12.

———— (1979) Energy Development in the Western United States: Impact on Rural Areas. New York: Praeger.

MURDOCK, S. H., L. L. JONES and F. L. LEISTRITZ (1980) "The Texas Assessment Modeling System (TAMS): a case study in model adaptation." Proceedings of the Conference on Computer Models for Forecasting Socioeconomic Impacts of Growth and Development, University of Alberta.

MURDOCK, S. H., F. L. LEISTRITZ, L. L. JONES, D. ANDREWS, B. WILSON, D. FANNIN, and J. DE MONTEL (1979) The Texas Assessment Modeling System: Technical Description. Technical Report 79-3. College Station: Texas Agricultural Experiment Station.

Murphy and Williams, Consultants (1978) Socioeconomic Impact Assessent: A Methodology Applied to Synthetic Fuels. Washington, DC: U.S. Department of Energy.

OLSEN, R. J., G. W. WESTLEY, H. W. HERZOG, Jr., C. R. KERLEY, D. J. BJORNSTAD, D. P. VEYT, L. G. BRAY, S. T. GRADY, and R. A. NAKOSTEEN (1977) Multiregion: A Simulation-Forecasting Model of BEA Economic Area Population and Employment. ORNL/RUS-25. Oak Ridge, TN: Oak Ridge National Laboratory.

PINDYCK, R. S. and D. L. RUBINFELD (1976) Econometric Models and Economic Forecasts. New York: McGraw-Hill.

REEVE, R., R. WEAVER, and E. NATWIG (1976) The Navaho Economic-Demographic Model: A Method for Forecasting and Evaluating Alternative Navaho Economic Futures. Salt Lake City: Utah State Planning Coordinator.

SHRYOCK, H. S. and J. S. SIEGEL (1973) The Methods and Materials of Demography. Washington, DC: Government Printing Office.

STENEHJEM, E. J. (1978) Summary Description of SEAM: The Social and Economic Assessment Model. Argonne, IL: Argonne National Laboratory.

10

Community Needs Assessment and Techniques

○ ○ ○ ○ ○ ○ ○ ○ ○ ○ ○ ○ ○ ○ ○ ○

RABEL J. BURDGE

○ ○ ○ ○ ○ ○ ○ ○ ○ ○ ○ ○ ○ ○ ○ ○

● The purposes of this chapter are (1) to provide the reader with an understanding of exactly what needs assessment is, (2) to illustrate the process and the techniques for collecting needs assessment information at the community level, (3) to show how needs assessment information may be interpreted, (4) to discuss how needs assessment information fits into the SIA-EIA process and other planning activities, and (5) to provide an example outline of a needs assessment report. Information in this chapter is needed by social impact assessors, community and regional planners, professional and lay community leaders, extension advisers, and others who wish to understand social impacts and planning at the community and regional levels.

A Short History of
Needs Assessment Studies

The formal process of determining what people needed was originally developed by local teachers and school superintendents as an aid in planning courses for elementary and secondary schools. Soon county agents, forest rangers, nurses, public health workers, and others, upon arrival in a new community, asked their client groups what major problems they faced. Based on the professionals' assessment of the needs of the local population, programs were designed and implemented in line with concerns of the client group. Historically, "needs assessment" was as casual as a "windshield survey" or as systematic as careful consultation with identified community leaders and important government workers (Beal and Hobbs, 1964). The assessment by the field professional was satisfactory in the absence of clear legislative direction. However, beginning in the 1960s, regulatory statutes in transportation, health, and land-use planning, as well as the federal land management agencies, required that the expressed needs of the clients, the community, or the impact area be considered. The directive for agencies to include local as well as national interests in the needs assessment process provided the impetus for social scientists to develop innovative methodologies for gaining public input. As the methods to tap needs became increasingly sophisticated, the requirement of including needs assessment as a step in the planning process became established. The National Environmental Policy Act (NEPA) specifically mandates needs assessment both in the initial environmental assessment and the subsequent full-scale Environmental Impact Statement.

Defining Needs Assessment Activity

As a tool in the planning process, public assessment activities provide an initial look at the thinking of a client population about a problem area. Put another way, assessing needs means finding out what people think they need, want, or desire in a particular program area. The planner or the change agent then sets about to design that program, or at least to modify existing ones in line with expressed public input. In the case of social impact assessment, the question is whether or not the proposed project or change in policy will meet the needs identified by the affected population.

When available, planning standards, such as the acres of park land or number of hospital beds per thousand population, represent a way of determining the difference between "haves" and "needs." For example, information on changes in the number of students per classroom teacher, incidents of violent crime, or persons admitted to mental institutions indicate changing needs. More police or teachers may be added or subtracted depending upon the direction of the indicated needs. Needs assessment activity provides a systematic way to account for the needs of different client groups during the planning process.

Developing a Needs Assessment Report:
General Steps

From our definition, a needs assessment program is a research and planning activity designed to determine a community's needs and utilization patterns in a variety of service areas (Warheit et al., 1977: 4). The purpose of social impact studies is to answer the following question: Will there be a measurable difference in the quality of life in the community as a result of what the proposed project is doing or might do in the future?

A careful examination of these research and planning activities shows how needs assessment and social impact assessment are interrelated not only by law, but by planning necessity. It is not possible to conduct impact studies without first gathering baseline data on the community — to include needs and utilization patterns of a wide variety of services of those living in the area. Table 10.1 provides a schematic overview of the needs assessment process.

The Community Overview

A description of the community is the first step in a comprehensive community needs assessment analysis. The purposes of this phase are (1) to obtain information on the sociological, demographic, economic, and geographic patterns of persons living in the area where the likely impacts will occur, and (2) to secure historical data on the network of federal, state, and local agencies in the community that might provide insight into community needs.

The needs assessor will first identify the data sources available, their format, accessibility, and the costs of procurement and analysis. This step is very important since the nature, availability, and costs of securing, analyzing, and presenting the data are important factors in deciding on the extent of the needs assessment effort. Much useful information is available from a variety of sources at minimal costs. Table 10.2 lists some suggested starting points.

Specifically, information ought to be gathered on community needs as revealed in the sociological and demographic characteristics of the community (often labeled "secondary data"). Data on age, race, sex, ethnicity, family income, per capita income, marital status, family structure, housing characteristics, population density, mobility, migration and distribution, labor force characteristics, and educational levels can be obtained from census reports. The 1980 U.S. Census has a "neighborhood" feature, which

TABLE 10.1   Summary View of the Needs Assessment Process

(1) Community Overview Studies

Focus: The sociological-demographic characteristics of the community or area to be affected:

(a) the community's population characteristics, such as age, race, sex, income, employment, housing, migration, and education

(b) available historical information on the sociological, demographic, economic, and geographic characteristics of the total community prior to the impact event

(2) Needs Assessment

Focus: Determining the specific needs of the community:

(a) the needs and service patterns of specific populations and sociodemographic groups in the community

(b) comparative analysis of the goals, activities, and client patterns of local agencies with the needs and service patterns of those in the community

(c) obtaining citizen views of the impact event

(d) utilizing needs assessment in planning and mitigating the effects of the impact event

(3) Social Impact Studies

Focus: Specific subgroups within the community, such as age, race, sex, ethnic, and occupational groups, who are likely to be affected:

(a) data for comparative analysis of needs and service utilization of subgroups in the community

(b) monitoring the general sociodemographic, economic, and sociological changes in the community during the impact event

(c) Data on changing conditions uncovered by local health and social service agencies

SOURCE: Adapted and modified from Warheit et al. (1977: 8-10).

allows summary tabulations on clusters of census blocks and tracts. These special runs are available at nominal cost from regional census centers. Vital statistics can provide information on morbidity, mortality, and incidents of disease. Some local and regional planning councils can supply information on land use and population changes. Next, the needs assessor must match needs or standards to available supply as reported by various agencies and businesses. However, in developing "secondary data" for the community overview considerable sociological detective work is required. A list of human service agencies functioning in the community can be obtained from councils of social agencies or similar groups. The objective is to develop an overall profile of community needs based on information other persons and agencies have collected about specific needs.

Obtaining Community Input in the Needs Assessment Process

As suggested in Table 10.1, it may be necessary to go beyond census data and agency records to assess the needs and concerns of the community, particularly under the conditions of anticipated rapid change associated with either growth or decline. Seven approaches that may be used in combinations, jointly, or in the suggested sequential pattern are described here. The various approaches are outlined and a review and critique of their design is offered. The materials listed in the references at the end of the chapter provide details on implementation and interpretation. The seven ways of obtaining direct public input are through key informants, advisory groups, community forum, nominal group exercise, Delphi technique, questionnaire surveys (including community surveys, community leader studies, community-regional independent surveys, and synchronized policy issue studies), and jury panels.

Each of the following approaches, except jury panels, requires increased amounts of time, provides more details as to the amount of different needs, and requires increased cost as measured by both professional and volunteer time and increased breadth in representativeness of the community or region under study. While each method in the list is progressively more complex, it provides a better assessment of the needs of the community. The community overview study provides the foundation for applying each of these techniques. Many may be used in combinations to provide a better view of a community's perceived needs.

KEY INFORMANTS AND EXPERT INPUT

Experts or key informants are persons from both the public and private sectors having knowledge of the community under study. They are selected by the needs assessor because they have a broad knowledge of the community, its services, and most of all its history. Other ways of using expert opinion, discussed later in this section, are through the "nominal group technique" and the "Delphi technique." Expert input can also be

TABLE 10.2   Census, Agency Records, and Secondary Sources
             for Needs Assessment Data

Census and Agency Records

- public libraries
- offices of city, county, or regional planning commissions
- county extension offices
- school district offices
- college or university departments (sociology, anthropology, education, planning, public health, library)
- financial institutions
- utility companies
- chambers of commerce
- agencies and organizations responsible for health, rehabilitation, law enforcement and protection, and recording vital statistics

Secondary Sources

- museums, libraries, and church records
- newspaper archives
- county offices that record land tenure changes, titles, sales, marriages, divorces, deaths, criminal offenses, and employment
- school and hospital registers and files
- planning commissions
- political institutions and organizations
- utility companies
- financial institutions
- businesses
- community organizations with special interests
- individuals' photograph albums, diaries, or collections
- family clippings, obituaries, and mementos

SOURCES: Butler and Howell (1980: 6-7) and Burdge and Johnson (1977: 257-274).

institutionalized by establishing formal task forces or advisory groups (Cohen et al., 1977; Warheit et al., 1977: 20.22). Expert input can be helpful in some of the following ways:

(1)   identifying issues for community or general population surveys
(2)   building awareness and understanding of community problems
(3)   helping the needs assessor to discover populations and organizations that should be involved in planning
(4)   building support for program implementation

(5) evaluation of proposed solutions to community problems
(6) assisting the needs assessor in establishing priorities among program alternatives.

By way of caution, key informants may represent only personal and local interests, and not those of the general population. However, with careful planning, the quality of this type of needs assessment approach can be quite good. Key informants are easy to use and incur the smallest monetary costs of any of the alternatives.

ADVISORY GROUPS (AND TASK FORCES)

It is often useful for a project to have a formal advisory group selected by the needs assessor from among members of voluntary, service, business, and conservation organizations within a community or region. The advisory group can be chosen from some of the following organizations and groups:

(1) *Service organizations*: Civic clubs, such as Rotary or the Kiwanis, provide a place to present a proposed development or management plan. Because these organizations include individuals from different parts of the community, they provide a good "first reaction" as to problems a proposed development will likely face in a community.

(2) *Business organizations*: Groups such as the chamber of commerce and the board of realtors can provide information on how they see their community being affected by changes in business activity brought about by the proposed development.

(3) *Conservation organizations*: Groups such as the Issak Walton League, rod and gun clubs, the Audubon Society, Boy Scouts of America, and others provide clues as to important environmental and aesthetic impacts.

The selection of persons to make up task forces or advisory groups requires that diverse views be represented. Those selected are asked to meet together and can be useful in some of the following ways:

(1) identifying methods for conducting a needs assessment
(2) identifying various population and organizational groups that should be involved in a community needs assessment
(3) assessing potential impacts of a development
(4) collecting information
(5) evaluating a community program or policy
(6) giving technical assistance or advise (Butler and Howell, 1980: 12)

COMMUNITY FORUM

A community forum is based on one or more public meetings to which people are invited to express their opinions about a proposed project, management plan, redesignation of resource utilization, or a listing of the major problems facing the community (a needs assessment). The community forum is an offshoot of the idealized New England town meeting, where everyone knew everyone else and most were unafraid to express their opinions in public.

Community forums differ from public hearings in that a deliberate attempt is made to tap all segments of a community and the organizer of the community forum always distributes information in advance. Strengths of the community forum as a way of obtaining needs assessment information include the following:

(1) Much information can be obtained about citizen and community viewpoints in a short time and at minimal expense.

(2) Community forums can be useful in identifying problems, locating needs, or suggesting issues that were not uncovered by experts or the advisory groups.

(3) In the absence of a full-scale needs assessment survey, it does give all citizens an opportunity to be heard.

(4) It provides visibility to the proposed environmental impact through pre- and post-community forum media exposure.

NOMINAL GROUP PROCESS

The nominal group process is a structured problem-solving or idea-generating strategy in which individuals meet in a face-to-face nonthreatening group situation. First, the leader presents the topic or issue to the group and instructs members to write as many responses or ideas as possible. Next, in a round robin all ideas and issues are listed and then are clarified and discussed. A secret vote allows the ideas to be ranked in importance. The nominal group process assures a balanced input from all participants and takes advantage of each person's knowledge and experience. In the needs assessment setting, it is useful for generating and clarifying ideas, reaching consensus, setting priorities, and choosing among proposed actions. Most important, it allows individual generation of ideas without undue influence by a dominant group member (for further discussion of this process, see Delbecq et al., 1975; Butler and Howell, 1980).

The needs assessor might use the nominal group technique in the meeting of a community advisory group or task force. A possible agenda would be (1) to determine what community problems are of greatest immediate concern; (2) to decide on a needs assessment strategy for dealing with identified problems; and (3) to design improved community services or programs.

DELPHI TECHNIQUE

The Delphi technique is another way of obtaining group input for ideas and problem solving. Unlike the nominal group process, the Delphi technique does not require face-to-face participation. The approach utilizes a series of carefully designed questionnaires interspersed with information summaries and feedback from preceding responses. A panel of respondents is chosen that best represents the views of the community (Delbecq et al., 1975).

The process begins with the initial development of a questionnaire focusing on suggested needs in a specified area. Each panel member then responds to the questionnaire independently and returns it. The initiators of the questionnaire summarize responses, develop a feedback summary, and submit a second questionnaire to the panel. After reviewing the feedback summary, panel members independently list priorities in needs assessment areas in the second questionnaire. Sometimes a third round is conducted and, on rare occasions, a fourth. The final summary represents the ranking of community needs.

In assessing community needs, the Delphi technique could be used for many of the same tasks as the nominal group process — determining and ranking community problems, setting goals, designing needs assessment strategies, planning a conference or community forum, developing improved community services, or evaluating alternative plans for community development. However, because most of the people in a community will be together geographically, it may simply be easier to call a meeting.

The Delphi technique has the advantage of allowing people to assess possible community needs under less time pressures, and, most important, to seek out information before responding. The Delphi technique allows the inclusions of responses of persons who do not live in the area. The procedures are detailed in Delbecq et al. (1975) and the advantages and disadvantages in Butler and Howell (1980: 17).

QUESTIONNAIRE SURVEYS

Questionnaires are very good at finding out what people think are important community needs and problems. They may also be designed to supply information on attitudes, beliefs, behaviors, and attributes in response to specific questions. Some examples of needs assessment information obtained through questionnaire surveys are as follows: (1) alternative solutions to community problems; (2) community and area reaction to problems and, most important, proposals for action; (3) information on citizen knowledge, attitudes, opinions, and beliefs in order to identify and rank community needs; (4) citizen awareness of community problems; (5) changes in the community's position on a variety of community issues; and (6) citizen attitudes or reactions to alternative community development proposals.

Surveys have the advantage of providing representative input by reaching all affected populations. Furthermore, trends established through surveys can be compared to other data bases, such as the U.S. Census. However, cost may be a problem because experts may be needed to develop the survey instruments, train interviewers, conduct interviews, and analyze results. Fortunately, the use of community volunteers can reduce the costs of questionnaire surveys and legitimize the use of the results by local persons. Research has demonstrated that development initiatives that include citizen participation have a better chance of being adopted (Koneya, 1978).

The five types of surveys detailed here utilize different combinations of respondents to obtain public input to needs assessment and community problems. The types of surveys to be discussed are (1) community surveys using citizen-developed agendas, (2) community surveys using standardized agendas, (3) community leader studies, (4) community-regional independent surveys, and (5) synchronized policy issue studies.

Community surveys using citizen-developed needs assessment agendas. Community surveys are studies of all or a sample of persons in a community. In the case of citizen-developed agendas, community volunteers do the entire needs assessment, from questionnaire formulation through report writing. The local needs assessor could assist the community in developing agenda items and in designing the research process. Obtaining opinions on perceived needs from as many members of the community as possible is an important as obtaining a representative sample. Face-to-face interviews are preferred because they increase contact among community members. Here the research process is almost as important as the results, for solutions to problems may flow from a heightened sense of community awareness and involvement (Blake et al., 1977).

Community studies using standardized needs assessment agendas. Sometimes a community will want a needs assessment study, but will not have time to conduct the process. In such cases, university or agency sociologists may be brought in to provide technical assistance in some or all phases of the questionnaire survey. Rural sociologists have developed standardized needs assessment questionnaires and are knowledgeable in sampling techniques, interviewer training, data analysis, and write-up (Hobbs, 1977; Ryan, 1980). Local people could do the interviewing, using either the face-to-face format or "drop-off" questionnaires. When a needs assessment study is initiated locally, the sample must be representative because the results will be presumed to reflect the needs of the entire community.

Local community studies utilizing standardized need assessment questionnaires have the advantage of being locally initiated because the community decides what problems are to be addressed and local people actually collect the information. The needs assessor can utilize the latest technology in data collection, thereby improving turn-around time and minimizing the possibility of breakdown in the research process.

Community leader needs assessment surveys. The community leader approach to needs assessment determination focuses on the elected, appointed, professional, or volunteer positions in a community or region. Either a sample or all of the community leaders might be chosen. Issues dealing with the needs assessment, the environmental impacts of a proposed development, or other community problems are formalized in a survey research instrument. The needs assessor may initiate the study with technical assistance available from a research sociologist associated with an agency, or local college or university. Telephone or self-administered questionnaires or face-to-face interviews are used, depending upon the numbers and the geographical limits of the study. This approach has the advantage of obtaining uniform responses to needs assessment questions, and it can be done with standardized surveys and may not require the presence of the needs assessor in the community.

Information from community leaders may be used as a way to identify opposition and support for proposed development (Basson, 1970). In addition, leaders may be informed about environmental impact issues and thus may be in a position to respond knowledgeably to the complex issues that go together to make policy. However, research efforts that focus only on leaders may be open to the charge that the "real" needs and preferences of the general population are not being identified. Substantial research by rural sociologists has demonstrated that community leaders differ from the general population in their perception of what should be done in the community (Miller, 1953). Interviews with community leaders could be a first step in gaining public input to needs assessment alternatives prior to either the community-regional independent survey or the synchronized policy issue survey described in the next sections.

Community-regional independent needs assessment surveys. Community-regional independent surveys differ from community questionnaire surveys only in that the studies are conducted independently of community input. They are similar to public opinion-type polls, but include needs assessment topics.

The format of independent, community, and multicounty surveys can include questions on any number of issues. The results may be used for identifying, comparing, and ranking problem areas. Topics selected for inclusion in these surveys may not always be applicable to each local community. Because of the expense incurred in contacting large numbers of people, data gathering is limited to some combination of the telephone and mailed questionnaire approaches (Dillman, 1978). Successful independent surveys dealing with needs assessment priorities for program development and government spending have been completed by rural sociologists in the states of Washington, Arizona, Colorado, Indiana, Illinois, Michigan, Kentucky, Pennsylvania, North Carolina, and Florida (for example, see Burdge et al., 1978; Burdge and Warner, 1975; Beaulieu and Korsching, 1979; Moore and Ishler, 1980; Dillman et al., 1974).

The community-regional independent survey has the advantage of providing reliable information on a variety of needs assessment issues in a short time. Because the samples are large, comparisons are possible with other communities, counties, and even states (Christenson, 1976). In states and regions where large needs assessment surveys have been completed, the social assessor will have a broad view of area needs.

At the community level, the independent survey is useful in comparing and identifying problems and establishing needs assessment preferences. It can provide an indication as to citizen attitudes toward development projects in general. However, a common complaint about questionnaire surveys (public opinion-type polls) is that citizens do not have enough information about the variety of alternatives to make intelligent responses (Dillman, 1977).

Synchronized policy issue studies. Two rural sociologists (Dillman, 1977; Wardwell and Dillman, 1975) have combined elements of the nominal group technique and community surveys into an approach called "synchronized policy issue studies." Their objective was to make information obtained from questionnaire surveys an integral part of the planning process. Briefly put, the approach involves obtaining information on problem areas, program alternatives, or preferences from community leaders through the use of the nominal group technique or through interviews with community leaders (Garkovich, 1979; Cohen et al., 1977; Goudy and Wepprecht, 1977). Information obtained from the leaders is then used as the basis for developing items to be included in a needs assessment questionnaire survey of the general population. After the information from the survey has been gathered and tabulated, the policymaking group (community leaders, task force members, council representatives, planning boards, or the like) modifies and finalizes policy recommendations based on its evaluation of the public's response to the questionnaire survey. If time allows, reformulated policies based upon the nominal or delphi techniques could again be put before the general population through another questionnaire survey.

This back-and-forth procedure can be applied at the community level, as reported by Garkovich (1979) in the case of Jessamine County, Kentucky. It has also been used at the state level, as reported by Wardwell and Dillman (1975). The improvements in administering and coding telephone and self-administered questionnaires allow needs assessors to analyze citizen responses to policy alternatives within a short time — often overnight.

Synchronized policy issue surveys require both financial and time commitments on the part of the sponsor and a sociologist to work closely with leaders in translating the needs assessment issues into questionnaire form. The approach combines the specialized knowledge of the community leader (experts) study with the representativeness of a community-regional independent survey.

JURY PANELS

The final needs assessment technique to be discussed here is an experimental one labeled the "jury panel" (Heberlein, 1976). It combines random selections of persons from the community with techniques in group decision making. First, a random sample of the adult population in a community or region is chosen. Using the sequential random sampling technique, each person receives a priority, as in the call to jury duty. Persons are phoned in turn until the required number of "jurors" have agreed to participate. The "respondents" agreeing to participate in the needs assessment project receive a modest honorarium and expenses in return for two days of hearing about a proposed government action and providing information to the researchers on what they see as community problems. At the end of the period they are asked to give their "verdict" on what they see as major community impacts or needs. Since selection is random, it may be assumed that all class positions in the community are represented. The jury panel is an excellent way to obtain representative public input, at acceptable costs, and in a timely manner.

The "jury panel" technique has the disadvantage of requiring considerable advanced planning and a leader who is trained in group dynamics (Butler and Howell, 1980). This needs assessment technique has been tried at the Shawnee National Forest in southern Illinois and the Wisconsin Department of Natural Resources (Heberlein, 1976). The approach is promising but needs more test cases in order to be evaluated properly.

Assessing the Strengths and Weaknesses
of Needs Assessment Techniques

The previous section has introduced the reader to a variety of ways to obtain needs assessment information. Some needs assessment situations require secondary information only — others may require and use input from a variety of sources. The major constraints are the availability of time and the amount of detail contained in the needs assessment requirements. Table 10.3 represents an attempt to summarize in a very general way the overall strengths and weakness of each of the techniques. The techniques are ordered in the table according to the ease in obtaining the information. If time permits, questionnaire surveys of the community population are the best source of information, but they require knowledgable and well-trained sociologists. Nevertheless, a creative combination of the techniques provides an excellent picture of actual needs for the community under study.

Writing the Needs Assessment Report

A report of the needs assessment activity that provides a ranking of the major needs of the community will be required. At a minimum, the following five topics should be included:

(1) *Purposes of the needs assessment study:* Emphasis would be on the type of planning activity that mandated that the study be conducted, for example, social impact assessment.

(2) *Background of the study:* Any historical or legislative requirements may be included here, along with justifications for conducting the needs assessment research.

(3) *Design of the study:* This section should provide enough detail on the needs assessment techniques utilized to enable replication of the findings.

(4) *Presentation of the findings:* This section presents the data and the analysis, using graphics and tables for effective communication.

(5) *Listing priorities and recommendations:* Recommendations, naturally, would flow from the purposes and findings of the needs assessment study. To be of maximum value, the list of needs assessment recommendations ought to (1) be based on facts derived from the data; (2) be rank ordered in terms of a time-cost priority; (3) be achievable — some objectives at once, others over time; and (4) reflect the best interests of the persons in the community.

There is no guarantee that the needs assessment information will be used creatively for program and development evaluation, even when the data are presented graphically, dramatically, and powerfully. Neither is there certainty that the recommendations that logically follow from carefully designed data analysis will be adopted. But if the data are analyzed and presented poorly, and if the recommendations are carelessly and thoughtlessly prepared, the probability of effecting any decision regarding whether or not the project is to be built is greatly diminished.

Using Needs Assessment Information in the Social Impact Assessment Process

As mandated in the NEPA process, public input must be obtained "up front," before final decisions have been made. If the scoping process, as outlined in the 1978 EIS guidelines, is followed, a positive result may be the

TABLE 10.3 Summary Review of Major Needs Assessment Techniques

Needs Assessment Technique	Major Strength	Major Weakness
Secondary information	can be obtained quickly, with little time spent in the local community	does not include input from the impact population and requires good sociological detective work
Agency records	can be obtained quickly, but requires time in community	does not include input from the impact population and requires good sociological detective work
Key informant (expert input)	can be obtained quickly and provides contact with the community	may not be representative of community and produces limited perspective
Advisory groups (task forces)	includes input representative of community leadership	may not be representative of community and requires regular meetings
Community forums	can include all segments of population and large amounts of input in short periods	requires careful planning and may not be representative of minority viewpoints
Nominal group process	generates a large amount of ideas in short time	requires expert leadership and may be best as a consensus-seeking technique
Delphi technique	helps achieve consensus on community needs, particularly on technical issues	requires expert leadership and time-consuming questionnaire preparation

Questionnaire Surveys

Community studies (citizen-developed needs assessment agendas)	involves citizens in the needs assessment process	very time consuming; citizens may lose interest
Community studies (standardized needs assessment agendas)	involves citizens in some of the needs assessment process but eliminates technical drudgery	time consuming; citizens may think experts have major input
Community leader surveys	ensures representation of all community leaders; does not require face-to-face meeting	not representative of entire community and time consuming
Community-regional independent surveys	good for comparing community needs with adjacent areas; is representative	very expensive and requires highly trained research staff
Synchronized policy and issue surveys	combines nominal group technique with questionnaire surveys	requires cooperation between policymakers and experts in survey research
Jury panels	chooses an advisory group by random selection from the general population	requires experience in group dynamics and survey research; is untried

acceptance of the proposed action. Programs in social services, health care delivery, and environmental alteration, among others, require that the congruity between needs of the clients and proposed or ongoing programs be considered. However, the methods for establishing congruity with public needs are not specified. In the case of environmental impact assessment, the laws simply say that the affected human population be consulted about possible consequences. That statement was part of the initial EIS legislation (NEPA, 1969), but since the Council on Environmental Quality (CEQ) guidelines were issued in 1978, that relationship has been specified in more detail. In the initial problem identification and scoping processes (sometimes called "preassessment"), the social assessment member of the EIS team must determine what the needs of the impact community are and how the proposed development will affect those needs. The purpose of the preassessment stage is to determine whether or not the proposed development will have any real "environmental impact."

If it has been determined that a full-scale environmental impact statement is needed, then at the baseline data collection stage (sometimes called the "profiling" stage) a more detailed needs assessment survey is conducted. The requirement for public involvement also enters into the SIA process. Many of the needs assessment techniques outlined here may come under the category of public involvement and may be used in the stages where the persons who are affected will have a say in which of the alternatives are chosen.

A community needs assessment is an excellent means of involving the public in problem solving and developing local goals. There is a tendency for people to resist change — frequently because they have inadequate information, or because they have not been involved in making decisions. A needs assessment can therefore be viewed as a process of citizen involvement whereby people not only learn more about the situation, but also feel that they have had a voice in the outcome.

The case of Creston, Washington, is a good example of the multiple use of different needs assessment techniques to assess needs as a component of a social impact analysis.

Creston, Washington: Anticipating Social Impacts[1]

In 1976, the Washington Water Power Company announced plans to begin construction in 1983 on the first of four coal-fired generating plants in a rural area of eastern Washington near Creston. Over the decade 1983-1993, a sizable construction force would be working on the four projects, estimated to cost between $2 billion and $3 billion.

Creston is an agricultural trade center located in Lincoln County. The town is on a state highway approximately 56 miles from Spokane, the major eastern city in the state of Washington. In the case of towns such as Creston, faced with the impacts of growth, the National Environmental Policy Act and Washington state legislation provide a context for generating needed information and a framework for negotiating with an energy developer.

Creston and the surrounding county are quite typical of most North American communities that have a primarily agricultural base. Lincoln County reached its population peak in 1910 with 17,539 residents, and consistently declined in population to a low of 9,300 in 1975. The town has a fairly stable population of about 350. Creston is 20 miles from Davenport, a community of approximately 1,600 residents, which is the county seat and location of the hospital and major shopping area for northern Lincoln County.

There is some concern within the community of Creston about the proposed new energy facilities, the threat of railroad abandonment to the agricultural economy, the need for more paved streets, the need for improved mail service, and the need for a better water system. Prior to 1979, the community did not have a comprehensive plan that could be used as a guide for local decision making about the community's future.

In 1979, the mayor, in cooperation with members of the Creston Planning Commission, approached the area Extension agent about doing a needs assessment study. Such a study, they reasoned, could be a means for getting a broad base of citizen input into the planning process and could provide objective indicators of human needs within the community. Using the resources of Washington State University Cooperative Extension, a questionnaire survey was completed in 1979. Substantial information was generated on citizen attitudes about proposed goals for the community, perceptions about possible and actual community problems and knowledge, beliefs and attitudes about the proposed energy development, as well as other changes occurring in the area. The survey helped citizens become more aware of problems and possible solutions, and provided information to help planning commission members and elected government officials make better policy decisions.

As we have seen, the questionnaire survey is but one method of generating useful information about citizen needs in communities where development is expected. In the case of Creston, a committee of persons representing a cross section of the community was formed to help with the process of impact assessment and mitigation. The Creston Project Committee, as it was called, provided the dual function of an advisory group and a task force. The professionals and laypersons involved with the impact committee provided useful input and legitimation to the community. However, they did not have the expertise to assess and understand thoroughly the critical fiscal and sociocultural impacts that might occur as a result of the proposed energy development. At such a point other needs assessment techniques such as the delphi might have been included.

As pointed out in earlier sections of the chapter, information generated by advisory groups and task forces can be supplemented using other methods, and such groups can employ different techniques for generating the information that they will then evaluate. This chapter has emphasized combining existing sources of information such as census and agency records with new sources of information to aid in the planning process in communities such as Creston. The delphi method can be very useful for obtaining expert opinion on needs and problems related to the impacts of anticipated growth. The key informant method may be useful for identifying the unique needs of minorities, youth, or the elderly. Community forums will be helpful for informing people about growth-related issues and for generating further information about needs and perceptions. The nominal group process will be helpful in small-group settings for obtaining lists of problems, ideas, and proposals for action.

In the case of Creston, the results of these needs assessments techniques as well as the results of the earlier needs assessment survey could provide the information base for developing subsequent and more refined surveys that can be useful when tightening up policies and making specific recommendations (Dillman, 1977; Garkovich, 1979). As time permits, multiple methods should be used when carrying out a detailed needs assessment study — otherwise many people and potential problem areas fall through the slats.

Due to declining demand for electricity and excess capacity in other facilities, the Creston generating plants were never built. However, the problems identified during the needs assessment exercise helped the community develop plans for adjusting to change in the future.

Note

1. This section is adapted from Butler and Howell (1980: 16-18), with permission of the authors.

References

ALEXANDER, C. A. and C. McCANN (1956) "The concept of representation in community organization." Social Work 1, 1: 48-52.
BAILEY, K. D. (1978) Methods of Social Research. New York: Macmillan.
BASSON, P. (1970) "Planning and perception of needs in five Upstate New York counties." Journal of the Community Development Society 1, 2: 23-29.
BEAL, G. M. and D. J. HOBBS (1964) The Process of Social Action in Community and Area Development. Ames: Iowa State University Cooperative Extension.
BEAULIEU, L. J. and P. F. KORSCHING [eds.] (1979) Focus on Florida: The Citizens' Viewpoint. Gainsville: Center for Community and Rural Development-IFAS, University of Florida.
BLAKE, B. F., N. KALB, and V. RYAN (1977) "Citizen opinion surveys and effective CD efforts." Journal of the Community Development Society 8, 2: 92-104.
BROWN, D. (1972) "The management of advisory committees: an assignment for the "70's." Public Administration Review 32, 4: 334-342.
BURDGE, R. J. (1982) "Needs assessment surveys for decision makers," pp. 273-283 in D. A. Dillman and D. J. Hobbs (eds.) Rural Society in the U.S.: Research Issues for the 1980's. Boulder, CO: Westview.
——— and S. JOHNSON (1977) "Sociocultural aspects of the effects of resource development," pp. 241-278 in J. McEvoy III and T. Dietz (eds.) Handbook for Environmental Planning. New York: John Wiley.
BURDGE, R. J. and P. D. WARNER (1975) "Issues facing Kentucky." Department of Sociology, Cooperative Extension Service, Lexington, KY.
BURDGE, R. J., R. M. KELLY, and H. J. SCHWEITZER (1978) Illinois: Today and Tomorrow. Urbana: University of Illinois Cooperative Extension.
BUTLER, L. M. and R. E. HOWELL (1980) Coping with Growth: Community Needs Assessment Techniques. Corvallis, OR: Western Rural Development Center.
CHRISTENSON, J. A. (1976) "Public input for program planning and policy formation." Journal of the Community Development Society 7 (Spring): 33-39.
——— (1975) "A procedure for conducting mail surveys with the general public." Journal of the Community Development Society 6 (Spring): 135-146.
CLARK, R. N., G. H. STANKEY, and J. C. HENDEE (1974) An Introduction to CODINVOLVE: A System for Analyzing, Storing, and Returning Public Input to Resource Decisions. Portland, OR: Pacific Northwest Forest and Range Experiment Station.
COHEN, M. W., G. M. SILLS, and A. I. SCHWEBEL (1977) "A two stage process for surveying community needs." Journal of the Community Development Society 8, 1: 54-61.

DELBECQ, A., A. VAN DE VEN, and D. GUSTAFSON (1975) Group Techniques for Program Planning: A Guide to Nominal Group and Delphi Processes. Glenview, IL: Scott, Foresman.

DILLMAN, D. A. (1978) Mail and Telephone Surveys: The Total Design Method. New York: John Wiley.

——— (1977) "Our new tools need not be used in the same old way." Journal of the Community Development Society 8, 1: 30-43.

——— J. A. CHRISTENSON, E. H. CARPENTER, and R. M. BROOKS (1974) "Increasing mail questionnaire response: a four-state comparison." American Sociological Review 29: 744-756.

Federal Highway Administration, Socio-Economic Studies Division (1976) Effective Citizen Participation in Transportation Planning, Vol. II: A Catalog of Techniques. Washington, DC: U.S. Department of Transportation.

FERBER, R. E. (1980) How to Do Surveys. Washington, DC: American Statistical Association.

GARKOVICH, L. (1979) "What comes after the survey? A practical application of the synchronized survey model in community development." Journal of the Community Development Society 10, 1: 29-38.

——— and J. M. STAM (1980) "Research on selected issues in community development," pp. 155-186 in J. A. Christenson and J. W. Robinson, Jr. (eds.) Community Development in America. Ames: Iowa State University Press.

GOUDY, W. J. (1975) "Studying your community: community summaries." Sociology Report 128B, Iowa State University.

——— and F. E. WEPPRECHT (1977) "Local, regional programs developed from residents' evaluations." Journal of the Community Development Society 9, 1: 44-52.

HEBERLEIN, T. A. (1976) "Some observations on alternatives mechanisms for public involvement: the hearing, public opinion poll, the workshop and the quasi-experiment." Natural Resources Journal 16, 1: 197-213.

HENDEE, J. C., R. N. CLARK, and G. H. STANKEY (1974) "A framework for agency use of public input in resource decision making." Journal of Soil and Water Conservation 29, 2: 60-66.

HOBBS, D. (1977) "Surveying community attitudes: a technical manual for communities." Manual 108, Missouri Division of Community Development, Columbia.

KONEYA, M. (1978) "Citizen participation is not community development." Journal of the Community Development Society 9, 2: 23-29.

MILLER, P. A. (1953) Community Health Action. East Lansing: Michigan University Press.

MOORE, D. E. and A. S. ISHLER (1980) "Pennsylvania: the citizens' viewpoint." College of Agriculture, Pennsylvania State University.

RYAN, V. (1980) CD-Dial. Ames: Iowa State University Cooperative Extension Service.

SCHATZMAN, L. and A. D. STRAUSS (1973) Field Research Strategies for a Natural Sociology. Englewood Cliffs, NJ: Prentice-Hall.

U.S. Bureau of the Census (1975) Census Data for Community Action. Washington, DC: Government Printing Office.

——— (continuing dates) Census Reports and Current Population Reports (various topics). Washington, DC: Government Printing Office.

———— (continuing dates) City and County Data Books (various topics). Washington, DC: Government Printing Office.

WARDWELL, J. A. and D. A. DILLMAN (1975) Alternatives for Washington: The Final Report, Vol. 6. Olympia, WA: Office of Program Planning and Fiscal Management.

WARHEIT, G. J., R. A. BELL, and J. J. SCHWAB (1977) Needs Assessment Approaches: Concepts and Methods. Rockville, MD: National Institute of Mental Health.

WARREN, R. L. (1955) Studying Your Community. New York: Russell Sage.

WEBB, E. J., D. T. CAMPBELL, R. D. SCHWARTZ, and L. SECHREST (1966) Unobtrusive Measures: Non-Reactive Research in the Social Sciences. Chicago: Rand McNally.

WEBB, K. and H. HATRY (1973) Obtaining Citizen Feedback: Application of Citizen Surveys to Local Government. Washington, DC: Urban Institute.

11

Psychosocial Assessment

○ ○ ○ ○ ○ ○ ○ ○ ○ ○ ○ ○ ○ ○ ○ ○

JOHN W. LOUNSBURY, KENT D. VAN LIERE,
and GREGORY J. MEISSEN

○ ○ ○ ○ ○ ○ ○ ○ ○ ○ ○ ○ ○ ○ ○ ○

● This chapter reviews the conceptual issues and empirical findings of psychosocial assessment and discusses the prospects for advancing knowledge and practice in this area. While such variables as cost-benefit measures, community-level fiscal indices, and objective social indicators (such as population growth, labor force participation rates, and mobility patterns) have served as the foci of studies of social impact assessment (SIA), many researchers believe that the the field should also concentrate on the individual subjective level in investigations of potential social impacts (Deane and Mumpower, 1977; Lounsbury et al., 1977). We consider such an emphasis to be one of psychosocial assessment. More generally, we shall consider any type of social impact assessment that focuses on individual subjective states and attempts to relate them to structural conditions or processes to be psychosocial assessment. Our focus will be on social psychological variables, particularly attitudes, beliefs, values, intentions, and behavioral responses.

Most writers appear to agree on the following reasons that analysis of psychosocial variables is important to the larger process of social impact assessment. First, social psychological variables mediate the relationship between structural conditions and external events impinging on the individual and his or her unique personal experiences and responses. Estimating how a change in these structural conditions will affect individuals depends in part on understanding their psychosocial orientation toward these changes. Second, direct attention to psychosocial impacts can enable the assessor to separate project effects from change that may be independent of a project. For example, changes in caseloads at a community mental health center, shifts in divorce rates, increases in participation in alcoholism treatment programs, and elevated outmigration rates might reflect important impacts of a large-scale project on a community. Yet following these trends provides little information on why the changes are occurring and whether they represent responses to the project as a whole, specific aspects of the project, or community shifts that are related only indirectly or unrelated to the project.

Finally, much of the rhetoric justifying social impact assessment as a part of the broader environmental impact process is stated specifically in terms of subjective states such as "social well-being" or "quality of life" (Deane and Mumpower, 1977; Fitzsimmons et al., 1975). Intuitively, this make sense: As Lewis (1980) notes, "The objective study may be more impartial, synthetic, inclusive, and generalized, but it tells us little about what keeps a community together, how its people find meaning and purpose in life, their deeper social values and sentiments, or the things which make life worth living." Psychosocial assessment can provide information that helps answer the latter types of questions.

As an integrative focus for this chapter we will draw upon what has been broadly termed "attitude theory," under which we subsume the concepts of attitudes, beliefs and intentions, as well as associated behavioral responses. There are several considerations in favor of looking at psychosocial assessment from the standpoint of attitude theory. First, attitudes and related concepts such as values and beliefs are familiar to most researchers and practitioners. Moreover, these concepts encompass a large number of the variables critical to understanding social impacts. Both general response states (such as social well-being and alienation) and beliefs about specific aspects of a project (such as the expected safety of a nuclear power plant) can be studied usefully from an attitude theory perspective. Finally, there is already a large body of research findings related to the analysis of beliefs, attitudes, and intentions that can serve as a foundation for theoretical and applied analysis in psychosocial assessment.

An Attitude Theory
Framework for SIA

Three concepts that are often distinguished in attitude theorizing are attitudes, beliefs, and behavioral intentions. *Attitudes* have been defined in myriad ways, but there appears to be increasing agreement that they should be defined as a positive or negative evaluation of an object. In the present context, we shall consider a measure attitudinal if the measure places an individual on a bipolar affective dimension (for example, a dimension ranging from dislike to like or strongly disagree to strongly agree). For example, answering "strongly agree" to the statement "I like nuclear power plants" reflects a person's attitude toward nuclear power plants. The object of an attitude can be something specific and concrete, such as a new freeway that is under construction, or a planned future event, such as a proposed hydroelectric plant; The object may also be a more abstract process such as increased development of alternative energy sources such as solar power.

We shall use the term "belief" when the measure places the individual as a dimension linking an object to an attribute. Usually, the dimension on which a belief is measured is one of subjective probability. For example, an individual may believe that it is very likely that a proposed nuclear power plant will create more jobs for the community. Many subjective states can be represented by this type of statement, and thus beliefs represent the building blocks for more complex cognitive constructs (such as values, norms, and well-being).

Finally, a *behavioral intention* represents a person's intention to perform a behavior, or likely course of action on individual might take with respect to an object. The statement "I plan to sign a petition against the siting of a nuclear plant in this county" is an example of a behavioral intention.

One reason for studying attitudes, beliefs, and intentions is to predict behavior. Many researchers with only limited background in attitude-behavior studies are familiar with a few classic articles that stress the often inconsistent relationship between reported attitudes and observed behavior (for example, see LaPiere, 1934; Ehrlich, 1969). However, a great deal of research carried out in the 1970s extended examination of this issue beyond the original question of whether general attitudes predict specific behaviors (see, for example, Fishbein and Ajzen, 1975; Schuman and Johnson, 1976) and found that attitudes can be important predictors of behavior when properly conceptualized and measured.

Perhaps the most important criterion for examining attitude-behavior relationships is the extent to which the measures of each correspond along four dimensions: behavioral action, the target at which the action is directed, the context in which the action occurs, and the time at which the action is performed. As an example, if we wish to predict whether an individual will vote in favor of a referendum supporting the construction of a coal-fired power plant in his or her community, the attitude should be measured with respect to the same action (voting), target (referendum on coal-fired power plants), context (in that community), and time (at the time the referendum is planned to be held). Thus the investigator might attempt to maximize the prediction of actual voting patterns by assessing specific attitudes toward voting for the proposed plant in the community in the referendum to be held one year hence. Or the researcher may measure general attitudes toward the plant to predict behavior patterns with respect to the plant.

Attitudes may also be predictive not only of a single behavioral action, such as voting, but they may be predictive of a composite behavioral measure that incorporates a broad range of actions related to an attitude. For example, Fishbein and and Ajzen (1974) analyzed the relationship between a measure of attitude toward religion and 100 behaviors related to religious activity (such as attending church, praying before meals, and donating money to a religious organization). They found that the average correlation between the attitude measure and single behaviors was in the .12 to .15 range, whereas the average correlation between the attitude measure and a summated measure of all 100 behaviors was in the .61 to .71 range.

One implication of this type of finding in the SIA context is that general measures of attitudes toward a given power plant or even more global issues such as attitudes toward nuclear power plant construction in the United States may not predict specific behavioral acts such as voting in a referendum or signing a petition, but the attitudinal measure may be fairly predictive of aggregated actions or behavior in general with respect to construction of the particular plant (or nuclear power plant construction in the United States). In some ways, the ability to predict a composite of behaviors may be more important in assessing project effects than simply being able to predict individual behaviors.

Several models for predicting behaviors on the basis of attitudes, beliefs, and intentions have been developed and tested with a fair amount of success. Most widely tested is the model developed by Fishbein and Ajzen (detailed in their 1975 book and in Ajzen and Fishbein, 1980). We have included a schematic diagram showing the elements of their model in Figure 11.1.

This model posits that the best predictor of a given behavior is the individual's intention to engage in that behavior. Intentions are, in turn, a function of the attitude toward the behavior and the social norms or subjective social pressure felt by the individual for engaging in the behavior. It is important to note that the attitude component included in this model is attitude toward the behavior, not attitude toward some object toward which behavior is directed. Thus we would measure attitude toward signing a petition opposing a nuclear power plant rather than attitude toward the plant. The model includes a subjective norms component to help account for those situations in which pressure from others may be influencing the individual to act in a way that is contrary to his or her attitude (see Ajzen and Fishbein, 1980, for a more detailed discussion of the components and ways to measure them).

Interestingly, in this model attitude toward the behavior is a function of the perceived outcomes associated with a behavior and the positive or negative evaluation of these outcomes. Quite often a key interest in the SIA process is the perceived likelihood of various project outcomes and the perceived desirability of these outcomes. In many cases, analysis of these individual elements may be as important as the analysis of overall attitudes toward the project.

Identifying Important Attitudes and Beliefs in the SIA Context

What attitudes, beliefs, and intentions should be studied in an assessment of the impacts of a project? The most typical approach, and one that delimits the scope of inquiry considerably, has been to assess attitudes and beliefs that seem most likely to be affected by a project and that are viewed (by somebody) as important outcomes for groups affected by the project. Examples of attitudes and beliefs that have been studied include attitudes toward the use of groundwater in an analysis of watershed rehabilitation by Smith and Hogg (1971); attitude toward holding a referendum on a planned World's Fair (Meissen, 1981); belief in the likelihood of occurrence of a number of local impacts among residents of a community adjacent to a proposed nuclear power plant (Lounsbury et al., 1977); attitudes toward forced relocation (Napier and Moody, 1979; Fellman and Brandt, 1970);

attitudes toward health care (Kennedy, 1979); and feelings about stress and mental health (Weisz, 1979).

In the above-mentioned examples there is little doubt that the variables studied were reasonable ones to have chosen initially for analysis. Indeed, the fact that in most cases there were changes in the levels of the variables studied that appeared to be associated with the impact event argues for their inclusion. What is missing in this approach is an explicit statement of the decision rules that determined the choice of one variable and not another. As a result, the selection of the final study variables seems arbitrary and may leave out important attitudes, beliefs, and intentions that should be studied. For example, it is interesting to note that initial impact assessments of an energy boomtown failed to consider the special consequences that could befall wives of incoming workers (Davenport and Davenport, 1979). Later concern was precipitated by an increase in these women turning to professional help at local community mental health centers, with problems ranging from depression to physical abuse. Some of these problems might have been foreseen if attitudes toward the families of incoming workers had been ascertained in the preliminary social impact assessments.

There are several different approaches for selecting the variables to be studied. First, the selection of variables could proceed from the theoretical orientation and explicit hypotheses formulated for the study. Here the focus is on resolving theoretical issues, such as whether alienation occurs when the public is denied the opportunity to vote on or influence the development of a project. In such a framework the choice of variables serves to enhance theory. Most SIAs that we have reviewed, however, are directed toward policy decisions and not toward social science theories.

Along more pragmatic lines, the SIA researcher could use some form of systematic technique to elicit information from "experts" that could help identify important variables. Singg and Webb (1979), for example, outline the use of the Delphi technique to ask knowledgeable residents and elites from the impact area, as well as professional experts from selected disciplines, to identify potential impacts.

A more comprehensive approach to identifying significant impacts is provided by Finsterbusch (1980) in his relevance tree. The relevance tree is a hierarchical display of categories that classifies areas in which impacts can occur. The level of analysis starts with four divisions — households, communities, organizations/groups, and social systems/institutions. Each of these is divided into four sectors: economic, political, societal, and cultural (communities also have an environmental sector). Each sector is divided into more specific impact areas. The assessor uses the relevance tree

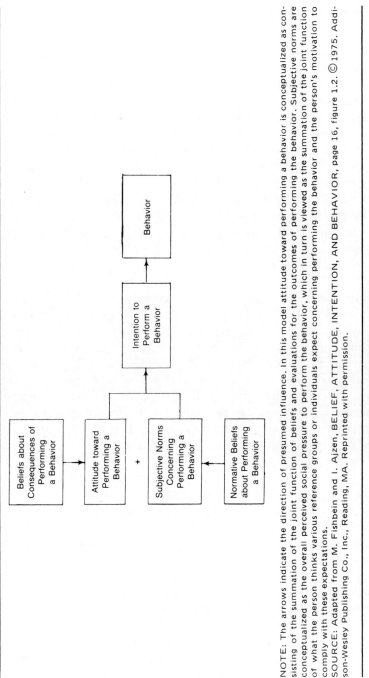

NOTE: The arrows indicate the direction of presumed influence. In this model attitude toward performing a behavior is conceptualized as consisting of the summation of the joint function of beliefs and evaluations for the outcomes of performing the behavior. Subjective norms are conceptualized as the overall perceived social pressure to perform the behavior, which in turn is viewed as the summation of the joint function of what the person thinks various reference groups or individuals expect concerning performing the behavior and the person's motivation to comply with these expectations.

SOURCE: Adapted from M. Fishbein and I. Ajzen, BELIEF, ATTITUDE, INTENTION, AND BEHAVIOR, page 16, figure 1.2. ©1975. Addison-Wesley Publishing Co., Inc., Reading, MA. Reprinted with permission.

Figure 11.1 Fishbein and Ajzen's Model for the Prediction of Intention and Behavior

as a stimulus to his or her imagination when creating a fairly inclusive list of potential impacts. Next, a much smaller list of potential impacts is selected for study on the basis of seven criteria: probability, number of people affected, extent of impact, causes of higher-order impacts, data availability, policy relevance, and public interest.

The relevance tree approach of Finsterbusch and simpler checklist approaches commonly used in SIAs are usually misleading in one important respect. They suggest that there are many important impacts to be considered. At the level of cognitive organization, however, only a small number of variables may have meaning to the individual. Fishbein and Ajzen (1975) suggest that as few as 5 to 9 beliefs about an object serve as the determinants of a person's attitude toward an object. For example, Sundstrom, Costomiris, et al. (1981) report on the survey results from a sample of 288 residents of Hartsville, Tennessee, which, at the time of the survey (1975) was the site of the world's largest planned nuclear reactor (for further information of the "Hartsville studies," see Schuller et al., 1975; Sundstrom et al., 1977). Based on a review of the existing literature and interviews with community elites and with representatives of the agency constructing the plant (the Tennessee Valley Authority), a list of 27 possible important effects was developed. Respondents were asked to rate the likelihood of occurrence of each event as well as the desirability of each event. To reduce the dimensionality of the set of items, a principal components factor analysis was performed on the perceived likelihood scores (there was too little variance on the "good" and "bad" outcomes to produce a meaningful factor analysis of the desirability scores). The results of this analysis are summarized in Table 11.1.

As can be seen in this table, five factors emerged, which were labeled "disruptive effects of growth," "hazards to health and environment," "increased business and development," "outside attention and recognition," and "economic benefits of growth." Although the specific content varies from item to item, we note that four of these factors correspond to equivalent second-level community impact dimensions in Finsterbusch's impact relevance tree; namely, the increased business factor and economic benefits growth factor correspond to Finsterbusch's economic category; the hazards to health and environment factor, corresponds to his environmental category; and the disruptive effects of growth factor contains elements similar to some of those found in Finsterbusch's political factor. This finding not only provides some empirical support for Finsterbusch's impact relevance tree, it tends to reinforce the previously suggested notion that

TABLE 11.1 Perceived Likelihood of 27 Potential Effects in the Hartsville Sample

Group of Effects	Effects	Likelihood Scores Mean	Standard Deviation
Disruptive	traffic congestion	1.88	1.17
effects	more taverns and bars	1.45	1.07
of	crowding in schools	1.63	1.10
growth	increased noise	1.50	1.09
	increased crime	1.20	1.17
	drugs in schools	1.30	1.19
	increased taxes	0.93	1.19
	housing shortages	1.76	1.02
Hazards	radiation hazards	0.03	1.41
to	air pollution	0.53	1.28
health	sabotage at the plant	0.50	0.76
and	foggy days	0.10	1.42
environment	pollution of lake	0.49	1.35
Increased	more store and shopping areas	1.19	1.05
business	more public entertainment	0.84	1.23
and	more recreation areas	0.88	1.16
development	more billboards	0.62	1.17
Outside	more tourism	0.63	1.36
attention	public recognition of the town	1.49	1.15
and	more opportunity to meet new people	1.66	1.02
recognition	industrial development	0.97	1.15
Economic	more jobs	1.43	1.05
benefits	better-paying jobs	1.30	1.15
of	better schools	0.34	1.41
growth	increased land values	1.44	1.19

NOTE: Response options for the perceived likelihood items were as follows: Certain = +3.0; very likely = +2.0; likely = +1.0; perhaps = 0; unlikely = −1.0; very unlikely = −2.0; almost impossible = −3.0.

a. Grouped on the basis of a factor analysis.

only a relatively small number of belief categories are salient for an individual's assessment of a project.

Attitudes and Beliefs by Stage of Project

Another approach to studying attitudes, beliefs, and intentions in an SIA is to reference them against the different stages of development of the project. Thus, for example, as a project develops and progresses through the stages of initial planning, site selection, negotiation, construction, and operation, there may be significant shifts in people's project-related beliefs and attitudes, particularly as they acquire new information about the project and experience different aspects of its consequences. As might be expected, the most common approach to studying psychosocial impacts at different stages of the life of a project has been to use two occasions of measurement: the first corresponding generally to the period of time before construction or peak development and the second occurring after a project has been completed or after construction work has subsided.

Napier and Moody (1979), for example, studied attitudes toward community variables among members of a small farming community before and after a large water impoundment was created. Initial measurement occurred during the land acquisition phase. Follow-up measurement occurred four years later at completion of the impoundment, after some 8800 acres of privately owned land had been removed from the tax rolls and 133 families had been relocated from the basin area. Contrary to the fragmentation of the community that the authors thought would occur, three of the five attitudinal variables were found to increase over time — community identification, feelings of integration with the community, and community satisfaction. As hypothesized, opposition to change and involvement in family interaction increased over time. Unfortunately, while the authors speculate on possible explanations for the increase in positive community attitudes (for example, more and better public services were provided, which may have resulted in more favorable attitudes toward community life), no evidence was presented to show that such factors were correlated with, or led to, attitude change. Nor was the analysis disaggregated by relocated versus nonrelocated residents, which might have shown more negative attitudes among those most directly affected.

One study that did focus on relocated residents was conducted by Burdge and Johnson (1973). They analyzed data collected before and after relocation from families and individuals who were forced to move because of the construction of the Carr Fork Reservoir. At the time of initial notification to residents about the reservoir (at which time residents knew few details about actual impacts), a majority of the sample of 400 residents was found to have generally positive or "acquiescent" responses on a reservoir development attitude scale. Approximately four years later, 300 of the displaced residents were resurveyed, at which time a majority of the sample held negative attitudes toward reservoir development. It appeared that most of the people who had been disrupted were disappointed with their experiences. One problem with the attitude measures collected is that they were somewhat general in nature and did not mention the Carr Fork Reservoir by name. For example, only 12 percent of the premigration sample agreed with the item "More dams are being built than are necessary for flood control," whereas 57 percent of the postmigration sample agreed with this item. There were few specific data concerning people's perceptions of the reservoir project and its attendant consequences, and how these change over time.

A study by Hughey (1981) provides one further example of studying attitudes and beliefs at various stages of a project. Extending the work of Sundstrom et al. (1977) and Lounsbury et al. (1977), he resurveyed 217 residents of Hartsville, Tennessee, to study potential changes in their attitudes and beliefs over a five-year period. The first set of measures had been collected in the summer of 1975, at the time of the initial announcement of the plant's siting; the second survey was conducted in the spring and summer of 1980, the year in which the construction labor force was at a peak. One of Hughey's analyses involved using the belief factor scores (see Table 11.1) to predict overall attitude toward the plant. In 1975 each of the five factors was significantly correlated with overall attitude toward the plant and, in a stepwise multiple regression analysis, it was found that two of the factors — hazards and economic benefits — accounted for 52 percent of the variance in global attitude toward construction of the plant. These factors were replicated and analyzed in the 1980 survey. Using the 1980 data with the replicated (from 1975) factors, 51 percent of the variance in overall attitude was accounted for by three factors — hazards, economic benefits, and social disruption. But perhaps the most interesting analysis performed by Hughey was one in which the panel members' 1975 scores on the belief factors were used to predict their 1980 attitudes toward the plant. In this case, four of the five factors correlated significantly with the 1980 global attitude score and 23 percent of the variance in 1980 attitude toward the Hartsville nuclear power plant was accounted for by two of the factors — hazards and economic benefits. Thus it appears that residents' beliefs about the likelihood of hazards to health and to the environment as well as the anticipated economic benefits of growth have a significant and fairly long-lasting effect in accounting for a person's attitude toward a nuclear power plant.

Intentions and Behavioral Responses in Psychosocial Assessment

One limitation of the line of research on the Hartsville plant, as well as most other studies of psychosocial impacts, is that intended and actual behaviors were seldom studied, particularly in relation to attitudes and beliefs. The questions of whether attitudes are associated with behaviors and what role intentions play in attitude-behavior linkages has, of course, stimulated an extensive body of literature in social psychology (see, for example, reviews by Wicker, 1969; Schuman and Johnson, 1976; Ajzen and Fishbein, 1977; Bentler and Speckart, 1979). Space does not permit us to summarize that literature here, but we do note that information about behavioral intentions and behaviors could have substantial value in the psychosocial assessment arena.

In one study, Little and Lovejoy (1980) obtained the responses of Utah and Arizona residents to the proposed Kaiparowits generating station, a nine-month, coal-fired electric generating station designed to serve the electric power needs of Arizona and Southern California. In addition to assessing global attitudes toward the project among 248 residents of 3 nearby communities (83 percent were in favor of it), Little and Lovejoy asked residents whether they would seek employment with the project (nearly 30 percent said they were planning to). Based on these data and on available employment statistics, the authors projected the total employment benefits (minimal) that could be expected to accrue to the communities. Unfortunately, the authors made no effort to relate the job-seeking intention measure to the attitudinal measure; but they did assess primary reasons for attitudes toward the Kaiparowits project. The main reasons listed for supporting it were "We need the power" and "Economic and employment benefits." The two major reasons for opposing the project were "We don't need the power" and "Will harm the environment." In this respect, Little and Lovejoy's study is consistent with the Hartsville studies in reaffirming the primary role of beliefs about economic benefits and environmental hazards as determinants of global attitude toward the impact event.

As part of another study to assess the social effects of an electrical load control program, Van Liere et al. (1982) examined intentions to participate in the program along with attitudes toward participation in the project and social pressure to participate. They found that these latter variables did predict intentions with moderate success ($R^2 = .38$ in one community and $R^2 = .30$ in the other community). It should be noted that in this study intention to participate was the key dependent variable, because the major interest at that stage of the project was to identify how much success the load management program would have in enlisting households to participate. Thus intentions can be important dependent variables in their own right, as well as independent variables used to predict other variables.

There is always the question of whether behavioral intentions predict subsequent behavior. A number of studies in other areas have shown that they do (see Ajzen and Fishbein, 1980). More relevant to the present topic is a study by Bowman and Fishbein (1978). They surveyed eligible voters in Oregon's 1976 general election on their intention to vote for or against a measure that would place restrictions on future power plants built in that state. As hypothesized, voting intentions were very strongly predictive of actual voting behavior ($r = .89$, $p < .01$). Additionally, Bowman and Fishbein found that attitudes toward the act of voting for the measure and beliefs about one's norm group's support for voting for the measure were significantly related to voting intention and voting behavior, but that the latter correlations disappeared when intention scores were partialled out. Overall, their results provide continuing support for Fishbein's general attitude model.

Global Levels of Support for or Opposition to Projects

At this point, we can make some tentative generalizations about overall levels of support for or opposition to impact events. Concerning projects that are designed to produce energy, it appears that at least two-thirds of the general public typically favor construction of these projects, *when the persons responding are not directly or immediately affected.* For example, in a national survey of the American public conducted by Louis Harris and Associates (1975), the following percentages of the total public favoring specific projects were observed: the Alaska oil pipeline, 81 percent; oil shale production in western states, 67 percent; building new nuclear power plants, 67 percent; off-shore (U.S. shores) drilling for oil, 66 percent.

Similarly, Little and Lovejoy (1980) found that 83 percent of the residents of Utah and Arizona counties favored construction of the Kaiparowits generating station. And the Hartsville studies discussed previously found that 69 percent of the residents of Trousdale County initially favored construction of the nuclear power plant near Hartsville. However, in the five-year follow-up, only 35 percent of the residents favored construction of the plant (which appeared to be the result of negative experiences during the peak construction period and unmet expectations over time). Another study consistent with the commonsense hypothesis that negative experiences may reduce public support for a project is the previously cited study of forced relocation of residents in an impoundment basin, where opposition to general dam construction for flood control increased from 12 percent to 57 percent. Support for impact projects also differs among socioeconomic, political, and interest group categories. For example, as might be expected, environmentalists have been found to be opposed to nuclear power plant construction more frequently than have business leaders (in the above-mentioned Harris poll, the percentages were 8 percent of the business leaders opposed to new nuclear power plant construction versus 79 percent of the environmentalists opposed).

As a final note on global public attitudes concerning impact projects, we offer the suggestion that overall levels of public support may vary by type of project, particularly when the benefits and costs are less salient or less clear than in the case of energy-generating facilities. In his study of Knoxville residents' attitudes toward the proposed 1982 International Energy Exposition (later upgraded to the status of a World's Fair), Meissen (1981) found that only 39 percent of the sample favored holding the event. A year later, Massey (1982) found that support for the exposition was only 43 percent among Knoxville residents. However, in a third, follow-up survey conducted by Massey and Meissen (1982) during the fair, they found that nearly 60 percent of the Knoxville residents favored the event. The difference between the later positive findings and the earlier negative findings may reflect the changing expectations of residents about the positive features of the fair as they experienced it directly.

The Role of Knowledge
in Attitudes and Beliefs

An important consideration in any research on public opinion concerning impact projects is the level of knowledge people have about the project and its consequences. At the early stages of a project, there is usually considerable effort expended by the media and public relations units of the agency sponsoring the project to inform the public about what they can (or should) expect in the way of consequences and outcomes of the project. The knowledge obtained by an individual can be viewed as the starting point for his or her ensuing beliefs and attitudes toward the project. One obvious line of inquiry concerns the sources of information utilized by individuals and the relative credibility of various sources of information about a project. Another logical area of interest to the social impact researcher is the knowledge base itself. For example, are individuals sampled well-informed or poorly informed about the project? And does an individual's knowledge base influence his or her attitude toward the project? Albrecht (1972: 4) reports on the responses of local citizens in two southern Utah counties toward proposed power plant construction and concludes: "Our data show very clearly that even in areas where the people will be most affected by the plants, the knowledge level upon which the attitudes are based is very low." He found that many people were not knowledgeable about the number of persons who would be employed by the plants, the amount of water (a variable resource in that area) the plants would use, what would be done with the water used for cooling, and so forth. Ultimately, consideration of knowledge levels could influence not only practical interventions such as increased efforts to disseminate information, but also the development of theoretical models of attitudes and beliefs in SIA.

One study that focused on the role of knowledge was Lounsbury et al.'s (1979) analysis of knowledge levels among Hartsville residents at the time of the second community survey. Using a seven-item, multiple-choice scale dealing with factual items about the plant (such as the number of reactors to be built, the amount of acreage required for the site, and the size of the peak construction force), they found that there were no differences between high- and low-knowledge groups on overall attitude toward the plant, although the high-knowledge respondents did mention more things they would worry about as a result of plant construction. They did find that respondent knowledge served as a significant moderator of the relationship between the perceived likelihood of various effects and overall attitude.

Thus the correlations between overall attitude toward the plant and the perceived likelihood of social disruption, increased business and development, and outside attention and recognition were significantly higher among the high-knowledge groups (with r's of −.59, .33, and .36, respectively) than among the low-knowledge groups (with r's of −.41, .13, and .13, respectively). One way to view such results is to say that the attitudes of more highly informed residents are more predictable from their beliefs than are the attitudes of less informed residents. But, on a larger scale, one can see that quite different construct relationships and empirically verified principles might be found, depending upon the knowledge level of respondents. If one is interested solely in obtaining point estimates about community attitudes, one could disregard knowledge levels. However, if one is interested in maximizing predictability, one might wish to discard, ignore, or not collect data from respondents with little or no knowledge about a project. Or, one might try to improve knowledge levels prior to attitude and belief assessment. At this point, we can only conclude that the role of knowledge should be more fully explored in the study of impact-related beliefs and attitudes.

Assessing Well-Being and Other Internal States

To this point, we have focused primarily on beliefs, attitudes, and intentions that are specifically related to a project. Another broad category of beliefs, attitudes, and intentions that is important in the psychosocial assessment process is that of internal states that reflect the personal well-being of individuals. These include alienation, subjective well-being, personal satisfactions, locus of control, and perceived loss of freedom.

While these attributes are being widely studied in the disciplines of sociology and psychology, there has been but scant attention paid to them by researchers who have studied psychosocial impacts. However, some initial efforts have been made to assess such variables as part of the potential and actual effects or residents of impact communities.

Freudenberg (1981) examined citizen responses to a survey conducted in a western community experiencing a "construction boom" and in three other "control" communities. Making separate analyses for men versus women and "newcomers" versus "oldtimers," he found no differences between the impact and control communities on a person's avowed happiness, overall life satisfaction and quality of life, feelings of accomplishment, and social integration. Only three out of twelve differences on alienation measures were observed. These three were all in the direction of male oldtimers in the boomtown experiencing greater alienation than male oldtimers in the control communities.

Napier (1972) studied the social-psychological responses of residents in two Ohio and two West Virginia communities that had been affected by the construction of a water impoundment. Comparisons were made between residents who had been subjected to forced relocation and those who had not been subjected to forced relocation. Napier also compared responses in the "initial-shock" period (at the stage of initial land acquisition) and the "postshock" period (at the later stage, when time relocation had been completed). The dependent variable in all comparisons was alienation from the community (as measured by feelings of powerlessness and estrangement from social systems in the community). Contrary to expectation, no differences were found between the located and relocated groups. The only observed difference was in the West Virginia communities, where there was an increase in alienation between the initial- and postshock groups. Napier suggests that the negative attitudes that did occur in the impact communities might have been directed more toward the external change agent than toward social relationships within the community.

Sundstrom et al. (1977) examined changes in personal life satisfaction and perceptions of "neighborhood life" among residents of Hartsville over a six-month period during the planning and initial licensing phase of the project to construct the Hartsville nuclear power plant. They found that a person's satisfaction with his or her own "life at present" and "life five years ago" both decreased significantly during that period. Also observed was a significant decrease in the extent to which neighborhoods were as "stable," "uncrowded," "close-knit," "quiet," "pretty," and populated with "people similar to me " — all of which were positive features of community life for the overwhelming majority of Hartsville residents.

Finally, Meissen (1981) found that the single highest correlate (r = .67) of attitude toward the Knoxville World's Fair was local political efficacy (defined primarily in terms of the degree to which citizens perceived that they has a voice in determining whether or not the fair should be held in their community). He also found that a resident's feeling of political efficacy with regard to the fair was significantly correlated (r = .46) with the ratio of positive to negative community impacts that the resident saw as likely to occur as a result of the fair. Meissen interpreted these results as being consistent with alienation theory, particularly in terms of the impact of perceived powerlessness on citizen response to the project.

Analyzing Trade-Offs

The concept of trade-off is also important in the SIA process. A trade-off implies a compromise of exchange between two or more competing goals. When individuals express a trade-off preference, they are indicating the amount of one attribute they are willing to give in order to gain some amount of another attribute. Quite often, in analyzing social impacts, it is the residents' trade-off preferences that the analyst is most interested in learning. Although trade-off analysis has not been widely used in the area of psychosocial assessment, it would appear to be an important area for future research. The literature to date suggests that most impact projects are perceived as bringing highly salient and valenced outcomes of both a desirable and undesirable nature. Overall attitude toward such projects is almost certainly the result of a trade-off between these different types of outcomes. The analysis of trade-off preferences is potentially superior to other methods of assessing attitudes toward a project for the following reasons: (1) trade-offs may generate results based on more informed judgment since constraints are obvious; (2) preferences regarding future states, rather than preferences for existing states, are readily defined and studied; (3) trade-off questions may help educate the respondent about the contingencies associated with relevant choices; and (4) it may be possible to assess attitudes toward "intangible" costs and benefits that do not fit well in more objective cost-benefit equations (Robinson et al., 1975; Dowall and Juhasz, 1978; Hoinville, 1971; Rohrbaugh and Wehr, 1978).

The analysis of trade-off preferences requires two types of information. First, some set of attributes, goals, or dimensions important to the decision must be identified. Second, some method of measuring the degree to which individuals are willing to trade off one dimension for another must be established. Strategies for accomplishing these goals are quite varied. Robinson et al. (1975) review different "gaming" approaches, whereas MacCrimmon and Siu (1974) use interactive computer programs, Dowall and Juhasz (1978) have respondents map their preferences on two-dimensional graphs, and Rohrbaugh and Wehr (1978) ask subjects to rate the desirability of alternative scenarios that include various combinations of five dimensions. Most of these studies are not directly related to the SIA domain as part of a broader environmental impact statement, but the techniques are developed for planning processes similar to the ones used in social impact analyses. (For a list of studies in this area, see Van Liere and Roth, 1980.)

The most important uses of trade-off analysis are as follows: First, the analysis will usually result in descriptive information that summarizes the overall trade-off priorities for a community. Rohrbaugh and Wehr (1978), for example, were able to conclude from their analysis of five dimensions — environmental conditions, economic conditions, self-determination, public services, and sense of community — that most clusters of citizens opposed very large changes in any one dimension. They also determined that none of the main clusters of citizens was concerned with the issue of self-determination relative to the other four dimensions.

A second use of trade-off analysis is to identify particular categories of individuals having similar trade-off preferences. Rohrbaugh and Wehr identified six relatively distinct categories. The largest group contained about 28 percent of the sample, while the remaining five groups each contained between 7 percent and 9 percent of the sample. They are also able to discover that family size, years of county residence, and years of formal education were the only demographic characteristics among those examined to be significantly different among the trade-off groups. On the other hand, Dowall and Juhasz (1978) conducted a trade-off analysis using different measuring techniques and were able to identify what they termed "communities of interest." These communities of interest represented various clusters of trade-off preferences and could be labeled with such descriptive terms as "hedonists, pragmatists, future-environment worriers, job hunters, and individualists." Thirteen of these communities of interest were located in their study of residents' preferences for land-use planning in a mountain area of Colorado. Similar to Rohrbaugh and Wehr, Dowall and Juhasz were also able to generate useful demographic profiles of these various clusters of trade-off preferences.

Methodological Considerations

Our review of the emergent empirical literature on psychosocial assessment would not be complete without consideration of the methodological quality of studies in this area. Unfortunately, there is a lack of methodological rigor on several fronts, ranging from research design to measurement to analytic techniques. We will briefly consider some of the problems with previous research and prospects for future research with respect to what we term "research design and measurement" issues.

Concerning the research design employed by psychosocial assessment studies, we note that most designs could be characterized as "one-shot" cases studies, with a single occasion of measurement and no control of comparison group. The methodological deficiencies of this type of study are well known and the reader is advised to consult sources such as Campbell and Stanley (1966) or Cook and Campbell (1979) for further details. Another approach was to use a "before-and-after" design, employing measurement of variables of interest before and after (or during) construction. Such studies are interesting, but there is little way to tell if changes that were observed in terms of the variables studied were the result of the impact project or other factors occurring in the community (such as increased growth, or higher taxes) or external events impinging on the community (such as economic recession, or changes in national media support for nuclear power). The challenge confronting research in this area, as in so many areas of social science, is to find some way to estimate what effects are the result of the project itself and what effects are a function of other factors.

One approach to controlling for some of the regional and national factors that might contribute to changes in attitudes and beliefs would be to utilize comparison communities that are not affected by the project but could be studied so as to serve as control groups against which the changes in the host community could be compared. Naturally, there might be many threats to the validity of comparisons between the host and "control" communities, depending on the equivalence of the communities on other important variables, such as size, in- and outmigration rates, degree of industrialization, employment rates, income levels, housing availability, transportation systems, and demographic and personal characteristics of community residents (for which the latter category could include such variables as attitudes toward nuclear power, community growth, and concern for the environment). However, when efforts to ensure equivalence on such factors are coupled with multiple occasions of measurement at various stages of a project, the use of research designs with host and control communities could do much to advance our understanding of which psychosocial changes in host communities are the result of the project under study and which changes are likely to result from or be mediated by other factors internal or external to the community.

Another potential advantage of concentrating on studies that use multiple comparison groups is that we might learn more about the generalizability of findings from one setting to another. At this point, for example, we do not know if the Hartsville findings will generalize to any other nuclear power plant construction in any other communities. Moreover, at present we know little about the degree to which knowledge derived from one type of project, such as the construction of a nuclear power plant, can be generalized to knowledge obtained in the context of a different technology, such as coal-fired electrical generating stations or a reservoir construction project. Lest this prospect seem too hopeless, we should reiterate that support for the Fishbein model, to name one, has been found in areas as widely disparate as weight control, drug taking, voting, buying behavior, dating, and support for nuclear power plant construction.

We have also observed some common shortcomings in the studies reviewed from a measurement perspective. Information was seldom presented on the reliability of measures used in a study. For example, most authors failed to report any index of the internal consistency of scales used to measure an attitude or belief (for which, say, a split-half reliability or alpha coefficient could have been used). Nor was any information provided on the stability or repeatability of measures — for which even a simple test-retest correlation coefficient could have been used. Absence of information on how reliable the measures are poses several problems for interpreting the data obtained from these measures. To the extent that the measures are not reliable, we must place less confidence in the accuracy of results. This is somewhat less of a problem where the datum of interest is a point estimate such as a mean score of community opinion averaged across a large number of respondents, because any random errors of measurement will tend to cancel each other out. The larger problem confronts attempts to study the relationship of one unreliable measure to another unreliable measure, in which case the estimate of the relationship (for example, a simple bivariate correlation) can be be substantially inaccurate owing to the joint effect of the two sources of error. We recommend that researchers in this area at least attempt to estimate (by some means) the reliability of the measures they use and report these estimates. This would held others to better evaluate the quality of the measures as well as possibly allow them to use more refined techniques, such as the "correction for attenuation" (see Nunnally, 1978), to revise the correlation and regression estimates produced from these measures.

Further attention should also be given to the methods of collecting data in psychosocial assessment. There is substantial reliance on the method of self-report, which is quite appropriate for measures of attitudes and beliefs. However, we could find no research in this area that examined whether the mode of data collection (face-to-face interviewing, telephone interviews, questionnaire mail-outs, or survey drop-off techniques) makes any difference in the quality of data obtained. Nor do we know if it matters whether the interviewer or sponsor of the data collection is perceived to be supportive of, opposed to, or neutral with respect to a controversial project. One could imagine that different results might be obtained by interviewers representing a power company, an environmental protection group, or a university.

On the whole, there is considerable opportunity for future researchers who would study psychosocial impacts to improve the quality of the research designs that have been used to date and to further inquire into the influence of various measurement strategies and psychometric characteristics on the quality of the data obtained.

Conclusions

Psychosocial assessment requires a more systematic approach to the identification of study areas and the cumulation of empirical findings if a useful body of research is to be developed. Like the broader area of social impact assessment, psychosocial assessment should attempt to use multiple theoretical perspectives in the context of applied research and still provide information useful in planning and decision making. In this chapter we have utilized an attitude theory perspective as a framework for approaching the study of psychosocial impacts. Such an approach seems to be effective since it has allowed us to organize and interpret many different concepts and empirical findings.

Out review also suggests that the question of what variables to study in a psychosocial assessment has been answered in many ways by previous studies, but there has not yet emerged a set of criteria or guidelines for making such choices. Improved use of experts, nominal groups, and a relevance tree would be beneficial in this regard. Also, replication of studies and the diffusion of research findings should identify empirical patterns that suggest the most fruitful variables for analysis.

Several other areas for improvement were also noted: First, a full understanding of psychosocial impacts requires more information gathered over time, at several critical stages of a project. Second, more research is clearly warranted on the question of the distribution of important beliefs and attitudes in affected populations and control populations (along with changes in these beliefs over time). Third, there should be much more methodological rigor in measurement practices and in the research designs used to study psychosocial impacts. To a large degree, the advancement of knowledge in the areas mentioned previously will depend on the methodological strength of the studies conducted.

Finally, research should be undertaken that not only systematically identifies patterns of beliefs and attitudes and describes changes in these patterns over time, but also asks why these patterns exist and why they change over time. It is hoped that researchers who work in this area will contribute to the answers to these questions as well as raise new questions that challenge the state of the art of psychosocial impact assessment.

References

ALBRECHT, S. L. (1972) "Sociological aspects of power plant siting." Prepared for the conference, "Developing Utah's Energy Resources — Problems and Opportunities," Salt Lake City, May 25.

AJZEN, I. and M. FISHBEIN (1980) Understanding Attitudes and Predicting Social Behavior. Englewood Cliffs, NJ: Prentice-Hall.

———— (1977) "Attitude-behavior relations: A theoretical analysis and review of empirical research." Psychological Bulletin 84: 888-918.

BENTLER, P. M. and G. SPECKART (1979) "Models of attitude-behavior relations." Psychological Review 86: 452-464.

BOWMAN, C. and M. FISHBEIN (1978) "Understanding public reaction to energy proposals: an application of the Fishbein model." Journal of Applied Social Psychology 8: 319-340.

BURDGE, R. J. and K. S. JOHNSON (1973) Social Costs and Benefits of Water Resource Construction. Lexington: Water Resources Research Institute, University of Kentiucky.

CAMPBELL, D. T. and J. C. STANLEY (1966) Experimental and Quasi-Experimental Designs for Research. Chicago: Rand McNally.

COOK, T. D. and D. T. CAMPBELL (1979) Quasi-Experimentation: Design and Analysis Issues for Field Settings. Chicago: Rand McNally.

DAVENPORT, J. A. and J. DAVENPORT (1979) "A town and gown approach to boom town problems," pp. 127-142 in J. A. Davenport and J. Davenport (eds.) Boom Towns and Human Services. Laramie: University of Wyoming.

DEANE D. H. and J. L. MUMPOWER (1977) "The social psychological level of analysis in social impact assessment: individual well-being, psychosocial climates, and the environmental assessment scale," pp 132-152 in K. Finsterbusch and C. P. Wolfe (eds.) Methodology of Social Impact Assessment. Stroudsburg, PA: Hutchinson Ross.

DOWALL, D. E. and J. B. JUHASZ (1978) "Trade-off surveys in planning: theory and application." Environment and Planning 10: 125-136.

EHRLICH, H. (1969) "Attitudes, behavior, and the intervening variable." American Sociologist 4: 29-34.

FELLMAN, G. and B. BRANDT (1970) "A neighborhood a highway would destroy." Environment and Behavior 2: 281-301.

FINSTERBUSCH, K. (1980) Understanding Social Impacts: Assessing the Effects of Public Projects. Beverly Hills, CA: Sage.

FISHBEIN, M. and I. AJZEN (1975) Belief, Attitude, Intention and Behavior: An Introduction to Theory and Research. Reading, MA: Addison-Wesley.

———— (1974) "Attitudes toward objects as predictors of single and multiple behavioral criteria." Psychological Review 81: 59-74.

FITZSIMMONS, S. J., L. I. STUART, and P. C. WOLFF (1975) Social Assessment Manual. Cambridge, MA: Abt Associates.

FREUDENBERG, W. R. (1981) "Women and men in an energy boomtown: adjustment, alienation, and adaptation." Rural Sociology 46: 220-224.

Louis Harris and Associates (1975) A Survey of Public and Leadership Attitudes Toward Nuclear Power Development in the United States. New York: Ebasco Services.

HOINVILLE, G. (1971) "Evaluating community preferences." Environment and Planning 3: 33-50.

HUGHEY, J. B. (1981) "Longitudinal assessment of attitudes toward a nuclear power plant." Ph.D. dissertation, University of Tennessee.

KENNEDY, D. A. (1979) "Health care in boom town," pp. 19-30 in J. A. Davenport and J. Davenport (eds.) Boom Towns and Human Services. Laramie: University of Wyoming.

LaPIERE, R. T. (1934) "Attitudes versus actions." Social Forces 13: 230-237.

LEWIS, H. M. (1980) "Social impact: Ignored or mistreated component in environmental impact research." Human Services in the Rural Environment 5: 12-16.

LITTLE, R. L. and S. B. LOVEJOY (1980) "Energy development and local employment," pp. 169-190 in J. Davenport and J.A. Davenport (eds.) The Boom Town: Problems and Promises in the Energy Vortex. Laramie: University of Wyoming.

LOUNSBURY, J. W., E. SUNDSTROM, and R. C. DeVAULT (1979) "Moderating effects of respondent knowledge in public opinion research." Journal of Applied Psychology 64: 558-563.

LOUNSBURY, J. W., E. SUNDSTROM, C. R. SCHULLER, T. J. MATTINGLY, and R. C. DeVAULT (1977) "Toward an assessment of the potential social impacts of a nuclear power plant on a community: survey of residents' views." 265-277 in K. Finsterbusch and C. P. Wolf (eds.) Methodology of Social Impact Assessment. Stroudsburg, PA: Hutchinson Ross.

MacCRIMMON, K. R. and H. K. SIU (1974) "Making trade-offs." Decision Sciences 5: 680-704.

MASSEY, O. T. (1982) "An application of diffusion of innovation theory in the analysis of attitudes toward the 1982 World's Energy Exposition." Ph.D. dissertation, University of Tennessee.

———— and G. J. MEISSEN (1982) Personal communication, February.

MEISSEN, G. J. (1981) "A differential analysis of the perceived social impacts of a World's Exposition." Ph.D. dissertation, University of Tennessee.

NAPIER, T. L. (1972) "Social-psychological response to forced relocation due to watershed development." Water Resources Bulletin 8: 784-794.

———— and C. W. MOODY (1979) "The social impact of watershed development: a longitudinal study." Water Resources Bulletin 15: 692-705.

NUNNALLY, J. C. (1978) Psychometric Theory. New York: McGraw-Hill.

ROBINSON, I. M., W. C. BAER, T. K. BANERJEE, and P. G. FLASCHBART (1975) "Trade-off games," pp. 79-118 in W. Michelson (ed.) Behavioral Research Methods in Environmental Design. Stroudsburg, PA: Hutchinson Ross.

ROHRBAUGH, J. and P. WEHR (1978) "Judgment analysis in policy formation: a new method for improving public participation." Public Opinion Quarterly 42: 521-532.

SCHULLER, C. R., J. R. FOWLER, T. J. MATTINGLY, E. SUNDSTROM, J. W. LOUNSBURY, E. M. PASSINO, D. A. DOWELL, and G. J. HUTTON (1975) Citizens' Views about the Proposed Hartsville Nuclear Power Plant: A Preliminary Report of Potential Social Impacts. Oak Ridge, TN: Oak Ridge National Laboratory.

SCHUMAN, H. and M. P. JOHNSON (1976) "Attitudes and behavior." Annual Review of Sociology 2: 161-207.

SINGG, R. N. and B. R. WEBB (1979) "Use of Delphi methodology to assess goals and social impacts of a watershed project." Water Resources Bulletin 15: 136-143.

SMITH, C. L. and T. C. HOGG (1971) "Cultural aspects of water resource development past, present and future." Water Resources Bulletin 7: 652-660.

SUNDSTROM, E. D., LOUNSBURY, J. W., R. C. DeVAULT, and E. PEELLE (1981) "Acceptance of nuclear power plant: applications of the expectancy-value model." pp. 171-189 in A. Baum and J. E. Singer (eds.) Energy Conservation: Psychological Perspectives. Advances in Environmental Psychology, Vol. III. Hillsdale, NJ: Lawrence Erlbaum.

SUNDSTROM, E. D., J. W. LOUNSBURY, C. R. SCHULLER, J. R. FOWLER, and T. J. MATTINGLY (1977) "Community attitudes toward a proposed nuclear power generating facility as a function of expected outcomes." Journal of Community Psychology 5: 199-208.

SUNDSTROM, E. D., L. J. COSTOMIRIS, R. C. DeVAULT, D. A. DOWELL, J. W. LOUNSBURY, T. J. MATTINGLY, E. M. PASSINO, and E. PEELLE (1981) Citizens' Views About the Proposed Hartsville Nuclear Power Plant: A Survey of Residents' Perceptions in August 1975. Oak Ridge, TN: Oak Ridge National Laboratory.

VAN LIERE, K. D. and R. F. ROTH (1980) Public Perception of Environmental Tradeoffs: A Preliminary Bibliography. Monticello, IL: Vance Bibliographies.

VAN LIERE, K. D., D. R. PLOCH, M. S. KUHN, C. M. HAND, B. W. McCONNELL, and B. H. BRONFMAN (1982) Public Reactions to Load Management: A Summary of Baseline Community Data for the Athens Automotion and Control Experiment. Oak Ridge, TN: Oak Ridge National Laboratory.

WEISZ, R. (1979) "Stress and mental health in a boom town," pp. 31-48 in J. A. Davenport and J. Davenport (eds.) Boom Towns and Human Services. Laramie: University of Wyoming.

WICKER, A. W. (1969) "Attitudes vs. actions: the relationship of verbal and overt behavioral responses to attitude objects." Journal of Social Issues 25: 41-78.

12

Causes and Correctives for Errors of Judgment

O O O O O O O O O O O O O O O O O

JERYL MUMPOWER and
BARRY F. ANDERSON

O O O O O O O O O O O O O O O O O

● This chapter develops the following set of recommendations for improving the judgments that must be made in any social impact assessment:

(1) Learn to recognize when a judgment is required.

(2) Separate fact and value judgments. Assign the fact judgments to technical experts and the value judgments to sampled, elected, or appointed representatives of the public.

(3) Decompose each judgment problem into subproblems that are easy to think about.

(4) Take steps to ensure that probability judgments will be based as clearly as possible on numbers or estimated numbers of cases, rather than on salient, but uninformative, aspects of the problem at hand.

(5) Take steps to ensure that the cases considered will be representative of the situation being judged and not simply of the judge's past or current experience.

(6) Employ graphic aids to help the judge keep pertinent data in mind.

Authors' Note: Any opinions, findings, conclusions, or recommendations expressed in this chapter are those of the authors and do not necessarily reflect the view of the National Science Foundation.

(7) Obtain multiple judgments, either from the same judge or, preferably, from a number of judges. If a group is employed, take steps to minimize the negative effects of group interaction.

(8) Obtain the judgments in different ways, proceeding from different starting points.

(9) Average the repeated judgments for each subproblem.

(10) Combine the component judgments into an overall judgment by means of a model (adding, multiplying, and so on) judged to be appropriate.

These recommendations are arrived at by considering (a) the judgmental tasks involved in social impact assessment, (b) cognitive processes, (c) the quality of human judgment, (d) judgmental inconsistency, and (e) judgmental bias.

Judgmental Tasks in Social Impact Assessment

Social impact assessment (SIA) is necessarily based on human judgment. Defining and structuring SIA problems require judgments about what plans and scenarios to retain for further analysis. Projecting impacts requires technical judgments, involving expertise in a variety of fields. And selecting a recommended plan requires value judgments, by the decision maker, about the desirability of various impacts. The role of human judgment in SIA is pervasive. This chapter, however, will focus specifically on its role in projecting and evaluating impacts.

Judgment is involved in *projecting* impacts whenever experts are used to predict the effects of alternative courses of action, as is frequently the case. For instance, projections of the social impacts of alternative air pollution management plans may require social scientists, physicians, physicists, engineers, and others to go "beyond the data" in order to address policy-relevant questions for which scientific research has not provided definitive answers. Even in those instances in which impact projection is based on formal, analytic models, the role of judgment is important, although perhaps less apparent. The selection of a model, the choice of inputs to it, and the interpretation of its outputs are all ultimately based upon someone's judgments. Using regression techniques in a trend analysis projecting a number of visitors in a national park, for instance, involves judgments concerning whether linear extrapolation is appropriate, whether data for the last five years (or ten or twenty) should be used, and so forth. The use of formal models or "standard" techniques may obscure the role of judgment in projection, but judgment remains important, nonetheless.

The role of judgment in *evaluating* impacts is even clearer. Decisions must be made about whether projected impacts are good or bad and whether the beneficial outcomes outweigh the negative ones. In addition to judgments about "trade-offs," judgments frequently must be made about how to cope with uncertainty in projected impacts. If the analysis indicates that the health impacts of a waste disposal facility are probably insignificant, but that there exists a slim chance that they might be catastrophic, what implications does this have for the selection of a recommended alternative? Because there are no hard-and-fast, universally accepted rules or formulas to follow in deciding which plan is best, the use of judgment for evaluating impacts is unavoidable.

The process of projecting impacts is sometimes distinguished from the process of evaluating them on the grounds that projections should rely upon expert, technical judgment, whereas evaluations require judgments that are the appropriate responsibility of the public or its representatives. Though we, too, shall argue for an analysis of complex judgment problems into fact and value components, we shall have little occasion to treat these two kinds of judgments differently, since, so far as is known, the psychological processes underlying them are essentially the same.

Cognitive Processes

Certain fundamental cognitive processes appear to be involved in a very wide range of cognitive tasks. This should be no surprise, since it is the same brain that is at work on these tasks. It is instructive to examine the nature of these processes and to consider their deficiencies and ways to correct for them.

An important distinction among human thought processes is between those that are automatic, effortless, and unconscious and those that are voluntary, effortful, and conscious (Anderson, 1975; Luria, 1973; Posner, 1973). One way to demonstrate the difference between automatic and effortful processes is to set one against the other. In hidden-figures problems, for example, a smaller figure can be found within a larger figure, yet it is difficult to find. The reason for the difficulty is that the effortful processes used to arrange and rearrange mentally various parts of the larger figure, in the search for the smaller figure within it, tend to be opposed by automatic perceptual processes that arrange these parts differently. Similarly, when a person is trying to learn a new response, such as "chairperson," to replace an old one, such as "chairman," the effortful processes used to produce the new response are opposed by automatic associative processes that tend to produce the old one.

Automatic processes have two major weaknesses: They tend to make thought stimulus bound, and they tend to make it habit bound. Our thought tends to be stimulus bound in that it tends to be dominated by what can be represented by the automatic processes of perception. Out of sight is often out of mind. Judgments thus tend to be based only upon the stimuli that happen to be present when the judgments are being made (Fischhoff et al., 1978). Projecting the impacts of multifaceted interventions or evaluating the desirability of complex sets of outcomes may thus be unduly influenced by the specific aspects of the situation that circumstances make most salient. Our thought tends to be habit bound in that we tend to interpret and respond to stimuli only in accustomed ways. Thus judgments tend to be in terms of the familiar. In projecting uncertain future impacts, for example, this may result in scenarios that are not sufficiently different from the present.

Effortful processes have one major weakness: an extremely limited capacity. They can deal with, at most, some half dozen items at a time (see Miller, 1956; Broadbent, 1975). This is why simplifying strategies are often used to deal with problems of any complexity. As individuals try to cope with more and more information, they tend to switch from cognitive strategies that make full and systematic use of all available information to simpler strategies that use only some of the available information and that are less likely to lead to the optimal choice (Payne, 1976). Thinking carefully about the multitude of potential impacts of alternative plans, therefore, will almost always be quite difficult, as individuals try to deal with the limited capacities of their effortful cognitive processes, their desire to make the best possible decisions, and the need to conserve time and energy. (Portions of the foregoing discussion follow closely the discussion in Anderson, 1980: 8-13.)

The Quality of Human Judgment

As might be expected, the weaknesses inherent in automatic and effortful processes frequently lead to judgments that fall far short of the ideal. Evidence from numerous substantive areas suggests that expert judgment is often surprisingly poor. Research in psychology documenting the fallibility of expert judgment can be dated back to at least the 1950s, to studies comparing the predictive accuracy of clinical judgment versus actuarial methods for diagnosis. To the consternation of many, expert predictions lost these "contests" with actuarial methods.

Over the years, expert judgments in a number of fields have been shown to be fallible and subject to a variety of biases. In an extensive review focusing on forecasting in business, Hogarth and Makridakis (1981) reached similarly pessimistic conclusions about the accuracy of expert forecasts. Large errors in forecasts were characteristically found, and simple quantitative models generally outperformed judgmental predictions. Furthermore, research indicates that, with very few exceptions, the fallibility of predictive judgments appears to be even greater for probability estimates (as discussed in Lichtenstein et al., 1977), a discouraging finding for SIA, since predictions of social impacts are ordinarily made in the context of substantial uncertainty, where probabilistic predictions are appropriate.

Not only is there compelling evidence that individuals' predictive abilities are often quite poor, there is equally strong evidence that they do not recognize their own fallibility. Research has consistently found experts and nonexperts alike to be excessively confident concerning their judgmental prowess (Fischhoff et al., 1977).

Einhorn and Hogarth (1978; Einhorn, 1980a, 1980b) have explored possible explanations for such overconfidence in the face of empirical evidence pointing to its lack of justification. They have identified several contributing factors, including psychological biases toward evaluating one's performance on the basis of the absolute rather than the relative frequency of success. More important, they argue that the circumstances in which predictive judgments are made usually prevent individuals from ever learning that their judgmental ability is low, even if it is in fact altogether invalid. The central idea of their argument is that experience does not ordinarily provide the type of disconfirming evidence that would be necessary for learning about one's own judgmental limitations. Brehmer (1980) and Hammond (1978) have independently reached the same conclusion.

The implications of this body of research for SIA seem clear. Predictions of social impacts based in whole or in part on expert judgment are likely to be highly fallible, yet those making such judgments are likely to be confident about their validity. Although it is harder to assess the quality of evaluative judgments than the quality of expert predictions, there is no reason to believe that the processes we use to evaluate impacts are not subject to the same flaws as those we use to project them. It is all too easy to ignore judgmental weaknesses in an SIA, yet doing so may result in errors that seriously impair the quality of the SIA process.

Just as it is useful to distinguish between random error and constant error when considering sources of error in experiments, it will be convenient to draw a parallel distinction between inconsistency and bias when discussing sources of error in judgments.

Judgmental Inconsistency: Causes and Correctives

Inconsistency, or random error, in judgment is probably due to both the limited capacity of effortful processes, which can attend to only some of the aspects of any problem, and the stimulus- and habit-bound nature of automatic processes, which call attention to different aspects of the problem on different occasions. Judgmental inconsistency appears to increase with task unfamiliarity and complexity (Fischhoff et al., 1980) and with uncertainty (Brehmer, 1970, 1973).

Four types of correctives for judgmental inconsistency have been employed widely. Two of these, "bootstrapping" and the use of groups of judges, seek to counteract random error by increasing the number of judgments. Bootstrapping uses multiple judgments from the same individual; groups rely on judgments from multiple individuals. The third corrective seeks to reduce random error by using decomposition to reduce the complexity of the judgments an individual must make. The fourth uses graphic aids to memory to reduce variations in what is currently available in the individual's memory.

Multiple Judgments: Bootstrapping

Bootstrapping involves having an individual make judgments for each of a series of actual or hypothetical cases. If projecting impacts, the judge makes projections for cases drawn from a set in which the values of the predictor variables vary. For example, if projecting the safety of a highway design, a highway engineer might judge the safety of a series of hypothetical highways varying in terms of numbers of lanes, widths of lanes, speed limits, and so forth. Similarly, if evaluating impacts, the judge evaluates the desirability of cases drawn from a set in which the values of the outcome variables vary. For example, a state official evaluating the overall desirability of competing highway designs might judge a series of hypothetical designs varying in terms of their projected safety, cost, environmental impact, and so forth. On the basis of a series of cases and judgments, statistical techniques are used to develop a model that describes how the judge arrived at his or her judgments. Because the statistical model represents an average, much of the random error in individual judgments is canceled out. Using the model, rather than the judge, can thus improve the quality of judgments.

For SIA, the bootstrapping procedure may prove useful whenever a single expert must be relied upon to project a particular type of impact or a single decision maker must evaluate the projected impacts or alternative plans. Research suggests that it is ordinarily better to use the bootstrapping procedure to develop a model of the expert or decision maker on the basis of his or her judgments and then to use the model in place of the individual. Such a model preserves the knowledge or wisdom of the individual, while correcting for the judgmental inconsistency that can result in random errors in judgment.

Multiple Judgments:
Using Groups of Judges

An intuitively appealing procedure for responding to the problems associated with expert prediction is to obtain predictions from multiple experts. Several variants of this approach can be distinguished (for an extensive review, see Hogarth, 1977).

The simplest procedure for aggregating predictions from multiple (assuming their predictions can be expressed in some numeric form) is simply to compute an arithmetic mean. Predictions from such "statistical groups" are usually better than those of most of the individuals in the groups. Under conditions where (a) the qualify of individuals' judgments (for example, the correlations between their judgments and the criterion) and (b) the degree of similarity among experts (for example, the correlations among their judgments) are known or can be approximated, there are clear procedures for determining an appropriate group size and for selecting specific individuals for inclusion. The logic is similar to that involved in developing psychological tests. The validity of the group prediction, like the validity of a test, depends on three factors: (a) the quality of each expert's judgments ("item validity"); (b) the size of the group (which affects "test reliability"); and (c) the degree of uniqueness (or nonredundancy) of each individual's predictive ability. (It is reasonable to wonder about the "optimal" size of groups, or the appropriate minimum size. Unfortunately, there is no good and simple answer to this question, particularly since many extraneous factors, such as social, political, and monetary ones, also come into play. A *very* rough rule of thumb is that it may ordinarily be wise to try to increase group size up to the point where potential new group members can be expected to hold very similar views to individuals already in the group.)

Although the performance of groups may not be as good as that of their best member, identifying the best member before the fact is usually quite difficult, if not impossible. As odd as it may seem, when computing group predictions it is probably unwise even to weight individuals according to their presumed expertise (Hogarth, 1977). The penalties associated with inaccurate assessments of expertise are likely to be greater than those associated with simply giving equal weight to each individual (Dawes and Corrigan, 1974; Einhorn and Hogarth, 1975).

The discussion to this point has assumed that the group is merely statistical, that is, while the judgments of its members are pooled, the members themselves do not interact. This, of course, need not be the case. When the members of a group interact, considerations in addition to the statistical ones discussed so far enter the picture. Group interaction can benefit judgmental performance in some ways, yet in others it can be a detriment.

The primary problem associated with interacting groups of experts is that, although such groups presumably possess the potential for improved prediction (for example, a broader base of knowledge, skills, and abilities, plus opportunities for criticizing, correcting, and learning from one another), other concomitants of group interaction and discussion may interfere with realizing that potential (Hackman and Morris, 1975; Hogarth, 1977). For example, there is a large body of research concerning biases in group judgments resulting from social pressures to conform. In a similar vein, Janis (1972) has studied group dynamics that lead to what he has termed "groupthink." In short, although research suggests that establishing groups of interacting experts for making predictions and forecasts of impacts may be better than relying on individuals or statistical groups, there are numerous pitfalls attending this approach.

The *Delphi procedure* (Dalkey, 1969; Linstone and Turoff, 1975) has been proposed as one means for taking advantage of the potential benefits of groups while avoiding some of the dysfunctional effects of group interaction. In this procedure, experts do not meet together and do not learn one another's identities; feedback is in the form of statistical descriptions of group responses; and numerous opportunities are provided for reappraising and revising judgments iteratively. Though the strengths and weaknesses of the Delphi procedure remain topics of controversy, the method's simplicity and ease of use have made it quite popular.

The *Nominal Group Technique* (NGT) is another technique devised to incorporate the advantages and eliminate some of the disadvantages of group decision-making strategies (Delbecq et al., 1975). The salient features of NGT are (a) individual judgments by participants, in the presence of the group; (b) iterative feedback from a facilitator concerning patterns of group responses; (c) structured group discussion directed by the facilitator; and (d) mathematical aggregation of individual judgments to form a group prediction.

Still another approach is to use techniques (described below) for decomposing and analyzing judgments of each individual in a group of judges. The resulting individual models can be used as a basis for group discussion or may simply be statistically aggregated (Adelman and Mumpower, 1979).

For SIA, then, the research suggests that predictions of social impacts may often be substantially improved by using statistical or interacting groups, rather than by relying on a single expert. Although replacing single judges with multiple judges has the potential for helping reduce errors resulting from judgmental inconsistency, an improvement cannot be guaranteed. The use of multiple judges may sometimes compound, instead of alleviate, the errors associated with individuals' judgments. Users of group judgment techniques should be familiar with the types of problems that can accompany these techniques and try to guard against them.

Decomposition

Decomposition is the analysis of a problem into subproblems, so that the simpler subproblems can be worked on and their solutions then combined to yield a solution to the original problem. Decomposition is a judgment and decision aid that addresses the limited capacity of effortful processes.

A number of approaches to decomposition, most of which are more complementary then competitive, have been developed. These approaches frequently make use of the fact-value (or projecting-evaluating) distinction discussed earlier. As Hammond and Mumpower (1979) have pointed out, experts and public representatives are frequently required to make complex judgments or decisions that require simultaneous judgments about both technical and value issues. Such simultaneous, compound judgments can be expected to be cognitively more difficult and complex, and thus more likely to result in judgmental inconsistency, than those that have been decomposed into smaller, more homogeneous subproblems.

After the problem has been decomposed into a fact portion and a value portion, a number of methods are available for helping individuals make judgments about the resulting subproblems. These methods generally involve further decomposition. Two prominent psychologically based methods are the POLICY procedure, developed by Hammond and his colleagues, and the SMART procedure, developed by Edwards and his colleagues.

In the POLICY procedure (Hammond et al., 1975), which is available in the form of a computer program, the judge first makes judgments of hypothetical cases, just as was described earlier for the bootstrapping procedure. For example, in a study involving the effects of police handgun ammunition, medical and ballistics experts were asked to predict the average severity of injury that would result from use of each of a series of bullets, each of which was described in terms of its weight, velocity, kinetic energy, and so forth (Hammond and Adelman, 1976). Then a statistical analysis is performed and a mathematical model derived that describes the way the judge combines information to make a judgment. Ths model decomposes the judgments into *function forms* and *weights*. Function forms describe the functional relation between each type of information provided by the hypothetical cases and the individual's judgment (for example, the greater the weight of the bullet, the greater the severity of injury). Weights describe the relative importance placed on each type of information (for example, muzzle velocity is more important than diameter of bullet when predicting average severity of injury). This model, which "decomposes" how the individual makes his or her judgments into a set of more fundamental parameters, is displayed graphically to the judge, who decides whether he or she wishes to change the weights or function forms. The resulting model may then be used as a decision aid to help the individual make judgments or predictions.

The SMART procedure (Edwards, 1976, 1977) uses a somewhat different and simpler approach. It asks judges directly to specify how much *weight* they wish to place on each type of information they use in making a judgment. Individuals are asked to rank each dimension in terms of its overall importance and then to assign numerical values that reflect ratio values of importance. They are also asked to draw or choose a *value curve* that graphically describes the relationship between values on each dimension and the overall judgment.

In addition to these two techniques, many other useful aids are available. The *utility theory* approach (Keeney and Raiffa, 1976; Keeney, 1980), for example, is widely use for decomposing and analyzing both value and technical judgments. *Bayesian analysis* (Slovic and Lichtenstein, 1971) is an important and well-known tool for facilitating probability judgments by decomposing them into judgments of the probabilities of conditioning events and the corresponding conditional probabilities. Finally, any simulation model can be regarded as a technique for (a) replacing certain technical judgments with data, (b) decomposing other technical judgments, and (c) aggregating the two.

For SIA, use of decomposition methods and judgment aids such as POLICY, SMART, and the others may offer substantial advantages over more common practices, such as simply requesting experts to make global predictions of impact or using survey or interview techniques to elicit evaluation of plans. Decomposition of problems into subproblems reduces the ambiguity and complexity of the types of judgments that individuals are asked to make, thus reducing the chance that those judgments will be adversely affected by judgmental inconsistency. The use of judgment aids with these decomposed problems helps protect against errors that result from demands on the limited capacities of effortful cognitive processes. Although the more conventional methods have their place (for instance, interviews are appropriate in the early problem-structuring phase of a study, and surveys may be appropriate later, when critical issues of the problem have been very well defined), methods for decomposing problems and judgments into their component parts may provide better protection against some of the types of problems and errors that may adversely affect the quality of projections and evaluations in SIAs.

Graphic Aids

Graphic aids should reduce judgmental inconsistency by supplementing the limited capacity of the working memory that serves effortful processes. In addition to the graphic displays used by techniques such as POLICY or SMART, the most widely used graphic aids are decision trees and decisional balance sheets.

A *decision tree* (Raiffa, 1968) is a flow diagram of the significant events in a decision problem. Events under the decision maker's control are represented as decision forks, and events not under his or her control are represented as chance forks. The tree begins with a single decision fork, representing the overall decision, and branches out, through various decision and chance forks, to a number of endpoints, each representing a different possible outcome scenario.

A *decisional balance sheet* (Janis and Mann, 1977) is a listing of the pros and cons of alternative courses of action, often arranged in the form of a cross-classification table in which the row variable might represent the alternative courses of action and the column variable might represent the pros and cons of each.

For SIA, use of graphic aids to memory should help protect against judgmental inconsistencies resulting from the stimulus-bound quality of automatic processes and the limited capacity of effortful processes. It can help to ensure that the important aspects of the problem are kept consistently in mind while judgments of fact or value are being made.

Judgmental Bias: Causes and Correctives

Bias, or constant error, in judgment is presumably based on the same cognitive mechanisms as inconsistency, or random error. When the mechanisms operate in the same manner from judgment to judgment, however, the error is constant, and the nature of the mechanism may be revealed clearly enough to permit identification. It is thus possible to organize this part of the chapter in terms of presumed causal mechanisms. As will be seen, different techniques are appropriate for correcting constant error. Simply increasing the number of judgments and averaging them, for example, would have no effect on constant error.

In psychology, the emphasis has shifted in recent years from research on the overall reliability (consistency) and validity (consistency and freedom from bias) of human judgment to research concerning the nature of the processes underlying judgment (Einhorn and Hogarth, 1981; Slovic et al., 1977). A large number of cognitive biases adversely affecting human judgmental abilities have been identified or suggested. Hogarth and Makridakis (1981) have made a comprehensive review of biases potentially affecting predictive and forecasting judgments, citing 29 biases identified in the research literature.

Before considering specific biases and correctives for them, it is appropriate to mention a general corrective that is applicable to both identified and unidentified sources of bias: *triangulation.* Triangulation is the use of multiple methods for obtaining judgments in order to converge on more nearly correct judgments. It is more akin to systematic counterbalancing than to randomization. Concurrent use of both willingness-to-pay and willingness-to-accept-payment techniques would be an example, where overreluctance to pay in the first case could presumably be balanced to some degree by an overreadiness to accept payment in the second.

Counterbalancing to cancel out order effects is a special kind of triangulation. How a stimulus is judged very often depends on how early or late in the sequence it is judged and on what particular stimuli it follows (Baird and Noma, 1978). A corrective for this source of error is to vary the order in which impacts are evaluated.

The remainder of this section considers specific biases and methods for ensuring against them. The biases are grouped under three general judgmental heuristics, or simplifying "cognitive rules of thumb," that are thought to give rise to them.

Representativeness

Representativeness is a judgmental heuristic, identified by Kahneman and Tversky (1972, 1973), according to which the likelihood of an event is judged by the degree to which it resembles its parent population or reflects features of the process by which it was generated. The representativeness heuristic produces a number of judgmental errors. Perhaps the best known is the *base-rate fallacy*. Distributional, or base-rate, information consists of knowledge about the distribution of outcomes in similar situations. Singular, or case, information consists of evidence about the particular case under consideration. People tend to rely primarily on singular information, even when it is of little value, and to give insufficient weight to distributional information. Thus individuals thinking about the social impacts of a project would be inclined to place too much emphasis on what they know about the project in question and too little on what they know about the social impacts of similar projects. The tendency to neglect distributional information is believed to be enhanced by any factor that increases the perceived uniqueness of the problem, such as detailed acquaintance with the specific case or intense involvement with it (see Kahneman and Tversky, 1972: 451-452). Judgment elicitation procedures should ask judges to think about what they know about similar cases.

For SIA, the base-rate fallacy points to the importance of avoiding predictions that place too much emphasis on the particulars of the project in question and too little on what is known about the impacts of similar projects. For instance, predictions of the local economic and social impacts of building a large dam should be based not only on a careful analysis of the particulars concerning that dam (the projected total payroll, the number of new jobs to be created, the expected increase in population, and so on), but also on data about the pattern of effects that resulted from the construction of other large dams.

Another judgmental error that is believed to result from the representativeness heuristic is *nonregressiveness bias.* Nonregressiveness bias is the tendency to make intuitive forecasts in such a way that the extremity of the predicted value is "matched to" the extremity of the proposed action or event. Kahneman and Tversky give as an example a book editor who is extremely impressed by a manuscript. Regarding it as one of the top 5 percent he has received in recent years, he forecasts that it will be among the top 5 percent in sales. Although this approach to forecasting seems reasonable on its face, it is statistically inappropriate when predicting events that are uncertain or probabilistic. Predictions of such events should take into account their inherent uncertainty by making less extreme predictions (predictions that regress toward the mean) than those that would result from the intuitively appealing "matching" technique.

Recent experience with nuclear facilities may illustrate, in part, the nonregressiveness bias. Possibly, some of the surprise that greeted strong negative public responses to nuclear facilities was a result of implicitly predicting public perceptions of risk on the basis of engineering estimates of risk. It was assumed, at least by some, that because the engineering estimates of risk were extremely low, the public perception of risk would also be extremely low. The two variables are related, but not perfectly so. Failure to recognize the fallacy of matching the predicted level of one variable with the level of another variable with which it is not perfectly correlated can lead to surprises for impact assessors as well as for book editors.

Kahneman and Tversky (1979a) have recommended a set of procedures that should correct for the base-rate fallacy, nonregressiveness bias, and overconfidence (a topic to be discussed later). The central idea is (a) to estimate the base rate explicitly, (b) to estimate the degree of predictability associated with the singular, or case, data, and (c) to combine these two judgments statistically. Statistical techniques are also used to provide a basis for judging the appropriate degree of confidence.

An additional judgmental error that is believed to result from the representativeness heuristic is the so-called *law of small numbers,* which refers to the belief that small random samples will be highly representative of the populations from which they have been drawn (Tversky and Kahneman, 1971: 106). Statistical measures of sampling error should also provide appropriate correctives for this error.

For SIA, judgments should be based as clearly as possible on the numbers, or estimated numbers, of cases in the categories of interest. These can then be adjusted for the particular case at hand.

Availability

Availability is a judgmental heuristic, identified by Kahneman and Tversky (1973), in which a person evaluates the frequency or likelihood of events by the ease with which relevant instances come to mind. For example, one may assess the risk of heart attack among middle-aged people by recalling such occurrences among one's acquaintances; and it is a common experience for the subjective probability of having an automobile accident to rise temporarily when passing an accident on the road. The probabilities of widely publicized causes of death (such as cancer, fire, homicide, and accidents) tend to be overestimated, while those of poorly publicized causes of death (such as diabetes, asthma, lightning, and stroke) tend to be underestimated (Lichtenstein et al., 1978).

In SIA, availability might influence predictions directly or indirectly. A catastrophic earthquake in California might have a direct, although covert, influence on expert judgments concerning the likelihood of an earthquake affecting a proposed dam elsewhere. Even if one assumes that experts would not be influenced by such an event (a dubious assumption, on the basis of research to date), it seems likely that such a catastrophic event might indirectly influence the types of concerns judged appropriate for an SIA and the degree of attention given to them.

Recency bias may be a special case of availability bias. Recent events are more available for recall than are remote events, and recent cases tend to be weighted more heavily than those remote in time, remote cases often not being taken into account at all (Tversky and Kahneman, 1973). Judgment elicitation procedures that encourage the judge to take into account events remote in time, as well as recent events, should provide an appropriate corrective.

It has been found repeatedly that verbally expressed attitudes tend not to predict actual behavior unless the judged items are meaningfully related to the individual's experience (Gross and Niman, 1975; Wicker, 1969). This may be because not all the important factors that influence behavior in the actual situation are present in the judgment situation. Judgment elicitation procedures (including surveys) should help the individual (by means of photographs, examples, or instructions) to keep in mind the contexts in which the consequences being evaluated will actually be experienced.

Questions should be framed, insofar as possible, as concrete choices. They should be as specific and realistic as possible. And the individual should be motivated to treat the choices seriously.

Illusory correlation, the tendency to infer the existence of a relationship between variables that are, in fact, uncorrelated, may be based, at least in part, on availability. Illusory correlation is present in experts as well as in untrained persons, and it is relatively impervious to experience (Chapman and Chapman, 1967, 1969). Illusory correlation appears to be based in part on the greater availability in memory of confirming information (Tversky and Kahneman, 1974) and in part on the greater difficulty of seeing the implications of disconfirming information, even when it is available (Wason and Johnson-Laird, 1972). The appropriate corrective would seem to be to assess correlations statistically, rather than intuitively. Any of the appropriate statistical formulas will (a) require both confirming and disconfirming data (which may be in the form of either objective measurements or judgments) and (b) ensure comparable use of both kinds of information.

For SIA, procedures should guard against availability biases in selecting cases for consideration. In particular, they should ensure that cases that have not come to the judge's attention frequently or recently are given adequate attention. The context that the judge has in mind should approximate as closely as possible the context of the scenario being judged.

Anchoring and Adjustment

Anchoring and adjustment form a judgmental heuristic, identified by Tversky and Kahneman (1974), in which people make estimates by starting from an initial value (the anchor) and then adjusting it, usually to an insufficient degree, to yield the final answer. For example, judges asked to estimate the percentage of African countries in the United Nations starting with an initial value (known to the judge to be arbitrary) of 10 percent produced a lower estimate than subjects starting with an initial value (also known to the judge to be arbitrary) of 45 percent. Fischhoff and MacGregor (1980) found that slight changes in how formally equivalent questions were asked could change estimates of lethality for potential causes of death by as much as a factor of 60. In SIA, the anchoring and adjustment bias may be of greatest concern when using survey or questionnaire methods, either with experts or in the local community.

By providing different anchors, different judgment elicitation techniques can lead to different judgments. For example, fractile estimation (asking the individual to select values on the impact variable that correspond to specified percentiles of his or her probability distribution) yields probability distributions that are too tight. Presumably, adjustment from the percentiles presented as anchors is insufficient. On the other hand, probability estimation (asking the individual to assess the probability that the true value on the impact dimension will exceed some specified values) yields probability distributions that are too flat. Presumably, adjustment from the values on the impact dimension presented as anchors is insufficient. The corrective, in this case, would seem to be to employ both fractile estimation and probability estimation and to average the results.

It may be use of the anchoring and adjustment heuristic that accounts for the well-known *error of central tendency,* the tendency to give judgments that are too near the center of the distribution (Guilford, 1954). The farther the true value is from the center of the distribution, the greater is this tendency. One way to deal with this error is to have extreme impacts judged first, so the individual will be less inclined to "adjust out" from central values.

What may be a special case of the error of central tendency is the tendency for probability estimates to be too low for high-probability events and too high for low-probability events (Peterson and Beach, 1967; Kahneman and Tversky, 1979a). This fact may help to explain why public reaction to low-probability risks tends to be higher than what would seem to be consistent with normative theory: The public vastly overestimates the probabilities. It may also help to explain the tendency to be overly confident about the accuracy of one's predictions. When asked to establish a confidence interval by setting upper and lower limits on the predicted value, the judge tends to select an interval that is inappropriately narrow.

Another source of error in judgment that might be attributable to the use of an anchoring and adjustment heuristic is the memory for prior responses. If repeated judgments are being obtained about similar or identical impacts (in order to reduce judgmental inconsistency), the previous response may be given, or at least taken as a starting point for an adjustment process, on subsequent occasions. Use of graphic, as opposed to verbal or numeric, rating scales can reduce this problem, since it is more difficult to remember positions on a line than words.

For SIA, judgments should be obtained in more than one way, starting from different anchors. For example, one could ask for both the probabilities of given events and events with given probabilities, and one could ask both how much one would be willing to pay to obtain a benefit and how little one would be willing to accept in payment to forgo a benefit. Where repeated judgments are obtained, graphic rating scales can reduce the likelihood that previous judgments will be used as anchors.

Summary and Conclusions

This chapter began with a list of recommendations for improving the judgments that must be made in any social impact assessment. In what followed, we attempted to explain the reasons for our recommendations.

We first noted the central role that human judgment necessarily plays in SIA, particularly in projecting and evaluating impacts. We then discussed two fundamental types of cognitive processes that seem to be involved in a very wide range of cognitive tasks, presumably including those in SIA. The first type of process was characterized as automatic, effortless, and unconscious; the second, as voluntary, effortful, and conscious. We noted that each type of process has certain inherent weaknesses. Automatic processes tend to make thought stimulus bound and habit bound, leading us to respond to what is most apparent or salient in the situation and to respond in much the same way on repeated occasions. Effortful processes have a very limited capacity, restricting severely the number of items that we can think about at any one time.

We next presented evidence showing that the quality of human judgment often falls far short of the ideal, even for experts. We distinguished two primary sources of error in human judgment: inconsistency and bias.

Judgmental inconsistency was attributed to shortcomings of both automatic and effortful processes; it appears to increase for complex or unfamiliar tasks. We described four correctives for judgmental inconsistency: (a) bootstrapping, the replacement of the individual by a statistical model based on a large number of judgments made by the individual; (b) using groups of judges to obtain judgments; (c) decomposing judgment problems into simpler subproblems; and (d) using graphic aids to supplement the limited capacity of effortful processes.

Judgmental bias was attributed to the same cognitive mechanisms as inconsistency; however, because the error is constant, it is possible to hypothesize certain underlying heuristics (or cognitive "rules of thumb"). The *representativeness* heuristic results in a tendency to place too much emphasis on distinctive characteristics of particular events and too little on information about the general case. The *availability* heuristic results in a tendency to evaluate the frequency or likelihood of an event by the ease with which relevant instances come to mind. And the *anchoring and adjustment* heuristic results in a final judgment that is too close to the initial estimate. For correcting representativeness errors, it was suggested that the judge be encouraged to take into account what is known about the general case, including the relative numbers of instances in different categories, and that statistical techniques be employed. For correcting availability errors, it was suggested that the judge be encouraged to take into account events remote in time, as well as recent ones, preferably by means of a systematic sampling frame suggested by the appropriate statistical technique. For correcting various errors due to anchoring and adjustment, it was suggested that extreme cases be judged first and that graphic rating scales and triangulation, starting from different anchors, be employed.

In conclusion, the important role that human judgment plays in SIA has not been given adequate recognition. Inattention to the role of human judgment and to the need for correcting errors in judgment may lead to significant deficiencies in many impact assessments. As unwelcome as the additional burden of making the pyschology of judgment an integral part of SIA may be, failure to do so may be somewhat akin to performing engineering calculations with a defective computer.

References

ADELMAN, L. and J. MUMPOWER (1979) "The analysis of expert judgment." Technological Forecasting and Social Change 15: 191-204.

ANDERSON, B. F. (1980) The Complete Thinker: A Handbook of Techniques for Creative and Critical Problem Solving. Englewood Cliffs, NJ: Prentice-Hall.

——— (1975) Cognitive Psychology: The Study of Knowing, Learning, and Thinking. New York: Academic.

BAIRD, J. C. and E. NOMA (1978) Fundamentals of Scaling and Psychophysics. New York: John Wiley.

BREHMER, B. (1980) "In one word: not from experience." Acta Psychologica 45: 223-241.

——— (1973) "The effect of cue validity on interpersonal learning of inference tasks with linear and nonlinear cues." American Journal of Psychology 86: 29-48.

——— (1970) "Inference behavior in a situation where the cues are not reliably perceived." Organizational Behavior and Human Performance 5: 330-347.

BROADBENT, D. E. (1975) "The magic number seven after fifteen years," pp. 3-18 in A. Kennedy and A. Wilkes (eds.) Studies of Long-Term Memory. New York: John Wiley.

CHAPMAN, L. and J. CHAPMAN (1969) "Illusory correlation as an obstacle to the use of valid psychodiagnostic signs." Journal of Abnormal Psychology 74: 271-280.

———— (1967) "Genesis of popular but erroneous psychodiagnostic observation." Journal of Abnormal Psychology 72: 193-207.

DALKEY, N. C. (1969) The Delphi Method: An Experimental Study of Group Opinion. Santa Monica, CA: Rand Corporation.

DAWES, R. M. (1976) "Shallow psychology," pp. 3-11 in J. S. Carroll and J. W. Payne (eds.) Cognition and Social Behavior. Hillsdale, N.J.: Lawrence Erlbaum.

———— and B. CORRIGAN (1974) "Linear models in decision making." Psychological Bulletin 81: 95-106.

DELBECQ, A., A. VAN DE VEN, and D. GUSTAFSON (1975) Group Techniques for Program Planning. Glenview, IL: Scott, Foresman.

EDWARDS, W. (1977) "Use of multiattribute utility measurement for social decision making," pp. 247-275 in D. E. Bell et al. (eds.) Conflicting Objectives in Decisions. New York: John Wiley.

———— (1976) "How to use multiattribute utility measurement for social decisionmaking." IEEE Transactions on Systems, Man, and Cybernetics 7: 326-339.

EINHORN, H. J. (1980a) "Learning from experience and suboptimal rules in decision making," pp. 1-20 in T. S. Wallsten (ed.) Cognitive Processes in Choice and Decision Behavior. Hillsdale, NJ: Lawrence Erlbaum.

———— (1980b) "Overconfidence in judgment," pp. 1-16 K. R. Hammond and N. Wascoe (eds.) New Directions for Methodology of Social and Behavioral Sciences. San Francisco: Jossey-Bass.

———— and R. HOGARTH (1981) "Behavioral decision theory: processes of judgment and choice," in Annual Review of Psychology 32. Palo Alto, CA: Annual Reviews.

———— (1978) "Confidence in judgment: persistence of the illusion of validity." Psychological Bulletin 85: 395-416.

———— (1975) "Unit weighting schemes for decision making." Organizational Behavior and Human Performance 13: 171-192.

FISCHHOFF, B. and D. MacGREGOR (1980) Judged Lethality. Eugene, OR: Decision Research.

FISCHHOFF, B., P. SLOVIC, and S. LICHTENSTEIN (forthcoming) "Lay foibles and expert fables in judgments about risk," in T. O'Riordan and R. K. Turner (eds.) Progress in Resource Management and Environmental Planning, Vol. 3. New York: John Wiley.

———— (1980) "Knowing what you want: measuring labile values" in T. Wallsten (ed.) Cognitive Processes in Choice and Decision Behavior. Hillsdale, NJ.: Lawrence Erlbaum.

———— (1978) "Fault trees: sensitivity of assessed failure probabilities to problem presentation." Journal of Experimental Psychology: Human Perception and Performance 4: 330-344.

———— (1977) "Knowing with certainty: the appropriateness of extreme confidence." Journal of Experimental Psychology: Human Perception and Performance 3: 544-551.

GROSS, S. J. and C. M. NIMAN (1975) "Attitude-behavior consistency: a review." Public Opinion Quarterly 39: 356-368.

GUILFORD, J. P. (1954) Psychometric Methods. New York: McGraw-Hill.

HACKMAN, J. R. and C. G. MORRIS (1975) "Group tasks, group interaction processes, and group performance effectiveness: a review and proposed integration," in L. Berkowitz (ed.) Advances in Experimental Social Psychology, Vol. 8. New York: Academic.

HAMMOND, K. R. (1978) "Toward increasing competence of thought in public policy formation," in K. R. HAMMOND (ed.) Judgment and Decision in Public Policy Formation. Boulder, CO: Westview.
—— and L. ADELMAN (1976) "Science, values, and human judgment." Science 194: 389-396.
HAMMOND, K. R. and J. MUMPOWER (1979) "Formation of social policy: risks and safeguards." Knowledge: Creation, Diffusion, and Utilization 1: 245-258.
HAMMOND, K. R., T. R. STEWART, B. BREHMER and D. O. STEINMANN (1975) "Social judgment theory," in M. F. Kaplan and S. Schwartz (eds.) Human Judgment and Decision Processes. New York: Academic.
HOGARTH, R. M. (1977) "Methods for aggregating opinions," in H. Jungermann and G. de Zeeuw (eds.) Decision Making and Change in Human Affairs. Dordecht, Holland: D. Reidel.
—— and S. MAKRIDAKIS (1981) "Forecasting and planning: an evaluation." Management Science 27: 115-189.
JANIS, I. L. (1972) Victims of Groupthink. Boston: Houghton Mifflin.
—— and L. MANN (1977) Decision Making: A Psychological Analysis of Conflict, Choice, and Commitment. New York: Macmillan.
KAHNEMAN, D. and A. TVERSKY (1979a) "Intuitive prediction: biases and corrective procedures." Management Science 12: 313-327.
—— (1979b) "Prospect theory: an analysis of decision under risk." Econometrica 47: 263-291.
—— (1973) "On the psychology of prediction." Psychological Review 80: 251-273.
—— (1972) "Subjective probability: a judgment of representativeness." Cognitive Psychology 3: 430-454.
KAHNEMAN, D., P. SLOVIC, and A. TVERSKY (1982) Judgment Under Uncertainty: Heuristics and Biases. Cambridge: Cambridge University Press.
KEENEY, R. L. (1980) Siting Energy Facilities. New York: Academic.
—— and H. RAIFFA (1976) Decisions with Multiple Objectives: Preference and Value Tradeoffs. New York: John Wiley.
LICHTENSTEIN, S., B. FISCHHOFF, and L. D. PHILLIPS (1977) "Calibration of probabilities: the state of the art," in H. Jungermann and G. de Zeeuw (eds.) Decision Making and Changes in Human Affairs. Dordecht, Holland: D. Reidel.
LICHTENSTEIN, S., P. SLOVIC, B. FISCHHOFF, M. LAYMAN, and B. COMBS (1978) "Judged frequency of lethal events." Journal of Experimental Psychology: Human Learning and Memory 4: 551-578.
LINSTONE, H. and M. TUROFF (1975) The Delphi Method: Techniques and Applications. Reading, MA: Addison-Wesley.
LURIA, A. R. (1973) The Working Brain: An Introduction to Neuropsychology. New York: Basic Books.
MILLER, G. A. (1956) "The magical number seven, plus or minus two: some limits on our capacity for processing information." Psychological Review 63: 81-97.
PAYNE, J. W. (1976) "Task complexity and contingent processing in decision making: an information search and protocol analysis." Organizational Behavior and Human Performance 16: 366-387.
PETERSON, C. and L. R. BEACH (1967) "Man as an intuitive statistician." Psychological Bulletin 68: 29-46.
POSNER, M. I. (1973) Cognition: An Introduction. Glenview, IL: Scott, Foresman.

RAIFFA, H. (1968) Decision Analysis. Reading, MA: Addison-Wesley.

SLOVIC, P. and S. LICHTENSTEIN (1971) "Comparison of Bayesian and regression approaches to the study of information processing in judgment." Organizational Behavior and Human Performance 6: 649-744.

SLOVIC, P., B. FISCHHOFF, and S. LICHTENSTEIN (1977) "Behavioral decision theory," pp. 1-39 in Annual Review of Psychology, Vol. 28. Palo Alto, CA: Annual Reviews.

TVERSKY, A. and D. KAHNEMAN (1974) "Judgment under uncertainly: heuristics and biases." Science 185: 1124-1131.

——— (1973) "Availability: a heuristic for judging frequency and probability." Cognitive Psychology 5: 207-232.

——— (1971) "The belief in the 'law of small numbers.'" Psychological Bulletin 76: 105-110.

WASON, P. C. and P. JOHNSON-LAIRD (1972) Psychology of Reasoning: Structure and Content. London: Batsford.

WICKER, A. W. (1969) "Attitudes versus actions: the relationship of verbal and overt behavioral responses to attitude objects." Journal of Social Issues 25: 41-78.

13

Visual Quality and Visual Impact Assessment

O O O O O O O O O O O O O O O O

JAMES F. PALMER

O O O O O O O O O O O O O O O O

● It is clearly Congress's intent that aesthetic values be included in the preparation of policies and plans for managing our national landscape. In the language of the National Environmental Policy Act of 1969 (Sec. 4331), we must "use all practicable means . . . [to] assure for all Americans safe, healthful, productive, and esthetically and culturally pleasing surroundings."

It is an old saying that "beauty is in the eye of the beholder," the implication being that each individual's perception of visual quality is unique and that opinions of all individuals are equally valid. However, our everyday experience indicates that there is a broad consensus concerning landscape evaluations. This chapter describes the role of visual assessments and surveys the common methods used to assess visual quality. These are divided into two general approaches: (1) professional appraisals that incorporate standardized criteria to evaluate landscape attributes, and (2)

This chapter is a revised version of Palmer, J. F., "Approaches for Assessing Visual Quality and Visual Impacts," in K. Finsterbusch and C. P. Wolf (eds.), METHODOLOGY OF SOCIAL IMPACT ASSESSMENT, 2nd Edition. Copyright © by Hutchinson Ross Publishing Company, Stroudsburg, PA. Reprinted by permission of the publisher.

landscape perception methods that are based on public perceptions and evaluations of the landscape. The last section briefly describes how these methods are used for assessing visual impacts using professional appraisals, predictive models, and public evaluations.

Integrating Visual with
Other Assessments

In its broadest sense, impact assessment is intended to integrate all pertinent environmental information for use throughout the planning and design processes. However, in practice such assessments are prepared largely to justify decisions already made. In addition, they are not integrative but typically disaggregate knowledge by separating social from physical environmental impacts. As currently conducted, visual assessments are perfunctory and not well integrated with either physical or social assessments. This condition need not exist, since most decisions affecting the environment have visual implications and would benefit from incorporating visual image-based methods of data collection, analysis, and communication. This potential is briefly considered by reviewing the four general stages of the environmental decision-making process: (1) environmental inventory, (2) policy formation, (3) program planning or project design, and (4) postimpact evaluation.

Environmental Inventory

The primary purpose of preparing an environmental inventory is to document existing conditions and provide baseline data for making informed environmental decisions. Procedures to establish control points for monitoring visual landscape change are detailed by Litton (1973). Visual images are a useful form of documentation for many types of inventories. For instance, all historic preservation inventories require thorough photographic documentation (Derry et al., 1977), and the U.S. Forest Service now uses photographic representation for evaluating fire hazard associated with residual slash (Fischer, 1981).

Just as an inventory provides the necessary basis from which to make decisions about the natural or social environment, a visual inventory provides the basis for evaluating the visually related effects of these decisions. The scale of these inventories can range from national (Zube and McLaughlin, 1978) and multistate regions (Research Planning and Design Associates, 1972) to small towns (Palmer, 1982) or specific sites (Derry et al., 1977). While professional knowledge is required for some approaches (Smardon et al., 1982), others may reasonably be conducted by local volunteers with possibly minor technical assistance available from most local colleges (USDA, 1977).

Policy Formation

The primary concern of policy formation is the expression of public values. Visual assessment methods are useful both for establishing goals and objectives relating to visual quality and for visibly representing various environmental futures. For instance, the Natural Resource Planning Program's Citizen Committee in Dennis, Massachusetts, coordinated a policy planning study based on community evaluations of their photographic landscape inventory (Palmer, 1982). The results of that study led to a change in the town's landscape quality policies that eventually were implemented through zoning revisions and conservation acquisitions. Examples of other policy formation studies range from an investigation of the potential change in regional visual quality due to urbanization (Brush and Palmer, 1979), through an exploration of the image area residents held of an urban core city (Goodey et al., 1971), to a study of possible alternative futures for revitalizing a small town's Main Street (Willmott et al., 1982). All these studies have the common purpose of providing information at a predesign stage so that the direction of public decisions is more responsive to the public's needs and wishes.

Planning and Design

Planning and design are the processes by which the policy goals and objectives are implemented in response to specific conditions. It is at this stage that environmental statements are typically prepared. The role of a visual analysis will vary according to the circumstances being evaluated. For instance, it is the basis of a proposed program for designing the reclamation of orphaned coal mines in Appalachia (Cole et al., 1976). It also played a dominant part in the consideration of impacts on national wildlands from alternative air quality management plans (U.S. Environmental Protection Agency, 1979). In evaluating the siting of a power facility, visibility is one of many considerations in the landscape analysis (Minnesota Environmental Quality Control, 1976). More commonly, it is a reflective scenic evaluation of previously identified alternative designs, such as a major harbor redevelopment project (Blair et al., 1980). Visual imaging and presentation are normal activities used to evaluate alternative plans or designs for the physical environment. While these activities are necessary for professional practice, they are also eminently suited for communicating environmental conditions to a lay audience. The media used to portray visual effects can be as sophisticated as computer drawings (Myklestad and Wagner, 1976), but hand-drawn sketches and photographs are still the most frequently used media, and these skills are available in most communities.

Postimpact Evaluation

Postimpact evaluation of visual quality is analogous to monitoring any other environmental condition. It is typically conducted as a disconnected research project rather than as an integrated follow-up to an environmental decision. Such research projects range from public evaluations of the visual character of national park visitor centers (Zube et al., 1976) to timber management practices (Daniel and Boster, 1976). Under ideal circumstances, evaluation research of this type would be conducted willingly by lead agencies and the information used to improve existing conditions and plan future projects. However, the need for conducting visual assessments must be brought before the public before it becomes a widespread practice. The initial steps toward this end are the documentation of visual quality as legitimate grounds for legal consideration (Smardon, 1979) and the appearance of professionals prepared to represent visual quality considerations during litigation or mediation processes.

Professional Appraisal Approaches for Assessing Visual Quality

Professional appraisals assess visual quality by applying standardized criteria to describe visibility, landform and land-use pattern, landscape features, cognitive structure, or aesthetic composition. The scenic value of these criteria are primarily based on traditional values within the landscape architecture profession. However, they are supported to some extent by recent landscape perception research.

Description of Landscape Patterns

VISIBILITY ANALYSIS

Visibility analysis is the most objective method available to resource planners conducting visual assessments. Visible areas are determined using topographic data. The analysis is conducted in one of two ways, delineating either all views *from* a site or *to* a site. Composite maps can be constructed from a series of analyses. For instance, the length of time areas are visible from a proposed road could be mapped for cars traveling in either direction. Another example would indicate all areas within a specified radius from which a proposed project would be visible. Computer programs are available for making calculations that involve large areas (Aylward and Turnbull, 1977; Travis et al., 1975). Felleman (1982) has compared the results from various visibility mapping methods.

LANDFORM AND LAND-USE PATTERNS

The basic elements of the landscape's physical character are the form of the ground and the cover pattern of natural vegetation and human artifacts. These elements are easily identified from topographic maps and aerial photographs. Several approaches exist to combine landform and land-use descriptions and to assign a scenic value to each resulting landscape type.

The visual quality of the North Atlantic states from Virginia to Maine was assessed by Zube and his colleagues (Zube, 1970; Research Planning and Design Associates, 1972) using this type of procedure. They employed existing data and extensive aerial reconnaissance. A series of seven landform classes were identified: mountains, steep hills, rolling hills, undulating land, flat land, coastline, and composite forms. The land-use pattern was divided into seven units: forest-wildland, forest-town, farm-forest, farm, town-farm, fringe city, and intermediate-center city. Areas were rated for how well they exemplified the scenic qualities associated with their landform and land-use patterns. The landform quality ratings were adjusted using a weighting system that valued mountains over flatland. Conversely, land-use quality ratings were adjusted to be more highly valued in flatlands and less valued in mountains. The combined landscape value that was mapped for the entire region was the sum of these two weighted values.

LANDSCAPE FEATURE AND ATTRIBUTE INDICES

Another approach to assessing scenic quality is to inventory possible landscape features and attributes. This approach was first popularized by Lewis (1964), who mapped the presence of over 200 landscape resources. These included water resources (such as waterfalls and lighthouses), wetland resources (such as wildlife preserves), topographic resources (such as caves and ski trails), vegetation resources (such as virgin timber and unusual crops), historical and cultural resources (such as covered bridges), archaeological resources (such as a prehistoric cemetery), wildlife (such as deer yards) and tourist service facilities (such as camping sites). He found that these resources tended to concentrate along corridors that could serve as the basis for landscape conservation efforts.

Leopold (1969) also used this checklist approach to inventory the aesthetic quality of potential wild and scenic rivers. However, he assigned evaluation scores to each of his 45 characteristics. This approach was extended by Melhorn and his colleagues (1975). Their computer program, Landscape Aesthetics Numerically Defined (LAND), calculates an aesthetic index based on comparisons among several sites.

Description of Landscape Composition

COGNITIVE STRUCTURE

Lynch (1960) has developed a system to describe the public's image of a landscape. His research in several metropolitan areas indicates that there are five elements that structure our image: (1) paths are channels for movement; (2) edges are boundaries or breaks in continuity; (3) districts are areas that have some common, identifying character; (4) nodes are points of intensive activity; and (5) landmarks are features that provide orientation and identity. Major changes in the landscape can disrupt this structure and cause a disturbing sense of disorientation and loss of place. Lynch discusses how to use his system to assess imageability and ways to maintain visual structure and a sense of continuity in the face of landscape change.

Appleyard and others (1964) extended Lynch's concepts and developed a notation for describing visual structure experienced when traveling along a road. Halprin (1965) and Thiel (1961) have also developed notation systems to document motion. They have found such notations useful for documenting existing and proposed landscape designs that provide a kinesthetic experience (such as highways), and in making qualitative comparisons.

AESTHETIC COMPOSITION

The traditional theory of artistic composition also provides the basis for describing the landscape's visual qualities. Litton (1968) has been the foremost proponent of this approach as a visual management tool. Litton's terminology is incorporated in a U.S. Forest Service management handbook (USDA, 1973) that defines and illustrates basic landscape concepts (characteristic type, variety, and deviations), dominance elements (form, line, color, and texture), dominance principals (contrast, sequence, axis convergence, codominance, and enframement), and variable factors (motion, light, atmospheric conditions, season, distance, observer position, scale, and time). The Forest Service has operationalized these concepts to identify and map landscape variety classes and levels of scenic sensitivity (USDA, 1974). This inventory serves as the basis for assignment of visual quality management objectives: preservation, retention, partial retention, modification, and maximum modification.

The Bureau of Land Management uses a procedure similar to the Forest Service's to evaluate scenic quality and determine the impact of visual landscape changes (USDI, 1980a). Their procedure evaluates the form, line, color and textural qualities and changes in landform, water, vegetation, and structure. Scenic quality ratings for landform, vegetation, water, color, influence, scarcity, and cultural modification are used to determine scenic quality management classes.

The Bureau of Land Management and Forest Service visual management systems are economical in time and resources necessary for their application. However, their complex and comprehensive nature may have introduced significant amounts of subjectivity into an ostensibly objective process. Smardon and his colleagues have tested the reliability, validity, and generality of these systems and the results urge caution in their use (Feimer et al., 1981).

Landscape Perception Approaches for Assessing Visual Quality

The field of environment and behavior research is a multidisciplinary effort to understand how people cognitively grasp the everyday physical environment. It encompasses social science researchers interested in creating conceptual frameworks and developing theoretical constructs, as well as environmental designers and planners interested in problem solving that is responsive to the social context. As summarized by Craik (1968), the general research strategy is to (1) define the environment of interest; (2) identify the population that will observe the environment; (3) select a medium to present or simulate the environment; and (4) develop a procedure to record observer responses to the environment. This framework neatly organizes the method and issues necessary to understand public perceptions and evaluations of the landscape.

Environmental Displays

The researcher must first define the environment to be assessed and select those views that best represent the environment. Three strategies are commonly used: (1) random selection, (2) rational selection, and (3) public selection.

Random selection. If the selected views will form the basis for statistical analysis, then a random sample is preferred. The particular strategy depends on the objective of the analysis. Daniel and his colleagues have used random walks (Daniel and Boster, 1976) and aerial photos (Daniel et al., 1977) to sample views for mapping scenic quality.

An alternate sampling strategy is to focus on the observer's exposure to the environment. Palmer (1983) used this experiential approach to sample Appalachian Trail environments, where photographs were taken every half hour of hiking time along random bearings. Another experiential strategy was employed by Jones and colleagues (1975) to evaluate the visual impact of proposed power facilities. Their major criterion for view selection was potential public visual contact.

Rational selection. Most researchers employ some rational criterion for the selection of their landscape views. In their study of the Southern Connecticut River Valley, Zube and his colleagues (1974) photographed a large number of scenes generally accessible to the public. This large sample was reduced by a panel of judges, who selected the photographs best representing possible combinations of landform types and land-use patterns. While this sample is clearly not random, it does have the defensible advantage of economically representing the maximum possible diversity within the study area.

Public selection. Another approach may be more appropriate for studies that clearly focus on public perceptions and images. The scenes used in the study of Cape Cod reported by Palmer (1982) were selected by a panel of citizens asked to indicate a representative range of views on a local street map. Cherem (1974) employed an approach elegant for its simplicity: He provided a camera to a sample of observers and asked them to photograph scenes.

Observers

A primary reason for using the landscape perception approach for assessing environmental plans is that such plans must be firmly related to the user-public's perceptions and behavior if they are to be effective. It is normally not possible to ask every potential user's opinion. Total user-populations are frequently very large and difficult to identify. Therefore, researchers must find their observer groups in one of three ways: (1) by sampling randomly, (2) by sampling according to availability, or (3) by proposing a surrogate group.

Random samples. Preparing a random sample may be an additional expense and certainly requires additional preparation and planning. However, it is a necessary control for unforeseen biases and, where it has been used, the systematic and comprehensive nature of random sampling seems to have provided a basis for useful findings. For instance, a survey of households randomly selected from the three Virgin Islands was used to gather residents' attitudes toward the aesthetic qualities of potential development in the coastal zone (Zube and McLaughlin, 1978). Among the findings was that native residents did not share the landscape preservation values of the professional staff who were preparing the coastal zone plan. In another case, Palmer (1982) sampled the list of registered voters to study local citizens' assessment of visual quality. Again, local perceptions differed from a traditional planner's solution. The most important result, however, was the credibility gained for a broadbased quantitative assessment of subjective values.

Availability samples. Most visual quality research uses observers who are conveniently available. Frequently people are surveyed in public places. For instance, Kaplan (1978) evaluated three alternative park designs by placing photographs of models in a bank and a public library. Other sources of nonrandom public samples are concerned citizens groups, civic organizations, and public meetings.

Public media, such as television and local newspapers, can also be used to attract an observer group. In the early 1970s, the American Falls International Board had to decide whether to "renovate" Niagara Falls. They took advantage of media cooperation to distribute thousands of "ballots" to obtain public reaction to the proposed plans (Gaines, 1973).

Surrogate groups. Frequently, researchers sample an available subpopulation with the suggestion that they are surrogates for the population at large. For instance, Shafer and colleagues (1969) sampled 250 Adirondack campers to represent users of American wildlands.

Presentation Media

The visual quality of landscapes must be simulated if potential visual impacts are going to be assessed (USDI, 1980b). Among the media available for simulation are (1) sketches, (2) models, (3) computer graphics, (4) photographs, and (5) graphic montages. The use of simulation raises questions concerning the validity of such techniques. There are no comprehensive evaluations comparing perceptions of simulations and the "real world." However, existing research does tend to support the validity of simulation (Daniel and Boster, 1976; Shuttlesworth, 1980; Zube et al., 1974). Appleyard (1977), McKenzie (1977), and Sheppard (1980) have surveyed the issues involved with landscape simulation.

Sketches. Perspective sketches have been used to simulate existing or possible landscapes since the Renaissance. As a simulation technique, it can be relatively inexpensive and is uniquely suited for spontaneous presentations. Cuff and Hooper (1979) have found that "conglomerate" graphic interpretations may actually be better representations of our environmental impressions than are "realistic" representations, such as color slides.

Models. Detailed naturalistic models have been used on several occasions to explain complex environmental designs to the public. Both the visual and hydrologic effects of alternative management plans for Niagara Falls were tested using a model (Gaines, 1973). The public planning department in Stockholm maintains a scale model of the city. Every proposed project must first pass inspection in the context of this model. Appleyard (1977) tells of other cities that have similar regulations. Wilmont and Felleman (1983) have designed and tested an inexpensive gantry that guides an optical probe through a model to simulate eye-level views on film or video.

Computer graphics. Computer-generated graphics will become more common as greater use is made of computers in environmental design and planning. Their greatest advantage is that large numbers of views can be prepared rapidly at low cost. Computer simulation is also ideally suited for the generation and comparison of alternative proposals. For instance, the computer-aided ECOSITE program was designed as a surface-mine reclamation planning tool (Cole et al., 1976). It allows the designer to create potential landforms that may then be viewed from any vantage point. The Forest Service has developed a graphics program, PREVIEW, to portray topographic and land cover data (Myklestad and Wagner, 1976). While the symbols used to represent individual landscape elements are somewhat abstract, the overall effect is quite realistic.

Photographs. Researchers have obtained good simulation results with the full range of photographic media: color prints (Zube et al., 1974), color slides (Daniel and Boster, 1976), black-and-white prints (Shafer et al., 1969), black-and-white slides (Winkel et al., 1970), and offset printed copies (Kaplan, 1979), as well as color film with sound (Banerjee, 1977) and film and black-and-white video (McKechnie, 1977). The primary limitation of photographic media is the need for an existing environment. To simulate proposed environments, one must photograph models (Kaplan, 1978) or alter the photograph using montage techniques.

Graphic montage. Graphic montage techniques allow researchers to portray potential environments with the realism of photographs. The easiest approach is to make composites from several photographs such as Wilmott et al. (1982) used to assess alternative Main Street redevelopment proposals. Artist enhancement with retouching pigments and opaque watercolors can also be done using hand-drawn perspectives. Color reproductions of montages are included in the text of study reports involving proposed dams and reservoirs (Ady et al., 1979) and offshore liquefied natural gas terminals (Baird et al., 1979).

Response Formats

It is necessary for the researcher to establish a method to elicit observer descriptions and perceptions of the landscape. While there are well-established and widely recognized methods available, a host of conceptual and methodological issues are associated with their use (Craik and Feimer, 1979; Daniel, 1976; Wohlwill, 1976). These issues include the following: (1) the reliability that the results can be replicated; (2) the validity that the method measures what it purports to measure; (3) the sensitivity of the method to distinguish actual differences; (4) the generality of the method's application across diverse environments and observers; and (5) the utility of the method for the landscape planners and managers needing to assess visual quality and impacts. These issues have not been addressed comprehensively for any visual assessment response format. However, the past decade has seen repeated use of several methods without any obvious difficulties that would eliminate them from further consideration. These include methods for quantifying visual qualities, such as (1) rating scales, (2) Q-sorts, (3) rank ordering, and (4) checklists. They also include more holistic cognitive methods for systematically describing visual qualities, such as (5) similarity sorts, (6) observer-employed photography, and (7) cognitive maps. Certainly this list should not be considered exhaustive. There is still a need for the development of innovative methods. In any case, researchers would be well advised to use more than one approach and seek convergent results.

Rating scales. Rating scales are the most widely used method for describing landscape qualities. There are four formats: (1) bipolar scales such as Daniel and Boster (1976) use in the Scenic Beauty Estimation method; (2) Likert-type scales of agreement such as McKechnie's (1971) Environmental Response Inventory; (3) unipolar scales such as the Bureau of Land Management (Feimer et al., 1981; USDI, 1980a) uses in its Visual Resource Management Program; and (4) magnitude estimates such as Fines (1968) used by assigning a unit value to a control scene.

Q-sorts. A disadvantage to rating scales is that different individuals may not calibrate the scale in the same way. Daniel and Boster (1976) found this a serious enough problem that their Scenic Beauty Estimation method standardizes the raw rating values. The benefits from using a forced Q-sort procedure to evaluate landscape simulations rather than a rating scale are (1) greater sensitivity because the scale's whole range is being used, (2) an equivalent application procedure used by each observer, and (3) reliability equal to other rating methods (Pitt and Zube, 1979). This procedure has been adopted for use in the visual quality inventory of a citizen participation-oriented natural resources planning program (Palmer, 1982).

Rank ordering. A third approach for obtaining a quantitative evaluation of visual quality is for the observer to rank a set of landscapes from highest to lowest quality. Zube and colleagues (1974) used rank ordering to assess eight sites that were photographically simulated and also evaluated in the field. The obvious advantage of ranking is greater differentiation among scenes. However, ranking large numbers of scenes becomes unwieldy.

Checklists. Unlike rating or ranking procedures, checklists are used simply to record the presence or absence of objects or attributes. For instance, Craik (1972) has developed a landscape adjective checklist of 240 adjectives commonly used in everyday life to describe landscape (for example, hilly, grassy, sunny).

Similarity sorts. The four previous response formats direct the observer's evaluations to specific visual qualities. A researcher interested in providing observers with greater control in defining the relationships among landscapes should consider a free sorting procedure. Rosenberg and Kim (1975) review the use of sorting methods to investigate perceptions. Palmer (1978, 1982, 1983) has developed a procedure for creating a landscape taxonomy that is based on people's perceptions of similarity among landscape scenes.

Observer-employed photography. Another holistic and naturalistic approach to identifying the landscape qualities important to observers is for the observers to document them photographically (Chenoweth, forthcoming). This approach recognizes the observer as an informant and participant—a more active member of the research team than an interview respondent taking a paper-and-pencil test.

Cognitive maps. Sketch maps were first used by Lynch (1960) to understand how people relate different parts of their environment and how they place themselves in the landscape. Cognitive mapping and related methods are described in detail by Gould and White (1974). In its simplest form, observers are given a blank piece of paper and asked to sketch a map of the area being studied. Appleyard (1970) effectively used this technique during the early planning stages of a Venezuelan new town, Ciudad Guayana. He found it an important source of information concerning spatial relationships that are difficult to express verbally.

Approaches to Visual Impact Assessment

The previous sample of methods forms the tool kit available to someone planning to conduct a visual impact assessment. There are no standardized guidelines for the use of these methods, but past assessments seem to have followed one of three approaches: (1) professional appraisals, (2) predictive models, and (3) public evaluations.

Professional Appraisals

Most visual quality and impact assessments are conducted by landscape professionals according to established criteria using standardized procedures. The criteria are based on evaluations of landscape patterns and composition without reference to public perceptions. Early studies assessed the landscape quality of large regions based on landform and land-use pattern (see Linton, 1968; Research Planning and Design Associates, 1972), landscape features (Lewis, 1964), or professional aesthetic judgments (Fines, 1968). These studies were not directly concerned with visual impacts. However, they implied that areas of high scenic quality were more sensitive to negative visual impacts and that a potential existed for positive visual impacts in the areas of low scenic quality. The Forest Service developed the first widely used visual assessment system (USDA, 1974). It primarily stressed objective criteria based on physical characteristics of the land, such as landform, rockform, vegetation, and water forms. Visual impacts were considered as part of a sensitivity analysis based on distance and visibility from major travel routes and use areas, as well as proximity to water bodies. The aesthetic criteria developed by the Forest Service (Litton, 1968; USDA, 1973) were too complex for field application, though they dealt more directly with the visual qualities susceptible to impact. The Bureau of Land Management (USDI, 1980a) generalized and simplified these aesthetic criteria into a procedure for making professional appraisals (that is, high, medium, or low) of four qualities (form, line, color, and texture) inherent to three landscape components (land/water, vegetation, and structures). The visual impacts attributable to a proposed project are assessed by contrasting the ratings for the existing and proposed conditions.

Predictive Models

Predictive models have tended to be more a tool for research than for impact assessment. Their orientation is to predict scenic quality based on the presence of quantifiable landscape attributes. In some instances, scenic quality may be defined by professional judgment. However, public evaluations can also be used and correlated to physical landscape attributes. In this case, predictive models form a type of hybrid between the objective criteria of professional appraisals and the democratic orientation of public evaluations. This approach seems particularly appropriate to situations where several small projects are proposed for similar landscape settings. An early application of this approach was developed by Leopold (1969) to compare the relative uniqueness of several rivers. Hamill (1975) adjusted his model to distinguish between overall positive or negative uniqueness. Melhorn and his colleagues (1975) made further improvements. However, these studies all used professional evaluations of scenic quality.

Daniel and Boster (1976) conducted a long series of public evaluations of forest stands using the Scenic Beauty Estimation method. They now have sufficient data to begin development of a computer-aided management tool that would predict scenic beauty based on proposed management practices for specific forest types (Daniel and Schroeder, 1979). In another example, Brush and Palmer (1979) investigated the general visual quality impacts as the Northeast became more urbanized. They based their discussions on the landscape perception studies by Zube and his colleagues (1974; Palmer, 1978; Crystal and Brush, 1978).

Public Evaluations

The third orientation to visual quality assessments is based on public participation and input using landscape perception methods. For instance, the Soil Conservation Service in Massachusetts developed a natural resource planning program that made extensive use of local volunteers for its completion (USDA, 1977). The visual assessment component of this program was envisioned as a major source of citizen participation. Its application in Dennis, Massachusetts, contributed to the purchase of additional conservation areas and the creation of new zoning regulations in order to maintain locally valued visual qualities (Palmer, 1982). Dennis was named the All American City for 1978 by the National Municipal League of Cities and Towns in large part because of the citizen participation and visual assessment components. The American Falls International Board conducted a large public evaluation of alternative modifications to Niagara Falls (Gaines, 1973). It solicited thousands of opinions regarding the appearance of these various alternatives. Another example is provided by the coastal zone plan for the Virgin Islands that incorporated input from 723 randomly surveyed households (Zube and McLaughlin, 1978). Residents were asked questions relating to coastal aesthetics, the comparative importance of coastal problems, shoreline development alternatives, and the need for shoreline protection programs. Photographs were used to assist in evaluations of visual quality and development alternatives. The photographs proved a very useful tool for defining the environment being evaluated and as a positive interview stimulus for engaging participants with diverse backgrounds.

Conclusion

Clearly there is no single approach to assessing visual impacts. While there are legislative and administrative mandates, actually incorporating assessments of environmental values and amenities into the public decision-making process is a formidable task that requires considerable innovation and ingenuity. During the last half of the 1970s, two major conferences addressed landscape visual quality and impact assessment, producing compendiums with dozens of contributed articles (Elsner and Smardon, 1979; Zube et al., 1975). This same period saw critical examination of the issues involved with the measurement of visual quality (Craik and Feimer, 1979; Daniel, 1976; Wohlwill, 1976), the preparation of extensive literature reviews (Arthur et al., 1977), comprehensive bibliographies (Arthur and Boster, 1976; Hultman, 1976; Nieman and Viohl, 1975; Smardon et al., 1981), and field manuals conducting visual quality assessments (Smardon et al., 1982; USDA presented 1973, 1974, 1977, 1978; UDSI, 1980a; Whyte, 1977). This chapter has presented a survey of existing methods that have been or could be used to assess the landscape's visual qualities and potential visual impacts. It is intended as a sampler of techniques rather than as a definitive statement of the "best" approach. This variety is healthy and should be maintained in order to (1) encourage the development of new innovations that fully meet the public's mandate; (2) develop criteria for evaluating reliability, validity, sensitivity, generality, and utility of visual assessment methods; and (3) prepare a group of professionals capable of conducting the necessary analyses (Craik and Feimer, 1979).

References

ADY, J., B. A. GRAY, and G. R. JONES (1979) "A visual management study of alternative dams, reservoirs, and highway and transmission line corridors near Cooper Creek, Washington," pp. 590-597 in G. H. Elsner and R. C. Smardon (tech. coord.) Proceedings of Our National Landscape: A Conference on Applied Techniques for Analysis and Management of the Visual Resource. Berkeley, CA: Pacific Southwest Forest and Range Experiment Station.

APPLEYARD, D. (1977) "Understanding professional media: issues, theory, and a research agenda," pp. 43-88 in I. Altman and J. F. Wohlwill (eds.) Human Behavior and Environment: Advances in Theory and Research, Vol. 2. New York: Plenum.

—— (1970) "Styles and methods of structuring a city." Environment and Behavior 2, 1: 101-117.

—— K. LYNCH, and J. R. MYER (1964) The View from the Road. Cambridge: MIT Press.

ARTHUR, L. M. and R. S. BOSTER (1976) Measuring Scenic Beauty: A Selected Annotated Bibliography. Fort Collins, CO: Rocky Mountain Forest and Range Experiment Station.

ARTHUR, L. M., T. C. DANIEL, and R. S. BOSTER (1977) "Scenic assessment: an overview." Landscape Planning 4, 2: 109-120.

AYLWARD, G. and M. TURNBULL (1977) "Visual analysis: a computer-aided approach to determine visibility." Computer-Aided Design 9, 2: 103-108.

BAIRD, B. E., S. R. J. SHEPPARD, and R. C. SMARDON (1979) "Visual simulation of offshore liquefied natural gas (LNG) terminals in a decision-making context," pp. 636-644 in G. H. Elsner and R. C. Smardon (tech. coord.) Proceedings of Our National Landscape: A Conference on Applied Techniques for Analysis and

Management of the Visual Resource. Berkeley, CA: Pacific Southwest Forest and Range Experiment Station.

BANERJEE, T. (1977) "Who values what? Audience reaction to coastal scenery." Landscape Architecture 67, 3: 240-243.

BLAIR, N.G.E., I. M. ROBERTSON, and D. S. NEMENS (1980) Environmental Impact Statement on Alternative Uses for Terminal 91 (Piers 90/91): Appendix I: Visual Assessment of Alternative Uses for Terminal 91. Seattle: Port of Seattle.

BRUSH, R. O. and J. F. PALMER (1979) "Measuring the impact of urbanization on scenic quality: land use change in the Northeast," pp. 358-364 in G. H. Elsner and R. C. Smardon (tech. coord.) Proceedings of Our National Landscape: A Conference on Applied Techniques for Analysis and MAnagement of the Visual Resource. Berkeley, CA: Pacific Southwest Forest and Range Experiment Station.

CHENOWETH, R. E. (forthcoming) "Visitor employed photography: a potential tool for landscape architects." Landscape Journal.

CHEREM, G. J. (1974) "Looking through the eyes of the public, or public images of social indicators of aesthetic opportunity," pp. 52-64 in P. J. Brown (ed.) Toward a Technique for Quantifying Aesthetic Quality of Water Resources. Logan: Utah State University.

COLE, N. F., M. FERRARO, R. MALLARY, J. F. PALMER, and E. H. ZUBE (1976) Visual Design Resources for Surface Mine Reclamation. Amherst: Institute for Man and Environment, University of Massachusetts.

CRAIK, K. H. (1972) "Appraising the objectivity of landscape dimensions," pp. 292-346 in J. V. Krutilla (ed.) Natural Environments: Studies in Theoretical and Applied Analysis. Baltimore: Johns Hopkins University Press.

——— (1968) "The comprehension of the everyday physical environment." Journal of the American Institute of Planners 34, 1: 29-37.

——— and N. R. FEIMER (1979) "Setting technical standards for visual assessment procedures," pp. 93-100 in G. H. Elsner and R. C. Smardon (tech. coord.) Proceedings of Our National Landscape: A Conference on Applied Techniques for Analysis and Management of the Visual Resource. Berkeley, CA: Pacific Southwest Forest and Range Experiment Station.

CRYSTAL, J. H. and R. O. BRUSH (1978) "Measuring scenic quality at the urban fringe." Landscape Research 3, 3: 9-14.

CUFF, D. and K. HOOPER (1979) "Graphic and mental representation of environments," pp. 10-17 in A. D. Seidel and S. Danford (eds.) Environmental Design: Research, Theory, and Application. Washington, DC: Environmental Design Research Association.

DANIEL, T. C. (1976) "Criteria for development and application of perceived environmental quality indices," pp. 27-45 in K. H. Craik and E. H. Zube (eds.) Perceiving Environmental Quality: Research and Applications. New York: Plenum.

——— and R. S. BOSTER (1976) "Measuring landscape esthetics: the Scenic Beauty Estimation Method. Fort Collins, CO: Rocky Mountain Forest and Range Experiment Station.

DANIEL, T. C. and H. SCHROEDER (1979) "Scenic Beauty Estimation Model: predicting perceived beauty of forest landscapes," pp. 514-523 in G. H. Elsner and R. C. Smardon (tech. coord.) Proceedings of Our National Landscape: A Conference on Applied Techniques for Analysis and Management of the Visual Resource. Berkeley, CA: Pacific Southwest Forest and Range Experiment Station.

DANIEL, T. C., L. M. ANDERSON, H. W. SCHROEDER, and L. WHEELER III (1977) "Mapping the scenic beauty of forest landscapes." Leisure Sciences 1, 1: 35-53.

DERRY, A., H. W. JANAL, C. D. SHULL, and J. THORMAN (1977) Guidelines for Local Surveys: A Basis for Preservation Planning. Washington, DC: Government Printing Office.

ELSNER, G. H. and R. C. SMARDON [tech. coord.] (1979) Proceedings of Our National Landscape: A Conference on Applied Techniques for Analysis and Management of the Visual Resource. Berkeley, CA: Pacific Southwest Forest and Range Experiment Station.

FEIMER, N. R., R. C. SMARDON, and K. H. CRAIK (1981) "Evaluating the effectiveness of observer-based visual resource and impact assessment methods." Landscape Research 6, 1: 12-16.

FELLEMAN, J. P. (1982) "Visibility mapping in New York's coastal zone: a case study of alternative methods." Coastal Zone Management Journal 9, 3/4: 249-270.

FINES, K. D. (1968) "Landscape evaluation: a research project in East Sussex." Regional Studies 2, 1: 45-55.

FISCHER, W. C. (1981) Photo Guides for Appraising Downed Wood Fuels in Montana Forests: How They Were Made. Ogden, UT: Intermountain Forest and Range Experiment Station.

GAINES, J. (1973) "Should Niagara Falls look like this?" New York Times (September 9): sec. 10, p. 1.

GOODEY, B., A. W. DUFFETT, J. R. GOLD, and D. SPENSER (1971) City Scene: An Exploration into the Image of Central Birmingham as Seen by Area Residents. Birmingham, England: Centre for Urban and Regional Studies, University of Birmingham.

GOULD, P. and R. WHITE (1974) Mental Maps. Baltimore: Pelican.

HALPRIN, L. (1965) "Motation." Progressive Architecture 46, 7: 126-133.

HAMILL, L. (1975) "Analysis of Leopold's quantitative comparisons of landscape aesthetics." Journal of Leisure Research 7, 1: 16-28.

HULTMAN, S. (1976) Environmental Perception, Landscape, Forestry: An Annotated Bibliography. Stockholm: Royal College of Forestry.

JONES, G. R., I. JONES, B. A. GRAY, B. PARKER, J. C. COE, J. B. BURNHAM, and N. M. GEITNER (1975) "A method for the quantification of aesthetic values for environmental decision making." Nuclear Technology 25, 4: 682-713.

KAPLAN, R. (1979) "A methodology for simultaneously obtaining and sharing information," pp. 58-66 in T. C. Daniel et al. (eds.) Assessing Amenity Resource Values. Fort Collins, CO: Rocky Mountain Forest and Range Experiment Station.

――― (1978) "Participation in environmental design: some considerations and a case study," pp. 427-438 in S. Kaplan and R. Kaplan (eds.) Humanscape. North Scituate, MA: Duxbury.

LEOPOLD, L. B. (1969) "Quantitative comparison of some aesthetic factors among rivers." Geological Survey Circular 620. U.S. Department of the Interior, Geological Survey, Washington, DC.

LEWIS, P. H., Jr. (1964) "Quality corridors for Wisconsin." Landscape Architecture 54, 2: 100-107.

LINTON, D. H. (1968) "The assessment of scenery as a natural resource." Scottish Geographical Magazine 84, 3: 219-238.

LITTON, R. B., Jr, (1973) Landscape Control Points: A Procedure for Predicting and Monitoring Visual Impacts. Berkeley, CA: Pacific Southwest Forest and Range Experiment Station.

—— (1968) Forest Landscape Description and Inventories: A Basis for Land Planning and Design. Berkeley, CA: Pacific Southwest Forest and Range Experiment Station.

LYNCH, K. (1960) The Image of the City. Cambridge: MIT Press.

McKECHNIE, G. E. (1977) "Simulation techniques in environmental psychology," pp. 169-189 in D. Stokals (ed.) Perspectives on Environment and Behavior: Theory, Research and Applications. New York: Plenum.

—— (1971) Environmental Response Inventory Manual. Palo Alto, CA: Consulting Psychological Press.

MELHORN, W. N., E. A. KELLER, and R. A. McBANE (1975) Landscape Aesthetics Numerically Defined (LAND): Application to Fluvial Environments. West Lafayette, IN: Water Resources Research Center, Purdue University.

Minnesota Environmental Quality Council (1976) Environmental Report, Minnesota Power and Light Application for Certificates of Site Compatibility. St. Paul: Author.

MYKLESTAD, E. and J. A. WAGNER (1976) PREVIEW: Computer Assistance for Visual Management of Forested Landscapes. Upper Darby, PA: Northeastern Forest Experiment Station.

National Environmental Policy Act (1969) 42 U.S.C. sec. 4321 et seq.

NIEMAN, T. J. and R. C. VIOHL (1975) The Description, Classification, and Assessment of Visual Landscape Quality. Monticello, IL: Council of Planning Librarians.

PALMER, J. F. (1983) "A visual character approach to the classification of backcountry trail environments." Landscape Journal 2, 1: 3-12.

—— (1982) "Assessment of coastal wetlands in Dennis, Massachusetts," pp. 65-80 in R. C. Smardon (ed.) The Future of Wetlands: Assessing Visual-Cultural Values. Totowa, NJ: Allanheld, Osmun.

—— (1978) "An investigation of the conceptual classification of landscapes and its application to landscape planning issues," pp. 92-103 in S. Weidmann and J. R. Anderson (eds.) Priorities for Environmental Design Research. Washington, DC: Environmental Design Research Association.

PITT, D. G. and E. H. ZUBE (1979) "The Q-sort method: use in landscape assessment research and landscape planning," pp. 227-234 in G. H. Elsner and R. C. Smardon (tech. coord.) Proceedings of Our National Landscape: A Conference on Applied Techniques for Analysis and Management of the Visual Resource. Berkeley, CA: Pacific Southwest Forest and Range Experiment Station.

Research Planning and Design Associates (1972) North Atlantic Regional Water Resources Study: Appendix N, Visual and Cultural Environment. New York: North Atlantic Regional Water Resources Coordinating Committee.

ROSENBERG, S. and M. P. KIM (1975) "The method of sorting as as a data-gathering procedure in multivariate research." Multivariate Behavioral Resource 10: 486-502.

SHAFER, E. L., Jr., J. F. HAMILTON, Jr., and E. A. SCHMIDT (1969) "Natural landscape preferences: a predictive model." Journal of Leisure Research 1, 1: 1-19.

SHEPPARD, S.R.J. (1980) "Predictive landscape portrayals: a selective research review." Landscape Journal 1, 1: 9-14.

SHUTTLESWORTH, S. (1980) "The evaluation of landscape quality." Landscape Research 5, 1: 14-20.

SMARDON, R. C. (1979) "The interface of legal and esthetic considerations," pp. 676-685 in G. H. Elsner and R. C. Smardon (tech. coord.) Proceedings of Our National Landscape: A Conference on Applied Techniques for Analysis and Management of the Visual Resource. Berkeley, CA: Pacific Southwest Forest and Range Experiment Station.

———— S.R.J. SHEPPARD, and S. NEWMAN (1982) Prototype Visual Impact Assessment Manual. Syracuse: College of Environmental Science and Forestry, State University of New York.

SMARDON, R. C., M. HUNTER, J. RESUE, and M. ZOELLING (1981) Our National Landscape: Annotated Bibliography and Expertise Index. Berkeley, CA: Agricultural Science Publications, University of California.

THIEL, P. (1961) "A sequence-experience notation for architectural and urban space." Town Planning Review 32, 1: 33-52.

TRAVIS, M. R., G. H. ELSNER, W. D. IVERSON, and C. G. JOHNSON (1975) VIEWIT: Computation of Seen Areas, Slope and Aspect for Land Use Planning. Berkeley, CA: Pacific Southwest Forest and Range Experiment Station.

U.S. Department of Agriculture (USDA), Forest Service (1974) National Forest Landscape Management: The Visual Management System, Vol. 2. Agricultural Handbook 462. Washington, DC: Government Printing Office.

———— (1973) National Forest Landscape Management, Vol. 1. Agricultural Handbook 434. Washington, DC: Government Printing Office.

U.S. Department of Agriculture (USDA), Soil Conservation Service (1978) Procedure to Establish Priorities in Landscape Architecture. Technical Release 65. Washington, DC: Government Printing Office.

———— (1977) "A natural resources planning program handbook." USDA Soil Conservation Service, Amherst, MA. (draft)

U.S. Environmental Protection Agency (1979) Protecting Visibility: An EPA Report to Congress. Research Triangle Park, NC: Author.

U.S. Department of the Interior (USDI), Bureau of Land Management (1980a) Visual Resource Management Program. Washington, DC: Government Printing Office.

———— (1980b) Visual Simulation Techniques. Washington, DC: Government Printing Office.

WHYTE, A.V.T. (1977) Guidelines for Field Studies in Environmental Perception. Paris: United Nations Educational, Scientific and Cultural Organization.

WILLMOTT, G. J., R. C. SMARDON, and R. A. McNEIL (1982) Consensus Seeking for Waterfront Revitalization Through Visual Stimulation in Clayton, New York. Syracuse: College of Environmental Science and Forestry, State University of New York.

WILMONT, G. and J. FELLEMAN (1983) The SUNY/ESF Environmental Simulator Technical Report. Syracuse: College of Environmental Science and Forestry, State University of New York.

WINKEL, G. H., R. MALEK, and P. THIEL (1970) "Community response to the design features of roads: a technique for measurement," pp. 133-145 in Transportation Research Board, Socioeconomic Considerations in Transportation Planning. Highway Research Board 305. Washington, DC: Transportation Research Board, National Research Council.

WOHLWILL, J. F. (1976) "Environmental aesthetics: the environment as a source of affect," pp. 37-86 in I. Altman and J. F. Wohlwill (eds.) Human Behavior and Environment: Advances in Theory and Research, Vol. 1. New York: Plenum.

ZUBE, E. H. (1970) "Evaluating the visual and cultural landscape." Journal of Soil and Water Conservation 25, 4: 137-141.

———— and M. McLAUGHLIN (1978) "Assessing perceived values of the coastal zone," pp. 360-371 in American Society of Civil Engineers, Coastal Zone 78. New York: American Society of Civil Engineers.

ZUBE, E. H., R. O. BRUSH, and J. G. FABOS [eds.] (1975) Landscape Assessment: Value, Perceptions, and Resources. Stroudsburg, PA: Hutchinson Ross.

ZUBE, E. H., J. H. CRYSTAL, and J. F. PALMER (1976) Visitor Center Design Evaluation. Denver: National Park Service.

ZUBE, E. H., D. G. PITT, and T. W. ANDERSON (1974) Perception and Measurement of Scenic Resources in the Southern Connecticut River Valley. Amherst: Institute for Man and Environment, University of Massachusetts.

14

Evaluation Methods

O O O O O O O O O O O O O O O O O

KURT FINSTERBUSCH

O O O O O O O O O O O O O O O O O

● How should a public official make policy decisions? In this chapter I will discuss the ethical principles that should guide these decisions and review the many techniques for making decisions involving multiple criteria. This type of decision making is commonly called "multiobjective," but it is also sometimes called "valuing" or "evaluation."

This chapter describes ideal decision-making procedures; actual decisions will deviate from the ideal patterns because they will be influenced by political pressures, bureaucratic games and jealousies, misinformation or inadequate information, and practical compromises of many kinds. Nevertheless, there is much to be gained from knowledge of ideal procedures, because they provide a model for decision makers to emulate (or appear to emulate).

Principles Governing Public Policy Decisions

Policymakers are public servants commissioned to serve the public good. From the beginning of the history of American government the public good has been understood to be the purpose of government. In fact, the first

This chapter is a revised version of Finsterbusch, K., "A Survey of Methods for Evaluating Social Impacts," in K. Finsterbusch and C. P. Wolf (eds.), METHODOLOGY OF SOCIAL IMPACT ASSESSMENT, 2nd Edition. Copyright © 1981 by Hutchinson Ross Publishing Company, Stroudsburg, PA. Reprinted by permission of the publisher.

grievance hurled against the King of England in the Declaration of Independence was that "he has refused his assent to Laws, the most wholesome and necessary for the public good." Later the Constitution was established to "form a more perfect Union, establish justice, insure domestic tranquility, provide for the common defense, promote the general welfare, and secure the blessings of liberty." The five components of the public good asserted here are security, law and order, justice, liberty, and welfare. Since security and law and order are usually not critical issues in most policy decisions of government, the values of greatest concern to policymakers are generally justice, liberty, and welfare. The relative importance of these three values is hotly debated in current political philosophy, with the utilitarians emphasizing welfare, Rawls emphasizing justice, and Nozick emphasizing liberty.

Ideally, the policymaker will have the wisdom of Solomon and will make and implement just policies that maximize the general welfare without interfering with personal liberties. Unfortunately, most policy decisions cannot maximize all three values, and no one value is demonstrably superior to the others. Policy decisions, therefore, must take into account multiple values. The philosophical rationale for this practice is called "ethical pluralism" and the management science name for it is "multiobjective decision making."

The classical utilitarian principle is that the general welfare is maximized by providing the greatest happiness for the greatest number. This utilitarian principle of maximizing social utility can claim to be both rational and ethical. It claims to be rational because it involves maximizing net benefits. It excludes alternatives that produce fewer benefits for the same costs. These alternatives are inefficient and hence without rational justification. Rationality is to get more for less. The utilitarian principle also claims to be ethical because it advocates benefits to everyone equally and lets each person define benefits, happiness, or utility for him- or herself. Thus it is devoted to the fulfilling of people's needs and desires and thus devoted to their good as they define good. According to utilitarian assumptions the above considerations add up to the maximization of the social good and to a sound public policy ethic.

The utilitarian principle appears simple and easily understood, but actually it involves some extremely difficult issues to resolve. The following issues are particularly germane to public policy decisions: (1) How is utility or good measured? (2) Whose utilities are counted? (3) Does maximizing utility involve only consequences (or ends), or are means also evaluated? On these issues utilitarians vehemently disagree. Some would confine utility measurements strictly to pleasure and pain. Others intuitively feel that there is more to utility than pleasure. Much self-sacrifice and even pain are necessary for many achievements in sports and for self-actualization in general. Many would rather be a troubled Socrates than a contented pig. For them, therefore, utility is not simply a net pleasure measurement. Those taking the pleasure/pain position, however, would argue that self-actualization can be justified on the basis of pleasure/pain measurements, because self-actualization is likely to increase the net pleasure (pleasure minus pain) of humankind.

The second issue probably would divide many utilitarians from most policymakers. Many utilitarians include animals in the calculation of total happiness, though not on a par with humans. They find no reason to exclude any sentient or conscious beings from moral consideration. Others emphasize differences between humans and other animals and make these differences the basis for differential moral consideration. Utilitarians also debate whether future generations should be included in their happiness calculations. At this point the policymaker would object that he or she is the servant of a specific public, and that his or her obligations to nonmembers and future members are very limited, if not nonexistent, except as present members want to protect wildlife, nonmembers, and future generations. The policymaker would limit utility calculations to the members of the geopolitical units that he or she represents or serves. The policymaker has a good point, but the welfare of nonmembers and future members must not be entirely neglected. Many Americans have strong feelings that policies should ensure the "good" of the environment for nonmembers and future generations.

The third issue raises the debate between act-utilitarians and rule-utilitarians. The former argue that each act should maximize happiness, but the later argue that individual acts should not violate rules that are beneficial for society. For example, rule-utilitarians would argue against stealing even though a theft by a poor person of some easily replaceable goods belonging to a rich person might result in greater aggregate happiness. On the other hand, act-utilitarians believe that even venerable rules such as "do not steal" have adverse net effects in special circumstances, so they should not be given precedence over the general utilitarian principle.

Many additional complexities and issues could be raised in connection with the utilitarian principle, but space does not allow them to be taken up here. They raise problems with the utilitarian principle but do not nullify its usefulness for public policy decisions. In sum, policymakers should consider the sum total of all positive and negative consequences of an action mainly for the members of their geopolitical unit, but also for other humans, future generations, and even, to a much lesser degree, for animals. To make the job manageable, policymakers should approach the evaluation from the perspective of act-utilitarianism while being sensitive to the good and bad consequences of rules of procedure. Finally, in evaluating utilities the policymaker should try to let people speak for themselves instead of just evaluating their utilities for them. This procedure sidesteps the issue of what constitutes utility, that is, whether utility is simply pleasure minus pain or whether it also involves many intangibles.

A caveat must be introduced at this point. Many public policy decisions are functional in nature and are judged strictly on the basis of their efficiency. They exclude considerations of ultimate values and are limited to instrumental choices. For example, when certain Pentagon officials have to select a bomber to buy for the Air Force, they are expected to select the most capable of available bombers without raising questions of the rightness of increasing America's military power. This chapter deals with multiobjective decision making and applies to decisions that consider at least one value besides efficiency.

If policymakers were to be guided by a single principle, the strongest candidate for this role would be the utilitarian principle. The main objection of most nonutilitarians to the utilitarian principle is not that there are better candidates for the single guiding principle for policy decisions, but that no single principle is sufficient by itself. They plead for the consideration of additional principles to correct for the shortcomings of the "maximum good" principle. Its major shortcoming, according to most nonutilitarians, is its failure to deal with the possible unfairness of the distribution of costs and benefits. They argue that the utilitarian principle must be tempered by an equity principle. The most eminent proponent of this view is Rawls, whose ideas will be summarized next.

Rawls, in his *Theory of Justice* (1971), proposes a set of principles as an alternative to the utilitarian principle for guiding public policies. Nevertheless, the utilitarian principle of maximizing the welfare of the many is not rejected by Rawls, but only modified by considerations of liberty and equality.

Rawls argues that his view of the good society is the one that impartial observers would choose. He imagines what form of society rational self-interested people would choose if everyone were ignorant of the statuses they would have in the new society they were contracting together to create. He reasoned that they would want strong guarantees of personal freedom as long as this freedom was not used in ways that would be harmful to others. They also would want a system based on equality, except when certain inequalities would benefit everyone. The principle of maximizing welfare would supersede the principle of equality as long as no one was made worse off. He recognized, however, that sometimes some people of necessity must be made worse off in order to produce important benefits for the group. Society must be very careful to spell out a just principle for this situation, and Rawls argues that his "justice as fairness" principle is the one that impartial persons would choose. The main result of the justice as fairness principle is the protection of the disadvantaged. If some people had to be made worse off for the sake of the general good (maximum welfare), the sacrifice must not be borne by the least advantaged.

Rawls's analysis of the original position (time of choosing the institutions of the new society) leads him to formulate the following two basic principles for organizing society and therefore for guiding public policies:

> *First principle:* Each person is to have an equal right to the most extensive total system of equal basic liberties compatible with a similar system of liberty for all.

> *Second principle:* Social and economic inequalities are to be arranged so that they are both: (a) to the greatest benefit to the least advantaged, consistent with the just savings principle, and (b) attached to offices and positions open to all under conditions of fair equality of opportunity (Rawls, 1971: 302).

The first principle may be designated as equal and extensive liberties. The second principle may be designated as the combination of fairness to the disadvantaged and equality of opportunity.

In Rawls's ideal society, liberty in the sense of basic political rights and justice in the sense of equality of opportunity and positive treatment of the least advantaged set the parameters within which the utilitarian principle of maximizing welfare operates. When liberty and justice are assured, the utilitarian principle outweighs all other considerations. Incidentally, the just savings principle referred to in the above quote imposes an obligation on the present generations (without requiring unreasonable sacrifices) to accumulate capital and save resources for future generations.

In practice, the real issue between utilitarians and Rawls is that of the welfare of the disadvantaged. The other two components of Rawls's scheme are seldom bones of contention. Very few policy iniatives involve infringements on basic political freedoms and usually equality of opportunity is compatible with maximizing welfare. In practice, therefore, the main disagreement is whether to maximize general welfare even when the disadvantaged are harmed. A practical solution to the tension between the fairness and utilitarian principles is to mitigate the harm to the disadvantaged or to fully compensate it and then maximize general welfare.

Some political philosophers emphasize the value of liberty far more than does Rawls. He gives certain liberties priority over the maximizing welfare principle, including freedom to live, freedom from slavery and unjust domination, and freedom from unjust imprisonment. In practice he would accept the freedoms included in the Bill of Rights and the Fourteenth Amendment. Some philosophers, however, go further and include in the freedoms that have precedence over the general welfare the freedom from government interference in one's affairs except to prevent direct harm to others. These philosophers are libertarians and they argue for free markets and the minimal state. Free markets often are very productive and therefore are congruent with the utilitarian principle. Libertarians, however, think they should be maintained whether or not happiness is maximized thereby.

Nozick (1974) has developed the best-known statement of the libertarian view. He advocates a minimal state that is narrowly limited in its functions to national defense and the enforcement of criminal and civil laws that protect people from force, fraud, and theft by others. A more extensive state is wrong because it would violate the rights of individuals, even if it would produce greater general welfare. Nozick is especially concerned that the state does not redistribute holdings. As long as the people acquired their holdings in a just manner, it is unjust to take their holdings away from them and give them to others even if the others are unfortunate, poor, or disadvantaged. Only voluntary transfers or transfers that rectify past injustices are legitimate.

Most public servants would interpret their commissions as obligating them to promote all three values discussed above: the general welfare, justice/equity, and liberty. The philosophical position most congruent with this practice of public servants is ethical pluralism (also called "intuitionism"). As its name implies, it argues that no one principle should be given precedence over all other principles in all possible situations. The ethical pluralists acknowledge no absolute principles, but recognize that a number of important principles or values must be taken into account when judging the ethical rightness of a political action. When they are in conflict they must be balanced off (traded off) against one another and no one value be given absolute sway over the decision.

Obviously, the critical question for the ethical pluralist becomes, How are the conflicting values balanced off against one another? Can a "best" procedure be determined? I attempt to deal with this issue in the remainder of this chapter by reviewing a range of techniques for making policy decisions involving multiple objectives or values. I turn now to a discussion of the potential of democracy for achieving best choices by the standards of ethical pluralists.

The traditions of American society claim that democratic procedures are the best for multiobjective policy decisions, because nondemocratic procedures violate inalienable rights. Certainly, democratic procedures increase the legitimacy of the decisions, but attention must be called to two problems. First, since there are a variety of democratic procedures from which to choose, which is the best democratic procedure? Should everyone vote on all issues or should only those who are affected vote? Should all votes be counted equally or should votes be weighted somehow according to the extent of the effects for each voter? Should voters vote directly on issues or vote for representatives, and, if the latter, should representation be geographic or proportional to party vote?

The second problem is what should be done when a democratic decision is clearly the wrong decision. A democracy could vote to start an unprovoked war or to repress or liquidate an unpopular minority. In other words, should some principles have precedence over the principle or democracy? If so, when should they have precedence? The Bill of Rights is a notable effort to establish some principles above the principle of majority rule and works well in protecting basic liberties. How about other values, such as maximizing the general welfare? Should this or any other value have precedence over democracy? Obviously the issues are complex and we cannot offer final answers.

Four major positions in the philosophy of ethics have been identified, but how should policy decisions be made in the light of the contradictory prescriptions reviewed here? Though the debates between these positions cannot be settled here, some guidance can be provided until the debates are settled by philosophers (if they ever are). First, the ethical pluralist position emerges as clearly the superior position until one of the other positions becomes more firmly established. The major virtue of ethical pluralism is that it does not exclude any value. This feature is important while the philosophical issues remain unresolved. Its major fault is that it often leaves the decision undetermined because there is no perfect way to determine the relative weights for values. This fault, however, reflects the larger indeterminacy among the competing ethical positions and must be accepted for now.

The second guiding comment I offer about the debate over which ethical principle is preeminent is that all participants in the debate seem to assume the legitimacy of multiple values. For example, the major argument against utilitarianism and libertarianism is that following their prescriptions leads to situations that violate other praiseworthy values. The main defense of these positions is that rightly understood they are not as antithetical to other values as their critics suppose. Thereby the defenders admit that other values are important. Furthermore, the importance of multiple values is basic to Rawls's theory of justice. It includes the values of liberty, equality, fairness (a bias toward the welfare of the disadvantaged), and maximizing general welfare. Rawls's position is pluralistic, but he does not trade off these values; rather, he rank orders them. Most of his critics do not fault him for advocating multiple values. They are simply not convinced by his arguments that his rankings are universally valid.

The third guiding comment for policymaking in light of the lack of consensus among ethical philosophers is that public policies are mandated to be concerned with multiple values regardless of the present state of ethical discourse in philosophy. In other words, policymakers are required to be ethical pluralists. It makes sense, therefore, to approach the question of how to choose the "best" policies from the framework of the ethical pluralist.

In summary, the above discussion claims that no single principle has yet been established for guiding public policy decisions. No weighting or ordering of various values is supported by compelling philosophical arguments. Multiple values, therefore, must be considered in public policy decisions. Three values that are especially important are maximizing the general welfare, protecting the disadvantaged from bearing greater than average costs, and minimizing government infringement on the liberties of citizens. Finally, since multiple values should be considered in policy decisions, multivalue methods must be devised that weight the values or utilize the "choices" of the public.

The next section reviews the full range of methods for multiobjective (value) policy decisions. They assume an ethical pluralist framework, and can be used in combination or singly. In the subsequent section a combination of methods for policy decisions is proposed that includes democratic choice methods, weighting schemes, and limits on negative effects.

Methods for Making Multiobjective Policy Decisions

In this section nineteen methods are reviewed for reaching a policy decision involving multiobjectives and the consideration of nonmarket impacts, that is, impacts that are not measured in dollars. When all impacts have prices they can be equated and the decision can be based on benefit/cost calculations. Few social impacts, however, have prices, so the focus of the discussion is on evaluating nonmarket impacts.

Nonmarket impacts do not share a common metric. Therefore, they cannot be evaluated relative to each other without a special methodology that compares unlike values. Some methods translate the unlike values into a common, more general value scheme. Other methods assume that such translations cannot be made on a satisfactory basis and substitute for them "acceptable" decision-making procedures. Still others provide methods for ensuring that "bad" decisions are not made when it is impossible to determine the "best" choice.

Table 14.1 presents the nineteen evaluation techniques developed by social scientists to assess nonmarket impacts. Two generic sets of techniques can be identified. The first of these sets are the techniques for deriving a cumulative number for each option under consideration; these numbers provide a concise basis for selecting the "best" option. These common metric or weighting scheme techniques are sufficient in themselves for making a choice among alternatives (unless, of course, the absolute numbers derived are identical). The second set of techniques does not present cumulative numbers. Rather, these techniques provide information — in itself insufficient to make a decision — to be utilized within a decision process. The former techniques completely determine the decision; the latter are indeterminant in themselves, leaving the final decision to a process sometimes prescribed by, but not controlled by, the research team.

TABLE 14.1   Alternative Methods for Evaluating Nonmarket Impacts

(A) Common Metrics
    (1) objective metrics
    (2) subjective metrics

(B) Weighting Schemes
    (1) consensual weights
    (2) formula weights
    (3) justified subjective weights
    (4) subjective weights
    (5) inferred subjective weights
    (6) ranking
    (7) equal weight
    (8) multiple methods

(C) Discrete Dimensions Evaluation
    (1) lexicographic pruning
    (2) minimum criteria analysis
    (3) balance sheet

(D) Democratic Choice Methods
    (1) public choice
    (2) advisory committee choice
    (3) political process outcome

(E) Methods that Obviate Evaluation
    (1) standardize costs or benefits
    (2) minimize negative effects
    (3) compensation and mitigation

Common Metrics

OBJECTIVE METRICS

The ideal evaluation technique is one that can register all of the impacts of each alternative on a common objective metric. This ideal cannot even be approximated. The three major candidates for an objective metric are money, time, and energy, and money is the lead candidate. Money measures market impacts and, with ingenuity, many nonmarket impacts can be converted to dollar values. Everyone recognizes the problems and imperfections of all techniques for assigning prices to nonmarket impacts, but some argue that dollar valuations are the best among imperfect solutions in an imperfect world. At best such methods are explicit and the results are concrete. Therefore, they can be clearly debated. Others object by asking, "What price can you put on the loss of a life?" Since this question cannot be answered scientifically, the objection has weight. The courts, however, cannot wait for scientific answers, because they must price lives in order to settle liability claims. They generally value a life to be equal to the victim's expected future lifetime earnings. No one claims that this is the "true" value of a life; but it does allow the courts to make decisions. Policymakers must also make decisions involving loss of life. Should they also price lives? If so, at what price? Rhoads (1978) reviews the techniques for pricing lives and points to the wide disparity in their results, ranging from $16,500 to $1,500,000 (see also Etzioni, 1979; Thompson, 1980). Etzioni (1979) points out that the public supports some measures that save lives at a cost of millions of dollars per life saved and will not support other measures that save lives at a cost of only a few thousand dollars per life saved.

There are many specific techniques for assigning prices to nonmarket impacts. Two procedures with relatively general applicability are costing outputs and costing the negation of outputs. Schmid (1975) has the decision maker assign subjective values to specified amounts of various project outputs. The outputs of each project alternative are measured and multiplied by the subjective values to obtain a total benefit score for each project alternative. He divides the benefit score by the alternative's cost to obtain the benefit-cost ratio. He even computes implied prices for each output from the subjective values and the costs. A less subjective method of computing prices for project outputs is proposed by Melinyshyn et al. (1973: 4): The price of project impacts is equated to "the cost of preventing the impact, the replacement cost, or a value judgment." Subjective judgments are used only when no objective method is available.

SUBJECTIVE METRICS

Any set of events that scale unidimensionally when evaluated can be constructed into a subjective metric by standardizing and aggregating the evaluations by a sufficient random sample of a population. For example, Holmes and Rahe (1967) have established a Social Readjustment Scale for scaling all stressful life events. Many stressful events have been placed on the scale through national sample surveys — for example, the death of one's spouse is 100 and moving to a new home is 20 — and others could be added without disturbing these placements. If such a scale could be created for the most general dimension of all, general personal utility, it would bring the millenium for evaluation methodology. Unfortunately, no such metric exists and probably never will. Meanwhile, existing subjective metrics are not general enough to scale all impacts of complex policies. A subjective metric, therefore, cannot provide a complete evaluation framework at this time.

Weighting Schemes

Policy studies do not yet depend entirely on common metric techniques. These techniques are too imperfect and require much more development before they are fully acceptable. Weighting schemes, however, are less demanding than common metrics and are widely used. They do not directly score all impacts on a single metric. Rather all impacts are measured on indices appropriate to them, and then the indices are weighted relative to each other. Eight types of weighting schemes are discussed below.

CONSENSUAL WEIGHTS

Consensual weights represent a consensus among experts or an official determination of relative importance by an authoritative group. Consensual weights do not currently exist in the field of impact assessment. They are extremely difficult to establish. Consensually derived thresholds, however, are common. For example, 70 decibels is generally considered the threshold that should not be exceeded by highway noise levels and regulations now require that highways be designed to keep noise levels beneath this point. Consensual thresholds are common because they involve much less value conflict than consensual weights. The latter could significantly affect the distribution of costs and benefits of policy decisions, so consensus is difficult to achieve. Perhaps weights that derive from empirically ascertained trade-off curves for affected parties could someday be fashioned into consensual weights if results replicate closely in a variety of studies. There is no indication, however, that consensual weights will be developed soon.

FORMULA WEIGHTS

Formula weights are calculated by applying mathematical operations to quantified measures. For example, the weight for the ith impact might be expressed in the formula:

$$w_i = \sum_{j=1}^{m} P_{ij} \quad I_{ij} \quad P_{ij}$$

where P_{ij} is the number of people of category j to be affected by the ith impact, I is the average intensity of impact, and p is the average probability of impact. In other words, for each impact the size of every affected group is multiplied by the intensity and probability of impact on that group, and these scores are summed for all groups and for all impacts. These are extremely difficult scores to determine, so these formula weights are infeasible for most projects. The most difficult task seems to be the estimation of the average magnitude of impact for each affected group. The widely accepted scale of stressful life events mentioned above (Holmes and Rahe, 1967) may provide the base for an impact magnitude scale, but considerable research would be required to locate most project impacts on this or any other scale. For examples of formula weights, see Melinyshyn et al. (1973) and Baker et al. (1972).

JUSTIFIED SUBJECTIVE WEIGHTS

Subjective weights are commonly used in formal decision-making frameworks, but justification for the selected weights is rarely provided. We recommend greater use of justified subjective weights, because reviewers need to know on what basis the weights were devised. When the criteria for assigning weights are explicitly identified, critical feedback can lead to improvements and wider acceptance.

Justified subjective weights may be explicit weights that the research team selects on the basis of all of the information available to it. In this manner I have proposed weights for census area variables that were used in a highway location formula (Finsterbusch, 1977a). Explanations are provided for assigning large or small weights to variables. New information or good counterarguments would lead to revisions of the formula.

When outside experts are used to provide weights in a full Delphi process the individual experts must justify their weights and criticize the weights of those with whom they disagree. Thus Delphi involves critical feedback that results in revisions in individual judgments, generally in the direction of greater consensus. The Delphi technique, therefore, produces a group decision and arguments that can be synthesized into a rationalization of the group decision. For an example of the use of Delphi in creating weights, see Dean and Shih (1973).

SUBJECTIVE WEIGHTS

An extremely prevalent technique is subjective weighting. There are many variations of this technique, differing in terms of the elements weighted and the choice of weighting procedures. Subjective weights may be assigned to project objectives (Charnes and Cooper, 1961; Charnes et al., 1969; Hill, 1967, 1973; Falk, 1968; Rodding, 1975), analytical dimensions (MacCrimmon, 1973; Cohon and Marks, 1975; Dean and Shih, 1973; Breen and Covault, 1976; Pikarsky, 1967), impact categories, or the alternatives themselves. Subjective weights may be assigned by decision makers, expert judges, representatives of interested parties, or samples of the relevant general public. Subjective weights may be assigned by a simple score assignment process, a trade-off matrix, paired comparison trade-offs, indifference curves, or Delphi procedures. These 4 elements for weighting, the 4 types of assessors, and the 5 weighting procedures make 80 combinations. My comments will be limited to the 5 weighting procedures. (For reviews of subjective weighting techniques or descriptions of special methods, see Delft and Nijkamp, 1977; Rodding, 1975; MacCrimmon, 1973; Cohon and Marks, 1975; Keeney and Nair, 1975; Breen and Covault, 1976; Hill, 1973; David and Duckstein, 1976; Pikarsky, 1967; Edwards, 1979; Keeney and Raiffa, 1976; Hwang and Masud, 1979; Cook and Stewart, 1975; Starr and Zeleny, 1977; Lord et al., 1979; Haines and Tavainess, 1981; Duckstein and Kempf, 1981; Zeleny, 1974, 1980; Cohon, 1978; Keeney and Wood, 1977; Nijkamp, 1977; Anderson, 1981; Zionts and Wallenius, 1976. See especially Hwang and Masud, 1979, for a review of interactive methods involving progressive articulations of preferences.)

Subjective weighting procedures can be categorized into five general types: (1) point allocation, (2) trade-off matrix, (3) paired comparison trade-off, (4) indifference curves, and (5) Delphi weights. The first type of weighting procedure — the point allocation procedure — is the simplest. Judges are asked to score a number of items by one of many possible pointing systems. Three examples of point allocation scales are presented below:

(1)   A scale of a fixed number of points — the items are to be scaled on a 0 to X scale, e.g., 0 to 1.0, 0 to 10, 0 to 100, 0 to 1000, or on a minus to plus scale, e.g., ±1.0, ±10, ±100, ±1000.

(2)   Scale around a middle value — take a middle score item and score it at 100 and score all other items relative to this item as ratios.

(3)   Distribute a set number of points — the judge is given a budget or a prescribed number of points to allocate among the items (for example, see Pendse and Wyskoff, 1976; Stewart and Gelberd, 1976).

The second weighting procedure is the trade-off martrix. The judge is given a table with categories or points on one variable in the rows and the categories or points of another variable in the columns. The judge ranks the cells of the tables. This procedure is especially useful when the trade-offs between variables are not linear but a simple procedure is required. It grows out of the work on conjoint measurement in mathematical psychology (Luce and Tukey, 1964) and has been developed in market research (Green and Rao, 1971; Johnson, 1974).

The third subjective weighting procedure is the paired comparison trade-off. All items are first ranked, then adjacent pairs are traded off. The judge indicates the fraction of the first item that is equal to the second item and repeats the process down the ranking. Gardiner and Edwards (1975) prefer to start with the least important item (attribute) and assign ratio scores sequentially up the ranks with ratio checking for nonadjacent pairs. Another variant of the paired comparison method is to first pair every factor with every other factor and then have judges select the preferred factor in each pairing. Relative importance of a factor is then determined by the frequency that it is preferred over other factors (Falk, 1968). Bishop (1972) uses a graphical description called "factor profile" for nonmonetary impacts to facilitate paired comparisons of alternatives. On every dimension the largest score is set at 100 percent and the other scores are made percentages of the largest. Unlike Falk, Bishop does not have judges compare all pairs. Instead, the winner in one comparison is compared with alternatives until it loses. Conjointly, the economic factor is also compared. If the winner on the social criteria costs more than the other alternatives, then the judge must decide if it is worth the extra cost. (For a paired comparison technique too complex to be summarized here, see David and Duckstein, 1976.)

The fourth subjective weighting procedure is the creation of indifference curves or trade-off functions. The Priority Evaluator Technique (PET) developed by Social and Community Planning Research in London has been applied by Pendse and Wyskoff (1976) to water resource projects. It starts with perceptions of the existing situation and has respondents select improvements (with prices indicated) within a fixed budget. Improvements are traded off at several budget levels. This evaluation system provides points for graphing the curve. (See also Haines and Hall, 1974, for another trade-off function method called the "surrogate worth" trade-off method).

The fifth subjective weighting procedure is the use of Delphi techniques to evolve a set of weights from a group of judges. One of the previous four techniques may be used to obtain an original set of weights, but the judges would also provide the rationale for the weights they choose. Then the judges anonomously criticize each others' weights, and revisions are made on the basis of this feedback. The revised weights are averaged to make group weights (see Linstone and Turoff, 1975).

INFERRED SUBJECTIVE WEIGHTS

When a certain type of judgment is made repeatedly, the judges' subjective weights may be inferred from past choices using linear regression. The independent variables in the linear regression are the assessment dimensions (judges' criteria). The dependent variables being predicted are the judges' previous choices. The coefficients for the assessment dimensions are the implicit weights the judges use in their judgments. Dawes (1971) used this approach to determine an admissions committee's basis for the admission of students into a Ph.D. program. It turned out that his equations predicted success in graduate school better than the committee's ad hoc judgments, which sometimes suspended the normal criteria and made exceptions in specific cases.

Subjective weights can be inferred from data other than previous choices. Johnson (1977) applies linear regression analysis to judges' ratings of scenarios to discover the implicit weights for evaluation dimensions that the judges use. Johnson gives judges cards to rank and scale that have different scenarios on them. Each scenario has a unique set of performance levels on five dimensions. Through computer analysis of the scale scores for the various scenarios, the implicit weights the judges were using became clear. Crews and Johnson (1975) advocate a similar scenario-judging procedure but alter the mathematical model for determining the implicit weights by substituting exponential equations for the linear equations. A further modification is proposed by Stewart and Gelberd (1976), who found the parabola formula more congruent with their data.

RANKING

One of the easiest weighting systems is to rank objectives, dimensions, impacts, or alternatives. It is easy to judge whether one item is preferable to another and to establish a ranking on a particular dimension. When several dimensions are involved, however, rankings on individual dimensions are less likely to sum to the best choice than are ratio-scaled subjective weights.

EQUAL WEIGHTINGS

The ubiquitous equal weights are the simplest to use but also the least accurate. Equal weights often are used to avoid the recriminations to which subjective weights or rankings are open. It is cowardly, however, to treat dimensions of very unequal importance as though they were equal in order to avoid accusations of bias in assigning them weights.

MULTIPLE METHODS

Frequently, projects combine several of the above techniques in the evaluation of alternatives. One type of weighting may be used to combine impact variables into general dimensions and another type of weighting to compute a total score out of the dimension scores (see, for example, Pikarsky, 1967). Sometimes, however, more than one method is used for the same evaluations and the results are compared and combined into a compromise set of scores. Breen and Covault (1976) have judges weight the importance of evaluative dimensions and also weight a sample of specific projects. These projects are then scored on the dimensions and the results are multiplied by the dimension weights and summed to total project scores. The two sets of project scores are compared and the dimension weights are then modified by reducing the squared differences between the results obtained by the two methods.

Discrete Dimensions Evaluations

Common metrics and weighting schemes are methods for making scores for different dimensions comparable and combining them into an overall score. Discrete dimensions evaluations analyze the dimensions or impacts separately without systematically combining them. They do not, therefore, provide by themselves a choice between alternatives. Three methods for evaluating discrete dimensions are described in this section.

LEXICOGRAPHIC PRUNING

Lexicographic pruning is commonly used in everyday personal decisions and was first proposed as a policy evaluation method by the author (Finsterbusch, 1977b). It is most appropriate when one or two dimensions have overriding importance and a decision must be made quickly. Lexicographic pruning immediately eliminates from consideration all alternatives that are low on the key dimension. Only the top few alternatives on the key dimension are reviewed on the second most important dimension and the best alternative on these two dimensions is selected. The remaining dimensions are scanned briefly to see if the selected alternative has serious disadvantages that call into question its superiority. If so, then a full multidimensional evaluation would be conducted. Otherwise, the decision is quickly made largely on the basis of one or two criteria. For example, if an individual wants to build a cabin on a 100-acre parcel of mountain property, he or she chooses the spot with the best view and then judges whether the accessibility of that spot from the mountain road is adequate. If so, then the search is terminated and the selected spot is checked out on many additional factors to see if it has any special problems (such as swampy land) that indicate that the comparison of locations should continue.

Hwang and Masud (1979) present a lexicographic method that ranks the criteria and selects the alternative that maximizes the first criterion. Only if there is a tie is the second criterion used. If a unique solution is not determined by two criteria, then additional criteria are applied sequentially until a unique solution is determined (see also Fishburn, 1974). This method gives too much weight to a single criterion to have many policy applications.

MINIMUM CRITERIA ANALYSIS

Minimum criteria analysis does not decide between alternatives, but it does decide which alternatives are completely unacceptable. Minimum criteria are established for acceptability on all dimensions (unimportant criteria might have no minimum standard), and all alternatives are eliminated that fail to pass all these minimum standards. If no alternative passes the minimum standards, the decision maker must decide whether any of the standards could be relaxed. If not, then he or she must search for alternatives that pass the standards or abandon the project. If only one ⋅

alternative qualifies, it is accepted. If several qualify, the choice among them must be made by some other method.

The great value of the minimum criteria analysis is that it prevents aggregate evaluation scores from concealing fatal flaws. The alternative with the best overall score may be completely unacceptable on a single dimension. Certainly a highway project should have benefit/cost ratios greater than 1.0, reduce travel time, spare major historical landmarks, have community support, compensate the most adversely affected, and so on, and a minimum criteria analysis would reject alternatives that did not. I recommend, therefore, that minimum criteria analysis be used in all evaluations. (In some evaluation schemes the minimum criteria are included as constraints.)

Minimum criteria analysis can be used effectively with lexicographic pruning if a decision must be made quickly. First, eliminate all alternatives that fail to pass any of the minimum standards. Next, use lexicographic pruning to choose among the surviving alternatives.

BALANCE SHEET

The last method for discrete dimension evaluation is the balance sheet approach, which is commonly used in environmental impact statements and other evaluation studies. To be precise, it is the absence of a method. It is the decision not to combine various impacts into an overall score or to evaluate them systematically. Rather, all important market and nonmarket costs and benefits are presented on a "balance sheet summary" and the text discusses some of the good and bad aspects of each alternative.

Democratic Choice Methods

The above methods are oriented to a bureaucratic decision-making process that uses information on impacts to select the "best" alternatives. Some elements of the judgment of "the best" are necessarily subjective, but the methods try to infuse the judgment with as much rationality as possible. Some people, however, are critical of all bureaucratic approaches and advocate democratic choice methods. For them it is more important that the decision-making process is democratic than that it results in the "best" choice (within limits). In this section, therefore, we review evaluation methods that are based on this view.

It should be noted that all evaluation methods involve the public in some way or another. Public support is included in some studies as one of many evaluative dimensions. In all studies public comments and criticisms are invited and considered to some degree in the decision-making process. In a few studies surveys are used to determine public attitudes toward project impacts or goals and this information is used in the creation of weights (Wachs, 1968; Oglesby et al., 1970; Falk, 1968). But it is rare for a study to have the citizens actually choose the alternative. An unusual example of the public having the major role in the evaluation of plans and alternatives is the Boston Transportation Planning Review (Gakenheimer, 1974; Sloan, 1974), in which citizen participation was extensive and influential. As a result, an ambitious system of additional interstate highway construction in the Boston area was drastically cut back, mainly because the new highways would have had negative impacts on the corridor communities and because many questioned that additional highways in the area would have significant accessibility benefits.

Several studies have reviewed the utility of various citizen participation techniques for water resources planning (Bishop, 1970; Delli Prisoli, 1975; Wagner and Ortolano, 1975; Warner, 1971; Willeke, 1971; Wolff, 1971). Two other summaries of citizen participation, by U.S. Department of Transportation (1976) and Manheim et al. (1975), are focused on transportation projects. Types of citizen participation have been described by Arnstein (1962).

PUBLIC CHOICE: DIRECT DEMOCRACY

When a project largely serves a local area, the public could choose the alternative or decide many of the design characteristics either by vote or by surveys. But first the agency must protect whatever interests outsiders might have, especially the interests of taxpayers, by eliminating alternatives that are technically or economically unacceptable. Then the public could make the final choice among the acceptable alternatives.

ADVISORY COMMITTEE CHOICE: REPRESENTATIVE DEMOCRACY

When the project issues are complex and the decision must be guided by technical information, it is difficult to inform the public sufficiently to enable the citizens to vote their true interests. In such cases citizen advisory committees can be elected to represent the public to the agency. Advisory committees may be limited to an advisory role or they might have real power, as in the Boston Transportation Planning Study. They can be an effective mode of public participation because they can meet frequently,

digest the summaries of the analytical studies, develop working relationships with the research team and the agency and thoroughly communicate
their views to the agency. However, most advisory committees are not
elected but appointed, and they are often unrepresentative of the community. Sometimes they are stacked with people who have the agency point of
view. More often, they are made up of prominent persons known to the
community leadership who may represent a wide range of interests but
almost never accurately reflect the attitudes of the average citizen.

POLITICAL PROCESS OUTCOME: COMPETITIVE INTEREST GROUP DEMOCRACY

A small minority of planners argue that impact assessments and
evaluation methods should be designed to integrate with the political
process. For some, this means providing impact information and the
various trade-offs to the public (Cohon and Marks, 1973; Peterson and
Gemmell, 1977). For others, this means working with and expanding the
political process (Burke et al., 1973; Mumphrey et al., 1971; Manheim,
1973). Burke et al. (1973) would set up a public participation program for
politically relevant interested parties that emphasizes negotiations and
bargaining interactions by means of Delphi techniques and computer-
assisted problem-solving methods. Through this program influential interested parties determine project selection and design.

Burke et al. favor working with the existing power structure, but
Mumphrey et al. (1971) would open the planning process to all affected
parties regardless of their political influence. They accept the fact that
concessions or side payments will be made to powerful interest groups in
order to forestall opposition. They argue, however, that need or the extent
of disamenity impacts rather than political power should be the basis for
side payments. Their recommendations, it might be noted, conform to the
principles of Rawls's (1971) theory of justice.

Manheim (1973) recommends a more complicated designer/public
dialogue than do Mumphrey et al., but shares their concern for the
politically weak but affected parties. He would have the research team
represent them in the arranged negotiation process:

> As the representative of the responsible decision-maker in a public
> works project, the team implicitly also represents the interests of voice-
> less groups or interests which are not active participants in the inter-
> action process. In some situations, these may include the long-term

interests of a particular community, national interests, and others for which no representation may be available [Manheim, 1973: 12].

Methods that Try to Obviate Evaluation

There are several ways to take nonmarket impacts into account without evaluating them. These methods reduce the evaluative task, but do not eliminate it.

STANDARDIZE COSTS OR BENEFITS

If either the costs or the benefits of a project are made the same for all alternatives, the evaluation process is greatly simplified. If several alternatives have the same benefits (such as a highway that runs from town A to town B) but have different costs, one selects the least costly, or, when costs are constant, the alternative with the most benefits. Usually this involves choosing between various combinations of benefits. Sometimes, however, adjustments can be made to make all benefits equal except one. Then the benefits do not have to be traded off and a best choice can be determined. Even when costs are not constant the best choice can be determined if all costs utilize dollar values (see Schmid, 1975).

MINIMIZE NEGATIVE EFFECTS

The second procedure for reducing the need to evaluate nonmarket impacts is to minimize them from the start. Highway location formulas serve this purpose (see Finsterbusch, 1977a). The more sophisticated formulas minimize relocation, negative proximity effects, and neighborhood disruption. By using such formulas and other highway location techniques (see Finsterbusch, 1976; Lane et al., 1975; Skidmore Owings and Merrill, 1975) alternatives are selected in the first place that have minimum negative impacts. Then appropriate design features can reduce negative impacts further. The more negative impacts are eliminated, the less they have to be evaluated relative to other impacts.

COMPENSATION AND MITIGATION

The third procedure for obviating evaluation is compensation — though establishing the compensation price is a type of evaluation. The point here is that those impacts that are compensated do not have to be evaluated relative to other impacts. Unfortunately, compensation is often not sufficient because it covers economic but not psychological and social costs (see Fried, 1963; Finsterbusch, 1976, for a discussion of the psychological and social costs of relocation), and, as Downs (1970) points out, even many of the economic costs of residential displacement are generally not compensated.

Recommended Package of Evaluation Methods

Evaluation is the final act in the decision-making process, but it should also occur in earlier stages of the study. We recommend at least three assessment cycles, each involving the identification of alternatives, the estimation of impacts, and evaluation. The first two assessment cycles work on the principle of elimination and the last assessment cycle works on the principle of selection. The first two cycles should narrow the field of alternatives down to the most promising two to five. In these rounds the focus is not on choosing the best but on eliminating all but the very good alternatives. In the first assessment cycle minimum criteria analysis and crude weighting methods are used. Among the criteria used should be the general welfare, justice or fairness in the distribution of costs and benefits, and minimum infringement on liberties. In the second assessment cycle all publicly unpopular alternatives are eliminated and weights that reflect the political realities are used to eliminate others. Again welfare, justice, and freedom are taken into account. In the beginning of the final assessment cycle negative effects are minimized and compensation and mitigation plans are developed. Then the final evaluation should use two separate methods. First, the research team calculates overall desirability scores for alternatives using justified subjective weights that seek to advance the values of welfare, justice, and liberty. Second, the research team obtains votes for alternatives or subjective weights for impact dimensions from the relevant publics. Both results are presented to the decision maker(s), who makes the final choice and reaps the political consequences. Thus the following evaluation system is recommended:

First assessment cycle: Eliminate unacceptable alternatives.
minimum criteria analysis (C2)

Second assessment cycle: Reduce to a few promising alternatives.
public choice (D1) to eliminate publicly unacceptable alternatives
ranking (B6) or subjective weights (B4) with easily measured impacts
to reduce alternatives to a few

Third assessment cycle: Select the best alternative.

minimize negative effects (E2)
compensation and mitigation (E3)
justified subjective weights (B3) seeking welfare, justice, and liberty
public choice (D1)

Decision maker decides following the results of either B3 or D1.

References

ANDERSON, B. F. (1981) "Cascaded tradeoffs: a multi-objective, multi-publics method for alternatives evaluation in water resources planning." Report for the Bureau of Reclamation, August.

ARNSTEIN, S. (1962) "A ladder of citizen participation." Journal of the American Institute of Planners 35 (July): 216-264.

BAKER, J. K. et al. (1972) "Measuring impacts of water resource developments on the human environment." Water Resources Bulletin 10 (February): 10-21.

BISHOP, A. B. (1972) "Approach to evaluating environmental, social, and economic factors in water resources planning." Water Resources Bulletin 8 (August): 724-734.
——— (1970) Public Participation in Water Resources Planning. Ft. Belvoir, VA: U.S. Army Engineer Institute for Water Resources.

BREEN, F. L., Jr. and D. O. COVAULT (1976) "Priority analysis and ranking of highway improvement projects." Traffic Quarterly 30 (October): 615-631.

BURKE, R., III et al. (1973) "Water resources and social choices." Water Resources Bulletin 9 (June): 433-447.

CHARNES, A. and W. W. COOPER (1961) Management Models and Industrial Applications of Linear Programming, Vol. 1. New York: John Wiley.

CHARNES, A. et al. (1969) "Static and dynamic assessment models with multiple objectives and some remarks on organization design." Management Science 15, 8: B365-B375.

COHON, J. L. (1978) Multiobjective Programming and Planning. New York: Academic.
——— and D. H. MARKS (1975) "A review and evaluation of multiobjective programming techniques." Water Resources Research 11 (April): 208-220.
——— (1973) "Multiobjective screening models and water resource investment." Water Resources Research 9 (August): 826-836.

COOK, R. L. and T. R. STEWART (1975) "A comparison of seven methods for obtaining subjective descriptions of judgmental policy." Organizational Behavior and Human Performance 13: 31-45.

CREWS, J. E. and G. P. JOHNSON (1975) "A methodology for trade-off analysis in water resource planning." Journal of the International Society for Technology Assessment 1 (June): 31-35.

DAVID, L. and L. DUCKSTEIN (1976) "Multi-criterion ranking of alternative long-range water resource systems." Water Resources Bulletin 12 (August): 731-754.

DAWES, R. M. (1971) "A case study of graduate admissions." American Psychologist (February): 180-188.

DEAN, J. H. and C. S. SHIH (1975) "Decision analysis for the River Walk Expansion in San Antonio, Texas." Water Resources Bulletin 11 (April): 237-244.

———— (1973) "Subjective decision-making for urban water resources development." Water Resources Bulletin 9 (October): 942-949.

DELFT, A. van and P. NIJKAMP (1977) Multi-Criteria Analysis and Regional Decision-Making. Leiden, The Netherlands: Martinus Nijhoff.

DELLI-PRISOLI, J. (1975) "Public participation: between myth and reality." Communicator, Great Lakes Basin Commission (May).

DOWNS, A. (1970) "Uncompensated nonconstruction costs which urban highways and urban renewal impose upon residential households," pp. 69-106 in J. Margolis (ed.) The Analysis of Public Output. New York: Columbia University Press.

DUCKSTEIN, L. and J. KEMPF (1981) "Multicriteria Q analysis for plan evaluation," pp. 87-99 in P. Nijkamp and J. Sprank (eds.) Multiple Criteria Analysis: Operational Methods. Hampshire, England: Gower.

EDWARDS, W. (1979) "Multiattribute utility measurement: evaluating desegregation plans in a highly political context," pp. 13-54 in R. Perloff (ed.) Evaluator Interventions: Pros and Cons. Beverly Hills, CA: Sage.

ETZIONI, A. (1979) "How much is a life worth?" Social Policy (March/April): 4-8.

FALK, E. L. (1968) "Measurement of community values: the Spokane experiment." Highway Research Record 229: 53-64.

FINSTERBUSCH, K. (1977a) "Formulas for locating highways in urban areas." Presented at the annual meetings of the Society for the Study of Social Problems, Chicago, September.

———— (1977b) Methods for evaluating Non-Market Impacts in Policy Decisions with Special Reference to Water Resources Development Projects. Ft. Belvoir, VA: U.S. Army Engineer Institute for Water Resources.

———— (1976) A Methodology for the Social Impact Assessment of Highway Locations. College Park: University of Maryland and Maryland State Highway Administration.

FISHBURN, P. C. (1974) "Lexicographic orders, utilities and decision rules: a survey." Management Science 20 (July): 1442-1471.

FRIED, M. (1963) "Grieving for a lost home." pp. 151-171 in L. J. Duhl (ed.) The Urban Condition. New York: Simon & Schuster.

GAKENHEIMER, R. (1974) Techniques and Conflict: The Open Study in Urban Transportation. Cambridge: MIT Press.

GARDINER, P. C. and W. EDWARDS (1975) "Public values: multiattribute utility measurement for social decision-making," pp. 1-37 in M. F. Kaplan and S. Schwartz (eds.) Human Judgment and Decision Processes. New York: Academic.

GREEN, P. E. and V. RAO (1971) "Conjoint measurement for quantifying judgmental data." Journal of Marketing Research 8 (August): 353-363.

HAINES, Y. and W. A. HALL (1974) "Multiobjectives in water resources systems analysis: the surrogate worth trade-off method." Water Resources Research 10, 4: 615-624.

HAINES, Y. and K. TAVAINESS (1981) "Hierarchical-multiobjective framework for large scale systems," pp. 201-232 in P. Nijkamp and P. Sprank (eds.) Multiple Criteria Analysis: Operational Methods. Hampshire, England: Gower.

HILL, M. (1973) Planning for Multiple Objectives. Philadelphia: Regional Science Research Institute.

———— (1967) "A method for the evaluation of transportation plans." Highway Research Record 180: 21-34.

HOLMES, T. H. and R. H. RAHE (1967) "The Social Readjustment Scale." Journal of Psychosomatic Research 11: 213-218.

HWANG, C.-L. and A.S.M. MASUD (1979) Multiple Objective Decision Making: Methods and Applications: A State-of-the-Art Survey. New York: Springer-Verlag.

JOHNSON, J. M. (1977) "Policy capturing in energy," pp. 341-346 in K. Finsterbusch and C. P. Wolf (eds). Methodology of Social Impact Assessment. Stroudsburg, PA: Hutchinson Ross.

JOHNSON, R. M. (1974) "Trade-off analysis of consumer values." Journal of Marketing Research 11 (May): 121-127.

KEENEY, R. L. and K. NAIR (1975) "Decision analysis for the siting of nuclear power plants: the relevance of multiattribute utility theory." Proceedings of the IEEE 63 (March): 494-501.

KEENEY, R. L. and H. RAIFFA (1976) Decisions with Multiple Objectives: Preferences and Value Tradeoffs. New York: John Wiley.

KEENEY, R. L. and E. WOOD (1977) "An illustrative example of the use of multiattribute utility theory for water resource planning." Water Resources Research 13: 705-719.

LANE, J. S. et al. (1975) "The no-build alternative." National Cooperative Highway Research Program, December.

LINSTONE, H. A. and M. TUROFF (1975) The Delphi Method: Techniques and Applications. Reading, MA: Addison-Wesley.

LORD, W. B., D. H. BEANE, and M. WATERSTONE (1979) Commensuration in Federal Water Resources Planning: Problem Analysis and Research Appraisal. Research Report 7902 for the Bureau of Reclamation. Boulder, CO: LTW Associates.

LUCE, R. D. and J. W. TUKEY (1964) "Simultaneous conjoint measurement: a new type of fundamental measurement." Journal of Mathematical Psychology 1 (February): 1-27.

MacCRIMMON, K. R. (1973) "An overview of multiple objective decision-making," pp. 18-44 in J. L. Cochrane and M. Zeleny (eds.) Multiple Criteria Decision Making. Columbia: University of South Carolina Press.

——— and J. K. SIU (1974) "Making trade-offs." Decisions Sciences 5 (October): 280-304.

MANHEIM, M. (1973) "Reaching decisions about technological projects with social consequences: a normative model." Transportation 2: 1-24.

——— et al. (1975) Transportation Decision-making: A Guide to Social and Environmental Considerations. Washington, DC: Transportation Research Board.

MELINYSHYN, W., R. CROTHER, and J. D. O'DOHERTY (1973) "Transportation planning improvement priorities: development of a methodology." Highway Research Record 458: 1-12.

MUMPHREY, A. J., Jr., et al. (1971) "A decision for locating controversial facilities." Journal of the American Institute of Planners 37 (November): 397-402.

NIJKAMP, P. (1977) "Stochastic quantitative and qualitative multicriteria analysis for environmental design." Papers of the Regional Science Association 39: 175-199.

NOZICK, R. (1974) Anarchy, State, and Utopia. New York: Basic Books.

OGLESBY, C. et al. (1970) "A method for decisions among freeway location alternatives based on user and community consequences." Highway Research Record 305: 1-14.

PENDSE, D. and J. B. WYSKOFF (1976) "Measurement of environmental trade-offs and public policy: a case study." Water Resources Bulletin 12 (October): 919-930.

PETERSON, G. L. and R. S. GEMMELL (1977) "Social impact assessment: comments on the state of the art," pp. 347-387 in K. Finsterbusch and C. P. Wolf (eds.) Methodology of Social Impact Assessment. Stroudsburg, PA: Hutchinson Ross.

PIKARSKY, M. (1967) "Comprehensive planning for the Chicago crosstown expressway." Highway Research Record 180: 35-51.

RAWLS, J. (1971) A Theory of Justice. Cambridge, MA: Harvard University Press.

RHOADS, W. E. (1978) "How much should we spend to save a life?" Public Interest 51 (Spring): 74-92.

RODDING, W. (1975) Aggregation of Individual Preferences. Gottingen: Vandenhocek and Ruprecht.

SCHMID, A. A. (1975) "Systematic choice among multiple outputs of public projects without prices." Social Indicators Research 2: 275-286.

Skidmore, Owings and Merrill (1975) Environmental Assessment Notebook 2: Social Impacts. Washington, DC: U.S. Department of Transportation.

SLOAN, A. (1974) Citizen Participation in Transportation Planning: The Boston Experience. Cambridge, MA: Ballinger.

STARR, M. K. and M. ZELENY (1977) Multiple Criteria Decision Making. Amsterdam: North Holland.

STEWART, T. R. and L. GELBERD (1976) "Analysis of judgment policy: a new approach for citizen participation in planning." Journal of the American Institute of Planners (January): 33-41.

THOMPSON, M. S. (1980) Benefit-Cost Analysis for Program Evaluation. Beverly Hills, CA: Sage.

U.S. Department of Transportation (1976) Effective Citizen Participation in Transportation Planning. Vol. I: Community Involvement Processes. Vol. II: A Catalog of Techniques. Washington, DC: Socio-Economic Studies Division, Federal Highway Administration.

WACHS, M. (1968) "A survey of citizens' opinions of the effectiveness, needs, and techniques of urban transportation planning." Highway Research Record 227: 65-76.

WAGNER, T. P. and L. ORTOLANO (1975) "Analysis of new techniques for public involvement in water planning." Water Resources Bulletin 11 (April): 329-343.

WARNER, K. P. (1971) "A state-of-the-art study of public participation in the water resources planning process." National Water Commission.

WILLEKE, G. E. (1971) Some Formal Methods for Assessing Public Desires, Values, Opinions, Needs, Concerns, etc. Atlanta: Environmental Resources Center, Georgia Institute of Technology.

WOLFF, R. D. (1971) Involving the Public and the Hierarchy in Corps of Engineers' Survey Investigations. Stanford, CA: Department of Civil Engineering, Stanford University.

ZELENY, M. (1980) Multiple Criteria Decision Making: A Companion Test. New York: McGraw-Hill.

—— (1974) Linear Multiobjective Programming. New York: Springer-Verlag.

ZIONTS, S. and J. WALLENIUS (1976) "An interactive programming method for solving the multiple criteria problem." Management Science 22 (February): 652-663.

About the Authors

Barry F. Anderson received his Ph.D. in experimental psychology from the Johns Hopkins University in 1957. He taught and conducted research in cognitive psychology at the University of Oregon from 1963 to 1968, and has been affiliated with Portland State University since 1968. He has authored or coauthored four books and a number of articles and reports. From 1979 to 1981, he spent a sabbatical at the Center for Research in Judgment and Policy at the University of Colorado, where he consulted in the area of public policy decision making for the Bureau of Reclamation, the Fish and Wildlife Service, and the Rocky Flats Monitoring Committee (nuclear), assessing expert judgments and measuring public values.

Kristi Branch is receiving a doctorate in educational development and social change from Harvard University. She is currently the president of The Research Branch, located in Billings, Montana. She has been actively involved in the development of methodology for addressing the social and economic effects of large-scale development on rural communities. She is a member of the Four Nations Resource Communities Group and the principal author of the *Guide to Social Assessment: A Framework for Assessing Social Change,* which will soon be published.

Rabel J. Burdge is Professor of Rural Sociology, Environmental Sociology and Leisure Studies, in the Institute for Environmental Studies, University of Illinois — Urbana-Champaign. He is the author of *Coping with Change: An Interdisciplinary Assessment of the Lake Shelbyville Reservoir,* coauthor of *Social Change in Rural Societies: A Rural Sociology Textbook,* former editor of the *Journal of Leisure Research,* and founding editor of *Leisure Sciences: An Interdisciplinary Journal.* He has written extensively on needs assessment surveys, the use of public involvement in the decision-making process, the social impacts of environmental alteration, and outdoor leisure behavior. He currently serves as Vice-President of the Rural Sociological Society and was selected as the 1982 recipient of the Theodore and Franklin Roosevelt Award for Excellence in Recreation and Park Research given by the National Recreation and Park Association.

Michael J. Carley is the author of *Rational Techniques in Policy Analysis* (Heinemann) and *Social Measurement and Social Indicators* (Allen and Unwin). He currently works as a consultant in the fields of policy analysis and social impact assessment. Recently, he was a UNICEF consultant to the National Centre for Human Resources in Brazil, and he is currently advising the Canadian federal and territorial governments on impact monitoring related to oil and gas developments in the Arctic. He holds an M.Sc. from the London School of Economics and is completing his Ph.D. in regional planning at the University of British Columbia. He was formerly a Research Fellow at the Policy Studies Institute in London, and he will be returning to that post in 1984.

James A. Chalmers received his Ph.D. in economics from the University of Michigan. He is currently with Mountain West Research — Southwest, Inc., located in Tempe, Arizona. During the 1970s, he was responsible for developing empirical data bases and methodology to assess the economic and demographic impacts of large energy projects in rural areas in the West. More recently, he has worked on developing information systems and decision tools applied to the real estate industry.

Thomas Dietz holds a Ph.D. in ecology from the University of California, Davis. He is currently Assistant Professor of Sociology at George Mason University. In addition to research on theory and method in social impact assessment, he is conducting a study of the Washington risk assessment community. His previous publications include *Handbook for Environmental Planning* and articles in *Energy, Policy Sciences, Public Administration Review*, and *Environmental Management*.

C. Mark Dunning is a Sociologist in the Research Division of the Army Engineer Institute for Water Resources at Fort Belvoir, Virginia. His principle duties include conducting and managing research on socioeconomic factors in water resources development and performing policy analysis on issues affecting the Corps of Engineers. He is the author of several Corps of Engineers research reports, policy studies, and training publications. In addition, his articles have appeared in the *American Water Resources Association Journal* and publications of the Environmental Design Research Association. He has delivered guest presentations at Princeton University, the University of Missouri, numerous professional society and Corps of Engineers meetings, and for other DOD agencies on topics of socioeconomic effects assessment, forecasting, and community involvement methods. He received his Ph.D. in sociology from Washington University.

Kurt Finsterbusch is an Associate Professor in the Department of Sociology, University of Maryland, College Park. He has been working intensely in the field of social impact assessment since 1974 and has contributed extensively to the development of methods, theory, and substantive findings in SIA. He has studied the effects of highways and dams on neighborhoods and displaced households. His publications in the field of SIA include *Methodology of Social Impact Assessment,* edited with C. P. Wolf (1977); *Understanding Social Impacts* (1980); and *Social Research for Policy Decisions,* with Annabelle Bender Motz (1980). He also edited the Summer 1982 *Impact Assessment Bulletin* issue on social impact assessment. Recently he has extended his SIA work in two directions: the assessment of the effects of development projects in Third World countries and the assessment of future social conditions likely to evolve from trends in population, resources, environment, and technology.

Cynthia B. Flynn is President of Social Impact Research, Inc. She is a sociologist with an international reputation in socioeconomic research. Her work on the socioeconomic effects of the accident at the Three Mile Island Nuclear Plant has been published in three reports by the U.S. Nuclear Regulatory Commission. She is part of a national team that has been studying patterns of elderly migration in the United States for the National Institutes of Health since 1977. She has made substantial contributions to the development of new and better methodologies in the areas of socioeconomic impact assessment, demographic analysis, and survey methodology, and she is frequently invited to speak on socioeconomic impact assessment at national meetings.

James H. Flynn is Vice President and Director of Research of Social Impact Research, Inc. He has conducted numerous major community research projects, including in-depth studies of nuclear power station sitings in at Calvert Cliffs (Maryland), Surry (Virginia), and Oconee (South Carolina), reports of which were published by the U.S. Nuclear Regulatory Commission. He managed the evaluation of the Lawrence (Kansas) Police Department Integrated Criminal Apprehension Program (1978-1982), funded by the U.S. Law Enforcement Assistance Administration. He also managed socioeconomic work on Puget Sound Power and Light's Skagit/ Hanford Nuclear Plant Project, and recently conducted a community analysis for Shell Canada.

F. Larry Leistritz is Professor of Agricultural Economics at North Dakota State University at Fargo. He has completed extensive research regarding the economic and fiscal impacts of energy resource development in the western United States. From 1975 to 1978, he served as Associate Director of the North Dakota Regional Environmental Assessment Program, a state-funded research and policy analysis project for analyzing the impacts of energy development. In that capacity he was responsible for managing the development of the REAP Economic-Demographic Models, RED-1 and RED-2. He is senior author of *Socioeconomic Impact of Resource Development: Methods for Assessment* and coauthor of two other books. In 1978-79 he was a Visiting Professor of Agricultural Economics at Texas A&M University, where he advised in the development of the Texas Assessment Modeling System (TAMS). He received his Ph.D. in agricultural economics from the University of Nebraska — Lincoln in 1970.

John W. Lounsbury is Associate Professor of Psychology at the University of Tennessee, Knoxville. He is also President of Resource Associates, Inc., a firm that consults to organizations on human resource development and management issues. His current research interests include attitudes and beliefs in relation to social impact assessment, psychological linkages between work and leisure, and nonreactive measurement of morale in organizations.

Lynn G. Llewellyn received a Ph.D. in social psychology from George Washington University in 1969 and currently serves as Assistant Chief and Project Manager for Social Assessment, Division of Program Plans, U.S. Fish and Wildlife Service. Prior to joining the Service in 1975, he was a senior research psychologist with the National Bureau of Standards and was project leader on a study of the social and environmental effects of new and improved highways, the results of which were incorporated in a 1982 Federal Highway Administration publication: *Social Impact Assessment — A Sourcebook for Highway Planners*. He is a member of the American Psychological Association and serves as a consultant with the American Institute of Architects' Regional Development and Natural Resources Committee and the American Society of Civil Engineers' Committee on Environmental Quality.

Gregory J. Meissen is Assistant Professor of Psychology at Wichita State University. His research interest is in the area of social impacts of large-scale urban development and energy development in rural areas. He is also examining the conceptual linkages between community psychology and social impact assessment.

Annabelle Bender Motz received her Ph.D. in sociology from the University of Chicago and currently serves as Full Professor in the Department of Sociology, American University, Washington, D.C. She was formerly Scholar in Residence with the U.S. Army Corps of Engineers' Institute for Water Resources and recently served as an Adviser to the Environmental Protection Service, Ministry of Interior, Jerusalem, Israel. She is a member of the American Sociological Association, Sociologists for Women in Society, the D.C. Sociological Society, and the Eastern Sociological Society.

Jeryl Mumpower received his Ph.D. in social psychology from the University of Colorado, Boulder. He is currently a program manager for the Technology Assessment and Risk Analysis Group, Division of Policy Research and Analysis, National Science Foundation. He is coauthor (with Kenneth R. Hammond and Gary H. McClelland) of *Human Judgment and Decision Making: Theories, Methods, and Procedures.*

Steve H. Murdock received his Ph.D. from the University of Kentucky and is currently Head of the Department of Rural Sociology, Texas A&M University. In 1982, he received the Distinguished Performance in Research Award for his work in the Agricultural Complex at Texas A&M. He has completed extensive research on the social and demographic impacts of resource development in the United States. He is senior author of *Energy Development in the Western United States: Impact on Rural Areas,* senior editor of *Nuclear Waste: Socioeconomic Dimensions of Long-Term Storage,* and coauthor of a third book. His areas of specialization include socioeconomic impact analysis, demography, and human ecology.

James F. Palmer, Ph.D., is a Research Associate and Curriculum Director for the Program in Environmental Studies at the SUNY College of Environmental Science and Forestry in Syracuse. He holds professional degrees in landscape architecture and natural resource planning. He has recently participated in aesthetic resource assessment short courses sponsored by the National Trust for Historic Preservation and the U.S. Army Corps of Engineers. His current research concerns cross-cultural landscape perceptions and the role of nature in the lives of urbanites.

David Pijawka received his Ph.D. in geography from Clark University. He is currently the Assistant Director, Center for Environmental Studies, Arizona State University, and has a faculty appointment with the Center for Public Affairs. His areas of research include risk assessment and policy, impacts of technology, and public response to hazards. His book, *Nuclear Power: Assessing and Managing Hazardous Technology*, will soon be published.

Roy Roper is a graduate student in the Department of Anthropology at the University of Illinois. His research interests include the familial consequences of voluntary and forced relocation in water resources projects as well as the more generic issues of adult human development and life-course progression.

Kent D. Van Liere is Assistant Professor of Sociology at the University of Tennessee, Knoxville. His research interests have generally focused on attitudes and behavior in the energy and environment areas. His most recent research involves the prediction of conservation behavior using a "definition of the situation" approach to energy opinions. He is currently on leave from his university position and is working with the Strategic Planning Staff in the Office of Planning and Budget at the Tennessee Valley Authority.

C. P. Wolf is Research Professor of Social Science at the Polytechnic Institute of New York. He has been instrumental in developing social impact assessment as a professional field of investigation through his organizing, networking, and publishing. He has organized numerous conferences and meetings among social impact assessors. His edited volumes, *Social Impact Assessments* (1974) and *Methodology of Social Impact Assessment*, with Kurt Finsterbusch (1977, 1981), were perhaps the major publications in SIA in its early years. He has helped found several organizations and several sections in social science associations dealing with social impact assessment. The newsletter he created and edits, *Social Impact Assessment*, has been a major influence in the development of social impact assessment as an applied social science. He has been affiliated with the Institute for Water Resources of the U.S. Army Corps of Engineers, the Office of Technology Assessment of the U.S. Congress, and the Environmental Psychology Program of the City University of New York.